CW01430360

study in FRANCE
Handbook

Written and researched by
Louise Tucker

ON COURSE PUBLICATIONS

Publishers
Jeremy Hunt, Mike Elms

Editorial team
Louise Tucker, Cheryl Roberts, Yolande Taylor
David Pievsky

Design and layout
Colleen Chong, Angela Jenkins

The publishers and editors make strenuous efforts to ensure that the information in this guide is correct at time of going to press but can accept no responsibility for any errors or omissions. Colleges reserve the right to make changes to their curriculum, course content, and prices at any time.

ISBN 1 898730 23 7
© Elms Hunt International Limited 1999

On Course Publications
121 King Street, London W6 9JG UK
Tel: 0181 600 5300 Fax: 0181 741 7716
E-mail: mike@oncourse.co.uk
Web: www.oncourse.co.uk

Contents

FRANCE

Using the Guide

France is home to all things cultural and romantic, from art to wine, fashion to photography. If you want to learn more about it, there is no better way to do so than by going to the country, living and learning in situ. Constant linguistic and local challenges teach you so much more than a class at home. This guide is aimed at everyone who is interested in the language and culture of one of the most interesting and historic places in Europe. Whether you are a student or a holiday-maker, planning a trip to further a passion or profession, this country and its extensive education system has something to offer you.

Schools and individuals/establishments offering courses are listed according to subject and region. Each section includes an introduction, which offers an overview of classes available. There are descriptions of the different types of schools and certificates, the price range, the amount of experience and qualifications necessary, the level of French required, enrolment and payment details (although many of the smaller, non-academic courses do not have fixed schedules or payment options). Also included is a comaprison of the advantages of Paris versus the provinces. Every entry includes contact details, a description of the school (its location and, where possible, its objectives), a summary of courses available, enrolment and payment information, services provided (accommodation reservations, airport transfers), facilities available (for example whether there is a laboratory or access to audio-visual materials in the case of language schools). All prices are quoted in francs, as these are still far more widely in use than Euros.

Each chapter is also sub-divided according to region: Paris; the North-East (for example Alsace, Burgundy, Champagne); the North-West (Brittany, Loire Atlantique); the South-East (Provence, Côte d'Azur); the South-West (Poitou-Charente, Périgord, Pyrénées).

For those seeking more information, the Studying in France section (page 5-29) and individual subject introductions will be the best place to start, all of which provide information about what's on offer and the inspiration to get started. If you are thinking of doing a degree course, refer to the 'Universities' chapter as a starting point (although exchanges are dealt with separately, in the Exchange Schemes and Assistantships chapter see p47). There really is an incredible range of courses available in France: all provide both a linguistic and an intellectual challenge. Why not learn French through theatre, painting, or wine appreciation? The potential for improving your language skills is enormous, and it is not just limited to grammar classes.

France and
the French

FRANCE

France has much to boast of, leading the way agriculturally for Western Europe, and ranking fourth in terms of scientific research among OECD countries, after Japan, Germany and America. Having been the dominant political power in Europe under Napoleon, France is once again a major European power, gaining strength since 1945. It was one of the founder members of the European Community, as long ago as 1958. Additionally, it is one of the five permanent members of the United Nations Security Council.

France has several overseas departments, including French Guyana, French Polynesia, Guadeloupe, Martinique, Mayotte, New Caledonia and Reunion. Previous territory included Morocco, Tunis, Madagascar, French West Africa and French Equatorial Africa; these members of its African empire gained independence in the period following 1956, but this history explains the prevalence of French-speakers in some of these areas today. The large immigrant population in parts of France (particularly Paris) is mainly composed of people originating from these colonies and their descendants. However, there are increasing numbers of Eastern Europeans flowing into France in recent years, among them Poles. Unfortunately this can lead to

James Heath

5

racial tension, fuelled by the extremely right-wing *Front National*, whose leader, Jean-Marie le Pen, represents the very worst of nationalist and racist opinions.

VITAL STATISTICS

The Boss

France (as anyone who knows anything about history will be aware) is a Republic. Its constitution was adopted in 1958 and it gives the President (who is elected every seven years) important powers. The President chooses the Prime Minister and the PM is responsible both to the President and the Parliament. The Parliament holds legislative power, and consists of the National Assembly and the Sénat.

At present the President is Jacques Chirac, heading the *Rassemblement pour la République*. This party is politically right-wing, in contrast with the party of his predecessor, François Mitterand, who led the *Parti Socialiste*. One of the most prominent moves by Chirac has been to

abolish conscription, leading to protest from left-wing groups who perceive compulsory military training as a social leveller.

One unpopular move politically by France as a nation within the last five years was the testing of nuclear weapons in the South Pacific. Although there are several Green Parties in France, these tend to campaign on a local basis, and they generally do not attempt to take the government to task over nuclear issues. This is a country which relies on nuclear power to produce 70 per cent of its energy.

The Boundaries

The country is divided into 22 regions (such as Alsace, Provence/Riviera) and each one of those is sub-divided into two to eight '*départements*' (which is roughly equivalent to a county). Paris, for example, is one of the *départements* of the Île-de-France region, in which there are many *châteaux*. The 96 metropolitan *départements* all have a number which is used for the postcode (Paris is 75000) and car registrations (the last two digits of Paris-registered vehicle number plates will be 75). Just as bored children in America spot state plates on long car journeys, so bored French children spot *départements*.

The Population

France is four times the size of the UK – it is the second largest country in Europe after Russia. 73.4 per cent live in cities and it is still possible to find unpopulated countryside and rural peace, something which is increasingly difficult in Britain. The highest concentration of the population is in Paris, Lyons, and in the South-East. The country is very centralised (try crossing from East to West by train without going through Paris) which

Victoria Davies/Benoît Besnard

elsewhere. French drivers have a reputation for recklessness. Driving licences issued within the European Union and America are valid in France, although if you come across a policeman who prefers not to have to read English, an International driving licence can be advantageous. The previous French road etiquette of *'priorité à droite'* (give way to the right) has proved to be a major cause of accidents, and is thus being phased out. However, expect to come across it in built-up areas; a yellow diamond on a white background gives right of way, while the same sign with a black slash across it means that those vehicles coming from the right have the right of way.

The weather

Northern France has a climate which is similar to that of Britain (ie cool and wet). It is not until you are south of the Loire that it becomes significantly warmer, with short winters and hot

creates a clear dividing line between the capital and the provinces, in terms of government, lifestyle and personality. The provinces have very defined regional characters, which extend from the cuisine to the architecture and although there is a fierce sense of national identity across the country, each area is also strongly identified by its local differences. When considering where to study, this difference should be taken into account. An urbanite in love with New York or London may find Toulouse and Nantes rather sleepy.

The roads

Autoroutes (motorways) are convenient and quick, but boring to drive on. There are tolls on each route. It is probably best to avoid driving at peak times in the French holiday period (between mid-July and the end of August), as the majority of Parisians desert the city at this point and head

	Month Average Temperature range (degrees Centigrade)
Jan	3 – 12
Feb	4 – 12
Mar	7 – 14
Apr	13 – 18
May	14 – 20
Jun	20 – 27
Jul	21 – 28
Aug	22 – 28
Sep	19 – 26
Oct	15 – 22
Nov	7 – 16
Dec	5 – 14

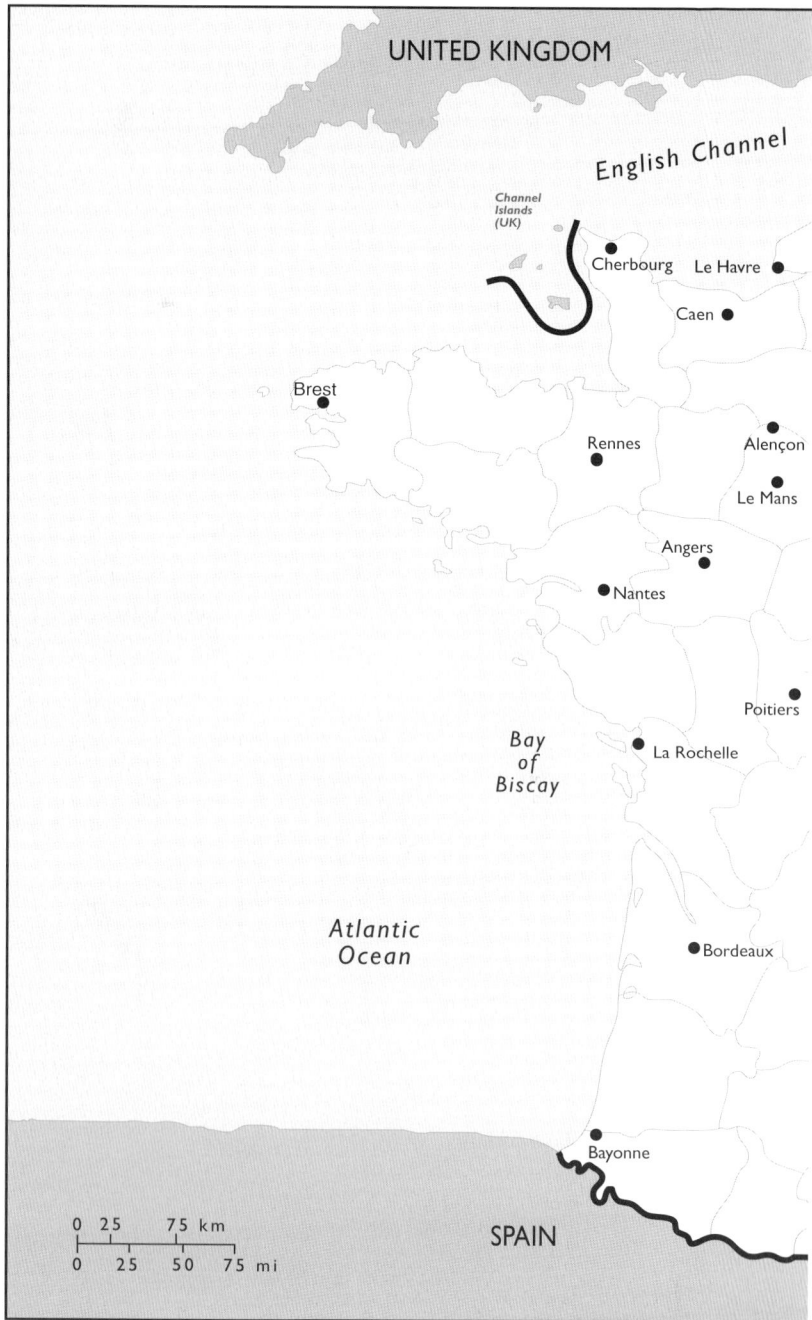

UNITED KINGDOM

English Channel

Channel
Islands
(UK)

● Cherbourg   Le Havre ●

Caen ●

Brest
●

Rennes
●

Alençon
●

Le Mans
●

Angers
●

● Nantes

Poitiers
●

Bay
of
Biscay

● La Rochelle

Atlantic
Ocean

● Bordeaux

Bayonne
●

0   25   75 km
0   25   50   75 mi

SPAIN

Calais

Brussels   NETH.

Lille

BELGIUM   GERMANY

Arras

Amiens

LUX.

Luxembourg

Rouen

Reims   Metz

Paris

Nancy

Strasbourg

Troyes

Mulhouse

Orléans

Belfort

Dijon

Tours

Bourges

Bern

Nevers

SWITZERLAND

Lac Leman

Clermont-
Ferrand

Lyon

Limoges

Saint Etienne

Grenoble

Perigueux

ITALY

Rodez

Avignon

Monte Carlo

Nice

Toulouse

MONACO

Béziers

Marseille

Narbonne

Toulon

Gulf of Lion

Perpignan

Mediterranean Sea

A brief history of time, French-style

France has a full-blooded, dramatic history. Its inhabitants have been subjects at some points, citizens at others. The 1789 revolution – Europe's first modern one – sits in the centre of French identity, and characterises France as a democratic nation.

1415 – Henry V of England wins a major victory against the French at Agincourt

1429 – Joan of Arc tried and executed by the English, turning her into a martyr

1436 – The English leave Paris, allowing the French monarchy to begin a centralising process which will create a more efficient nation-state

1562 – killings of Protestant worshippers begins a protracted war of religion

1572 – the massacre of St Bartholemew's Day kills thousands more Protestants

1598 – the Edict of Nantes helps to reconcile Protestants to France by granting them freedom of worship and other rights

1634 – Académie Française founded by Cardinal Richelieu

1643 – Louis XIV begins a 72-year reign. He is known as the Sun King for his extravagantly rich image

1648 – The Fronde rebellion, a protest against increasing central power, begins

1685 – Louis XIV revokes the Edict of Nantes, causing a war between France and Protestant powers

1715 – Louis XV, at the age of two, becomes king: the aristocracy take the opportunity of the regency to increase their powers

1751 – First volume of Diderot's *Encyclopédie*, a classic enlightenment text, is published

1771 – the *Parlement* of Paris is exiled following a legislative stalemate. This horrifies the nobles, and causes anti-monarchical feeling

1788 – catastrophic harvests and the monarchy's complete bankruptcy (deriving from ambitious and failed foreign war campaigns) combine to produce a constitutional crisis and the foundations of a revolution

1789 – The Bastille prison is stormed on the July 14, bringing the working classes directly into what would otherwise have been a liberal revolution. The Declaration of the Rights of Man, the nationalisation of church land, and the abolition of the privileges of the nobles all quickly follow

1792 – France is declared a Republic

1793 – As revolutionary radicalism develops, the former king Louis XVI is executed on January 31 after trying to escape with his family to Varennes

1794 – The Terror, during the revolution's darkest hour, rages amidst counter-revolutionary paranoia and fear of invasion

1804 – Napoleon is in power, giving himself the humble title of 'Emperor Napoleon I'

1815 – Napoleon is finally removed and replaced by Louis XVIII, inaugurating the restoration

1830 – Charles X overthrown, and replaced by Louis-Phillipe of Orléans

1848 – European revolutions, and in France the Second Republic is declared

1852 – A coup gives France another Bonaparte

1871 – The self-declared Paris Commune lives a short life before being retaken by governmental troops, with many lives lost in the process

1889 – La Tour Eiffel is built, and marvelled at

1894 – the Dreyfus case splits French public opinion on questions of anti-semitism and nationalism

1895 – Louis Lumière registers the patent for a Cinématographe Lumière: a flexible and transparent film with punched edges (unwittingly launching the career of thousands of sculpted beauties and action men for generations)

1904 – Pablo Picasso moves to Paris; there is now a museum devoted entirely to his work in this city

1914 – World War One begins, much of it to be fought on French soil, and with massive human costs

1940 – Hitler invades, defeats and divides France, setting up a satellite government based in Vichy.

1944 – Paris liberated, too late for those deported to concentration camps

1949 – Simone de Beauvoir publishes 'The Second Sex', contributing greatly to the feminist stance

1968 – The French Revolutionary spirit boils over once more, in the form of student riots

1986 – The Musée d'Orsay opens, in a converted railway station

1992 – EuroDisney is launched, at a location outside Paris

1995 – Jacques Chirac is elected President in May

1997 – Socialist government in landslide election victory under Lionel Jospin

1998 – France wins the World Cup, to national celebration

1999 – The Euro is on its way, ending centuries of financial independence within Europe…

summers, allowing full enjoyment of the beaches of the Côte d'Azur. (bearing in mind that other factors such as overcrowded campsites and overpriced access to the beach may conspire against you!).

Other useful information for prospective students

France is one hour ahead of Britain throughout the year, with the exception of a short period in October, when the two countries run on the same time. It is six hours ahead of Eastern Standard Time and nine hours ahead of Pacific Standard Time.

If you're a citizen of the European Union, you're eligible for subsidised meals, accommodation, and any other student reductions. If you're not a citizen of the European Union, but you are a full-time student in France, it's worth bearing in mind that as long as your visa is still valid you can get a non-EU work permit for the following summer. This would allow you to enjoy the country for a few more months,

while benefiting from a (slightly!) larger budget.

PARIS VS THE PROVINCES

Paris

The capital is, well, the capital. And it's Paris. The attractions of this city and its facilities (such as museums housing world-famous collections of art) are undeniable, but it isn't for everyone. Those who are looking for an all-inclusive package, including tuition, accommodation and meals will not find it in Paris (except in the case of language schools). This city, and, in fact, every city, is an option for those who are looking for a particular type of class and do not mind finding their own accommodation and meals. It is suitable for the *à la carte* tourist or academic student: those who have either very relaxed or very specific aims and schedules, able to slot in classes over a weekend or a month or planning to spend a year on a particular project. The advantage of Paris is that the central area is fairly compact; most of

The Arc de Triomphe

Fidelma Smith

the city is within the confines of the *péripherique* (ringroad).

The city itself is divided by the river Seine, which flows from East to West, and has two islands in the middle of it: the Île de la Cité and the Île St Louis (the latter is now one of the most exclusive residential areas in the city). The northern area of Paris is known as the *rive droite* (the Right Bank), and that lying south of the river is termed the *rive gauche* (the Left Bank). However, this does not mean that the character of the city can be as neatly subdivided; the atmosphere will vary between arrondissements, and even within the *arrondissements* themselves. The 1er and 2e arrondissements are somewhat sleazy (this is where the red-light district is); however, La Bourse (the Parisian Stock Exchange) is also located in the 2e arrondissement. The Pigalle area (between the 9e and 18e) is another sleaze centre, where cabarets such as the Moulin Rouge are situated; the area is a trendy night spot among people of design and advertising ilk. The 8e is where the Champs Élysées, the Arc de Triomphe, and the most expensive shops can be found. (The famous three-week *Tour de France* cycle race finishes with a few laps of the Champs Élysées). The poorest, decaying parts of the city tend to be in the northern and eastern areas, for example the Belleville and La Goutte d'Or; however, there are building programmes underway to try and improve the quality of the housing available.

If you fancy cooking yourself an alternative to French cuisine, the 13e is the place to go for Chinese supermarkets. It is likely, though, that the very reason you are in France is to acquire some knowledge of the legendary local cooking. Wine buffs and cooking fans will find half-day courses, evening wine-tastings and year-long professional programmes on offer all over Paris. However, there is just as much to tempt their palate, if not more, in the different regions of this gastronomic playground, especially given the rich cuisine of areas such as Normandy (which is where camembert and calvados originate from). Never order Coke with a gourmet meal, as this is something that the French cannot tolerate; when ordering wine in a restaurant, remember that the cheaper table wines are known as *vin de table* or *vin ordinaire*.

Should you find yourself wishing to go home after an evening out in Paris sampling several glasses of the variety of *vin* on offer, make use of the night buses, which run between 1.00am and

PUBLIC HOLIDAYS IN FRANCE

January 1 New Year

April 5 Easter (Pâques)

May 1 Labour Day

May 8 End of World War 2

May 13 Ascension Day

July 14 Bastille Day

August 15 Assumption of the Virgin Mary

November 1 All Saints Day

November 11 1918 Armistice Day

December 25 Christmas (Nöel)

5.00am from the *place du Châtelet* to various stops on the edge of the city. Maps of the bus routes can be obtained free from bus terminals, the tourist office, and métro stations. The Metro runs from 5.30am until 12.45am, and is usually busy enough to make it relatively safe. You may want to go further afield; the RER (Réseau Express Régional) suburban express lines run between 5am and 1am.

THE PROVINCES

If you decide against Paris, in the provinces the choice of where to go is defined by the attractions of a particular region, as much as by a desire to learn. Would you rather polish pronouns in St Malo or paint pictures in Antibes? The sights will be as much a temptation as the school. If you want to paint the sea it is obvious that you won't go to the Auvergne, but will the Atlantic or the Mediterranean inspire you? The weather may influence your perception of the area.

In foodie terms the cuisine taught in Provence will be very different to that taught in Burgundy. The former is renowned for *pistou* (a paste of olive oil, basil and garlic) and *aïoli* (a type of garlic mayonnaise); the latter region makes use of the red wines produced there, in dishes such as *boeuf bourguignon* and *coq au vin*. The Loire valley, on the other hand, has the appeal of the best wines and arguably the purest French accent. However, it may not be the local food that is of most interest; the added attraction may be the opportunity to participate in outdoor activities, such as surfing out of hours, in towns such as Biarritz, which hosts an annual surf festival. Skiers will want to have close proximity to the Alps, with its dramatic landscapes. Those with a penchant for history may prefer areas such as Brittany, which is rich in archaeological sites.

Another consideration to bear in mind is price. Once you head away from popular tourist spots and the capital into the countryside and hinterland,

James Heath

living expenses fall dramatically and it is much more likely that you will learn and/or practice your language skills away from all the other foreigners. Ultimately, the decision to choose Paris, Lyon or Rennes instead of Provence, Burgundy or Picardy will be based on the courses available and personal preference.

The North-East

This area includes the most heavily industrialised parts of the country, so that the attractions for visitors are somewhat limited; however, this is where the channel ports are located, so it is likely that at one point or another most people will pass through this region. Several of the battles through-out history have occurred here, namely the Battle of the Somme during the First World War, and even further back in time, skirmishes between the English and the French at Agincourt and Crécy. Boulogne is perhaps one of the nicer towns in the region, with plenty of fresh food and seafood on offer. Lille is the largest city in the north and is a

sprawl of heavy industrial plants; it suffers from poverty and racial conflict, although the heart of the city is more prosperous.

Alsace has its own distinct cuisine, with a strong German influence, best exemplified by *choucroute* (sauerkraut – pickled cabbage with meat added). Onions are a favoured ingredient. Typical wines from the area are white wines such as Riesling, and other alcoholic drinks produced locally include fruit brandies such as Kirsch, made from cherries. All these local delights may mean that you long for some fresh air and exercise; a good place to visit would be Franche-Comté and the Jura mountains, where there are large areas of lake and woodland. It is also possible to practice *ski du fond* here (cross-country skiing).

The North-West

Until the sixteenth century, Brittany remained independent from France; now it is a criminal offence to support Breton nationalism, although people

James Heath

still tend to view France as a separate entity somehow. This is the place to go for *crêpes* and *galettes* (the savoury version). There is also a fantastic array of seafood. The capital of Brittany is Rennes, which was damaged by fire in 1720 and had to subsequently be rebuilt. The Breton coastline is known as the Côte de Granit Rose, because of the pink granite boulders in the sea.

Nantes, originally the capital of Brittany, is supposedly a part of the Pays du Loire rather than Brittany, but its inhabitants still consider themselves affiliated to the latter. The fortunes of this city were obtained through the slave trade, shipbuilding, and in modern times, industrial growth. The Loire river crosses the city in five channels. The land between Nantes and the coast mainly consists of marshes; the smaller towns in the area have high rates of unemployment and are economically depressed.

The South-East

Geographically this region boasts the southern Alps as well as the Rhône Valley, where there are Roman cities such as Orange. However, having the Rhône within the region is a dubious boast, as water from the river is used to cool two nuclear power stations, and contains large amounts of industrial effluent. The region has plenty of charm in other respects though (such as the Côte d'Azur), so much so that it might be a dilemma to prioritise which parts of it to visit.

The second largest city in France, Lyon, is located in this region, and has hundreds of bars and restaurants to visit. The nightlife is good, whether your taste encompasses clubs, film, opera, jazz or theatre. In Provence huge quantities of wine are produced, originating from the First World War when the vineyards were planted to meet the demands of soldiers. The town of Orange has a memorable Roman theatre, with two important music festivals held in the summertime. There is also the medieval town of Avignon to visit, regarded as one of the major artistic centres of France; it tends to get extremely busy in the summer. Those who are more bloodthirsty can go to Arles and the Camargue to watch a bullfight; these differ from the Spanish events in that it is the bullfighters rather than the bull itself which gets hurt. In fact, before the bull retires it parades around the arena while people throw flowers.

The South-West

The Pyrenees are located here, the less developed cousin of the Alps. They range from the Basque-speaking west to the Catalan East; hikers can enjoy walks all the way from the Atlantic coast to the Mediterranean. The season for walking is from mid-June to September; at other times the ground will be covered in snow. The Basque people of this area share a common language with their Spanish neighbours, Euskera, and have a clear sense of separate identity. Euskera is of interest to linguists, because it is totally unrelated to other European languages, the majority of which are thought to have evolved from a language termed 'proto-Indo-European'. The game 'pelota' is played here, which is similar to squash but possibly even more dangerous, as players hit a hard leather-covered ball against a high wall.

The South-West is also the homeland of *foie gras* and *truffes* (truffles). Both luxury foods, they are prized the world over. The region produces good-quality red and white wine, so visitors are unlikely to be subjected to meagre fare.

THE FRENCH

Lifestyle

Those who have not visited France before may be somewhat taken aback when complete strangers kiss them on the cheeks on first meeting them. However, this is traditional French etiquette when greeting one another, and can in fact eliminate the awkward pauses that may happen in Britain, for example, in that moment of indecision of whether or not to proffer a hand to shake. Be warned that you may have to kiss people in this manner up to four times before the conversation can proceed...

Sex

The French are renowned for their liberal attitude towards sex, despite the fact that Catholicism is the predominant religion. The legal age of consent for gay people is 15. Nudity is not frowned on; expect to see topless women on the beaches, and even on television gameshows during prime-time television.

Leisure and Culture

• Television, as in England and the USA, is a very popular national pastime in France. There are four national public television channels: France 2, France 3, Arte and La Cinquième (educational channel). There are also three national private channels: TF1, M6 and Canal Plus (which supports the French film industry), and increasingly a profusion of satellite channels.

• French cinema is perceived as active and innovative. Only Hollywood produces more films annually than France. The French are proud of their films, and perhaps justifiably so. Certainly their films tend to have a directorial style that is more stylish than their competitors. France has produced successful film actors such as Bridgitte Bardot, Juliet Binoche, Gerard Depardieu, Jean Reno, Sophie Marceau, and directors such as Luc Besson and Jean-Paul Rappencau.

• France is host to over 250 music, dance and drama festivals per year. Teaching in these fields has increased over the past few years. Classical music has a very rich heritage, with 20th-century giants such as Claude Débussy, Maurice Ravel, Francis Poulenc, Oliver Messiaen and Pierre Boulez to boast of. Jazz is also very popular here and has been moulded

James Heath

The Louvre

into a distinctively French sound by musicians such as Django Reinhardt and Stéphane Grapelli (whose band was called 'Le Hot Club de Paris'). Popular music in France is still dominated by the American and the British bands, but the best of French pop resides in the 'alternative' sector, with strong Latin American and African influences.

• It's all very well eating delicious French food and drinking great wines, but if you want to be authentically French you'll need to be reading a French newspaper as well. Le Monde is a daily, serious, paper, Le Figaro is a right-wing competitor, while L'Humanité and Libération, as you can guess from the titles, aspire to more left-wing political visions. If this is all a bit serious-sounding, then just give in and buy the weekly Paris-Match, for the kind of light gossip about royals and the stars that you would find in Hello! magazine in Britain.

• France houses around 1,200 museums, drawing tens of millions of visitors each year. The Louvre, Versailles and the Musée d'Orsay alone welcome nearly 12 million people annually. Other less well-known museums, such as the Museum of Jewish History in Paris, are nevertheless excellent. Most cities outside Paris have at least one museum. In addition, more than 1,400 monuments are open to the public, the Eiffel Tower being the most popular attraction with 5.2 million visitors a year. Some 38,000 buildings are classified as historical monuments and are protected by the Ministry of Culture.

• The French National anthem is the 'Marseillaise', composed in Strasbourg in 1792, originally known as the 'Battle Hymn of the Army of the Rhine', it became the national anthem on July 14 1795. The motto of the French Republic is "Liberty, Equality, Fraternity", originating from the revolutionary ideals of 1789.

Religion

France is a secular state with the following representation of religious faiths: 81.4 per cent Catholics, 6.9 per cent Moslem, 1.6 per cent Protestant, 1.3 per cent Jewish, 0.7 per cent Buddhist, 0.3 per cent Orthodox, 8.1 per cent Other. You can sample the Catholic culture of France by attending a religious feast day.

Education

The French take education very seriously, spending in the region of £60 billion a year, 7.4 per cent of GDP and 37.2 per cent of the national budget. This represents about £1,000 for each resident in France and over £4,000 per pupil or student.

Sport

Whether it's the thrill of a capacity football stadium or the peaceful pace of a local *boules* contest, France will have something to offer you whatever your sporting interests.

• The most famous sporting event in France is probably the *Tour de France*, taking place in July, and broadcast across the world.

• Rugby and Football are also taken very seriously.

• If you like to participate rather than watch, then you can try boules for yourself, or take to the mountains for that expensive but rewarding ski-trip.

• Basketball is very popular in France and most municipal sports centres have a court.

• There are also plenty of swimming pools in the larger towns and cities.

Shopping

This is the land from which the word '*chic*' originated, and French fashion houses such as Chanel and Dior continue to go from strength to strength. The famous couturiers are to be found in rue du Faubourg-St-Honoré, avenue François 1er and avenue Victor Hugo. One surprise is that British designers (such as Stella McCartney and Steve McQueen) currently have a strong influence within the French fashion world. French women are meticulous about their appearance, priding themselves on dressing in smart and elegant clothes, with a touch of *parfum* and a hint of jewellery. The major department stores are *Galeries Lafayette* and *Au Printemps*. In January and July there are sales, with up to forty percent discounts on designer clothes.

For food shopping, the cheapest places are inevitably the local supermarkets, although fresh bread should be bought each day from the *boulangerie*, in typical French fashion. Quality cured meats and *paté* can be bought from a *charcuterie*, while a vast array of appetising cakes and pastries are available from *pâtisseries*.

Du pain...

The French are as fastidious about their food as about their fashion. From the extremely elaborate *haute cuisine* of the 19th Century, best represented in the food of Chef Escoffier, to the considerably less rich *nouvelle cuisine* which became trendy in the 1970s, food has always been a topic of hot discussion. Some French gastronomic habits may appear a little unusual to the unaccustomed, who are used to viewing snails as threats to the garden rather than the digestion, and whose experience of frogs is strictly limited to watching Kermit on the TV. However, put aside your cultural prejudices and you will discover a whole new world out there in terms of taste sensations.

Typically French products number more than the two most stereotypical ones just outlined; it is thanks to the French that we have the now ubiquitous *croissant*, as well as *pain au chocolat, baguettes, brioche, crêpes, paté de foie gras, petits fours....* Meals in general are not something to be rushed, and what better way to enjoy food than to send it on its way with several glasses of French wine.

Du vin...

Winemaking in France dates back to before the birth of the Roman Empire. There are several wine-producing regions in France, each with its own characteristic product, to be savoured with a particular kind of food. Among the most famous are Bordeaux, Burgundy, Champagne, (for whose golden bubbles we owe thanks to Dom Perignon, the first to produce the product of the same name. He used three varieties of grape and allowed the liquid to ferment in the bottle; for this he had to use especially strong glass bottles, imported from Newcastle) as well as Côtes du Rhone (where Beaujolais comes from). The type of grape and the climate of the area will influence the flavour and the quality of the finished product, which can vary from year to year. This is why the vintage of the wine is so important (the year in which the grapes from which it is made were harvested). On a wine label, also look at the name of the wine region; the more specific this is, the better the wine will be. The words 'Grand Cru'/ 'Premier Cru' denote the best wines. Another thing to look out for is the name of the property or producer of the wine (for example, Château/Domain/ Clos). The *appellation d'origine contrôlée* controls the amount of wine that a particular area can produce.

Et le fin...

This chapter can only offer a mere taster of a country which is rich in culture, history and refinements. From snow-capped Alps and chocolate box villages, to the beaches such as Cannes, (where the Hollywood Greats can strut their stuff); from film festivals to art festivals... there's something that should appeal to everyone. Follow in the footsteps of the great French artists (Monet, Renoir, to name the most obvious), or the great French philosophers (Jean-Paul Sartre, Rousseau, Voltaire), walk in the Tuileries or the Champs Élysées...or simply sit in a cafe and watch the world go by.

The French Education System

COURSES AVAILABLE FOR FOREIGNERS

Holiday courses and language schools are obviously designed with tourists in mind. However, there are several other options, which enable you to learn a new skill and improve your French. Enrol in a classic Parisian *atelier* for a week and paint. Attend a cooking class in a country hotel for a weekend and sharpen your knives and your knowledge. Or spend a year in a professional school, redirecting an existing career or training for a new one, whilst adding proficiency in a foreign language to your CV. Nearly every sector of French education is open to foreigners, depending on qualifications, experience and linguistic ability. Whether you want to follow a first degree, transfer for a year, or study for a Master's, there are academic or professional routes, in universities, art schools and vocational institutions. Exceptions include the *Grandes Ecoles*, which are practically closed to non-French applicants. There are also specific courses designed with international students in mind (for example, Insead's MBA; the nine-month bilingual or English programmes at the Ritz, ECSF and Cordon Bleu cooking schools; the one-year diplomas at Sciences Po).

STUDYING FOR A DEGREE IN FRANCE

France is one of the few Western countries which upholds the right of free education for all. It has a very complicated system of higher education that mirrors the different branches that are established after compulsory schooling. The choice of *baccalauréat*, the exam which is passed at the end of secondary education, determines the route a pupil will follow, whether vocational or academic. Post-18 further education is divided into public and private sectors, non-competitive entry and competitive entry. Universities are open to everyone with a *baccalauréat (bac)* or equivalent qualification. Almost every other school requires applicants to pass an entrance exam in addition to the *bac*. As a general rule, the cheaper the school and the easier it is to get in, the bigger the student intake, and consequently the lower the quality of teaching is likely to be. There are many public schools (especially in the art sector) which are practically free, but have a limited intake and a stringent selection procedure. Private schools have small intakes, tough entrance exams and, relatively speaking, expensive fees. The university sector is a veritable eye-opener for anyone used to the British or North American systems: huge classes; no social structure; practically non-existent student-teacher contact. However, what can you expect for the paltry sum of 500FF-1000FF per year?

What to Expect

Anglo-Saxon students used to leaving home for university will be surprised to discover that many university-age students in France live with their parents or, failing that, commute home every weekend. Universities do not offer the sort of entertainment or support networks found in the UK or America. Teaching is more impersonal due to much larger intakes, bigger lecture classes, less engagement between lecturer-student, and limited student participation. There is a greater reliance on exams, rather than continuous assessment, especially oral exams. For more detailed information about the university sector in France, see the 'Universities' chapter.

LANGUAGE SCHOOLS

Certificates

For those wanting to learn the French language, you need to consider whether what you want is an attendance certificate, or a Masters in FLE. FLE (*Français Langue Étrangère*) is an acronym you will encounter once you enter professional territory, but for those considering a summer course or a short

sabbatical it is only of interest for comparing the qualifications of the school's teachers. Most schools will offer in-house, non-examination certificates at the end of short courses. These provide varying degrees of information, from attendance to detailed breakdowns of a student's progress. Universities offer self-regulated examinations, either at the end of a semester or an academic year. These are recognised, especially in the ADCUEFE network, by similar institutions but, with the possible exception of those offered by the Sorbonne, they have no national or international recognition. The DELF (*Diplôme d'Étude de Langue Française*), DALF (*Diplôme Approfondi de Langue Française*), and the CCIP (*Diplômes de la Chambre de Commerce et d'Industrie de Paris*) are widely available national qualifications. The Alliance Française is the only language school which offers examinations recognised by ALTE, a European association which determines

the transferability of cross-cultural qualifications. It is worth checking whether a centre can administer external exams as well as prepare them, whether exam fees are included in the price, and whether the school is responsible for putting students forward.

Professional Associations

The ADCUEFE (*Association des Centres Universitaires d'Études Françaises pour Etrangers*) regroups 25 of the university centres and aims to ensure that the various diplomas on offer are all of an equivalent national standard which is recognised by all the members. Its priority is retaining and improving teaching quality.

SOUFFLE and the PETIT GUIDE are associations, like ADCUEFE, which offer an externally determined guarantee of quality. SOUFFLE, like the British association ARELS, is one of the founders of ELITE (European Federation of Associations for Teaching of Mother Tongues to Foreign Students) which imposes a charter of quality on all its members. Schools are checked at least once every five years by external examiners and each institution must satisfy certain requirements in terms of teaching and facilities in order to continue/gain membership. 18 centres in France meet SOUFFLE's requirements. Details can be obtained from the following address:

Jean Petrissans, SOUFFLE,
B. P. 133, 83957 La Garde cedex,
France
Tel: +33 4 94 21 20 92
Fax: +33 4 94 21 22 17
Web: www.mm-soft.fr.net/raw/souffle
Email: souffle@toulon.pacwan.net.

The PETIT GUIDE offers a similar professional guarantee but includes a greater number of schools. Researchers visit each school to determine the quality of the schools' teaching and facilities in order to provide comprehensive and comparable descriptions of each. The GUIDE is free of charge and written in five languages: English, French, German, Spanish and Japanese.

PETIT GUIDE, Ulysse
Communication, 21 avenue du professeur Grasset 34093, Montpellier cedex 5, France
Tel: +33 4 67 91 70 00
Fax: +33 4 67 91 70 01
Web: www.fle.fr
Email: ulys@fle.fr.

The DELF and DALF

Created by the Ministry of Education in 1985 (modified in 1992) the DELF (1st level) and the DALF (2nd level) are official national qualifications. A DALF certifies a level of French that allows a student to enter a French university without passing a language test.

Chambre de Commerce et d'Industrie de Paris (CCIP)

The widely-recognised CCIP exams test a student's aptitude in using French for professional purposes. They assume a good knowledge of the language and of the socio-economic culture as well as an understanding of France in general. Seven exams are available: three in business French (eg Practical Certificate of Commercial French) and four in professional French (eg French for Tourism; Legal French). Written tests are examined in Paris but oral tests can be taken in provincial centres.

Alliance Française

The AF offers four diplomas in General French, including Basic Practical French (CEFP) and the Superior Diploma in Modern French Studies, and three in specialised domains, including the Diploma in Business Translation and the Practical Certificate in Translation. The exams take place in AF schools worldwide.

The Sorbonne exams at the CCF are available both within the University and in several of the larger language schools. They are internally written and examined but internationally recognised.

Professorat

The AF and the Sorbonne offer one-year courses in Francais Langue Étrangère for future French teachers. The two centres' examinations are recognised as equivalent. The AF course is open to French and international students; prospective applicants need a qualification equivalent to the *baccalauréat* and must pass an entrance exam in French. Graduates of this course are not guaranteed employment but it is very likely that they will be offered a paid teaching practice in one of the Alliance's schools. It is also possible to take this course by correspondence. Shorter refresher courses, lasting from one week to one month, are available at the Alliance and in many of the schools listed.

The Institut Français

The Institut Français was set up at the beginning of the 20th century with the aim of promoting the language and culture of France throughout the world. There are now around 150 branches of the Institut spread around the globe. The Institut Français runs language courses, all conducted in French, and taught by experienced native French speakers. Other courses, for example, French current affairs, philosophy, history, and business studies are sometimes offered, although this varies from country to country. Some Instituts around the world produce in-house publications exploring topics of social and cultural interest relating to France. 'Tandem', a magazine written at the London branch, for example, is available at the well-resourced library which you can browse through at your leisure. Newspapers, magazines, literature and specialist books on topics such as philosophy or politics are also available there. There are books on a huge range of subjects in both English and French.

ENGLAND
Cultural Centre (library and cinema)
17 Queensbury Place
London
SW7 2DT

Language Centre
14 Cromwell Place
London
SW7 2DT

HOLLAND
Vijzelgracht 2a
NL – 1017 HR Amsterdam

JAPAN
15 Ichigaya Funagawara-Chô
Shinjuku-Ku
Tokyo 162

SCOTLAND
Centre Culturel et de Coopération Linguistique
13 Randolph Crescent
Edinburgh
EH3 7TT

SOUTH AFRICA:
6 Wolhuter Street
Market Theatre Precinct
PO Box 542, Newton 2113
Johannesbourg

USA
22 East 60th Street
NY 10022

Applying to Study

LANGUAGE

Is a good knowledge of French necessary?

Most prospective students will ask 'how much French do I need?' Obviously, language schools are open to everyone, from beginners to those with more advanced knowledge, but what about cookery courses or wine tastings, art studios or business schools? Each institution differs, depending on its size and status, usual intake and the type of course offered. Schools with a high intake of international students and holidaymakers will generally teach in more than one language or even exclusively in English, irrespective of size. Most cooking institutes, business schools and summer art courses fall into this category. Wine-tastings and classes (unless they are connected to an established cooking course) tend to be taught in French; there are some available, (those aimed at tourists or temporary visitors) where the staff can organise translators or interpreters if necessary. Art *ateliers* are interested in your use of a pencil, not a pronoun, and the very brave could start a class with no French at all. However, for the sake of survival, a minimum of niceties and conversation would help, if only to understand how much you are paying to enrol.

For those considering an international school, for a one-year fashion design course or a three-month stage make-up certificate, the same rules apply. French isn't absolutely necessary – most of these institutions regularly accept students who can barely say *bonjour* – but the investment in time and money that you are making means that you may as well profit from it as much as possible, by attempting to acquire some vocabulary at least.

Students applying to the French formal education system have to prove their level of French before their application will be considered. Transfer students, spending a year or Junior year abroad, will not have to do this, although it is obvious that if you're not a language student and not planning to enrol full-time in a language school, then the utility of enrolling in the university sector is questionable.

Levels of French

Each school entry in the Guide includes, where relevant, the level of French required. Be aware that schools that have little experience of accepting foreigners will also have little experience of gauging the linguistic skills necessary for following a course. Please refer to the key, for a further explanation of the terminology within the guide, which is used to denote the level of French required.

APPLYING AND ENROLLING

Applications and enrolment will be determined by the type of course. Most language schools will enrol a student on Friday and start teaching them on Monday (although this is generally not

Key to the terminology used to denote level of French required

None

Nada, *rien*, nothing. This is probably more difficult to achieve than fluency. How many anglophones have never eaten in a 'restaurant', attended a 'reunion' or 'rendez-vous', or wished their friends a 'bon voyage'? French words and syntax pepper the English language, and the more aware you are of this as a complete beginner, the less daunting the task might appear. You already know some vocabulary, now it's merely a question of grammar and accent... *bonne chance*.

Basic

The 'yes' and 'nos', 'hellos' and 'goodbyes', 'how much is... ? 'and 'where is... ?' level of language. The ability to ask a question but maybe not to understand the response. Numbers from one to three, food stuffs, drinks and dates still seem like lists to the student at this level, more than language to be used. Limited, need-to know tourist/infor-mation seeking/survival requests vocabulary. No awareness of what a tense is, let alone that there are different ones.

Conversational

The ability to ask a question, understand the response and have enough knowledge of vocabulary and grammar to construct a few more questions, a few more answers and a sub-clause or two for good measure. Numbers and dates, verbs and nouns are integral to the learner's comprehension, not rote tables to be remembered. Can move a conversation from 'where' and 'what' to 'why' and 'which'. Basic knowledge of present and past tenses.

Intermediate

The facility to move between tenses and sentence structures. Wide, non-tourist, non-information-centred vocabulary. Comfortable conversing in the present, imperfect and future tenses, using all parts of the language, including adjectives, pronouns and participles. Aware of the different formulaic patterns of French etiquette.

A level/post-secondary education

A very specific designation used in those instances where an official, recognised period of language study is expected for the application to be considered. Post-secondary implies that the student has passed the final high school/secondary diploma in their home country. It also suggests a comprehensive grammatical and theoretical knowledge, more than practical, oral abilities.

Advanced

The ability and facility to use all parts of the language including difficult tenses, the subjunctive and idioms. Extensive vocabulary, covering everything from information to insight. Comfortable with French in all social and professional situations and with the cultural connotations of the language. Likely to have studied French culture in depth either as a visitor or student.

Fluent

Near-native competence and com-prehension. Switching between mother tongue and foreign language without difficulty. May have gaps in vocabulary, grammar and accent but none which prove obstacles to communication.

the case for beginners' classes, which tend to start once a month or once every two weeks). Summer schools will fill up much faster than language courses throughout the academic year, and early enrolment (at least a month in advance) is recommended. Cooking and painting courses will tend to fill up quickly in holiday periods and most of these have a simple application procedure, filling in a form and, of course, sending a deposit cheque.

Academic courses will run on a much stricter schedule. University admission for foreigners begins in November of the preceding year. Art schools begin the application procedure for first-time students, or transfers, in January. Extremely competitive programmes such as Insead's MBA and Sciences Po's *certificat* have complicated procedures

and high standards: applicants are advised to start as early as possible. The nine-month cooking programmes have selection procedures but applicants are more likely to be turned away for lack of space. Again, apply early.

UNIVERSITIES: THE APPLICATION PROCESS

First year students

French universities are open to international applicants with a qualification equivalent to the *baccalauréat* (ie. any final secondary exam which allows university entry in the student's home country) and a recognised level of French. Prospective candidates must request an application dossier between November 15th and the January 15th, and return it by January 31st. These are available from the chosen university, or the Cultural Services of the French Embassy in the home country. Information requested will include a copy of the diploma certificate and its translation (done by an official, legally recognised, service) and proof of the applicant's ability in French. The officially-recognised test of French language takes place in embassies worldwide in mid-February. This is mandatory for anyone without demonstrable proof of their ability in the language. Candidates can only apply to one university. If they are not accepted in the institution of choice, they can request a dispensation (from the Ministry of Education before July 10) to apply to another university.

Visa status must be considered when applying. Candidates already residing in France with a valid 12-month visa/*carte de*

John James

séjour can apply direct to the University. Candidates residing abroad, or in France without the required visa, must apply through the Cultural Service of the French Embassy in their home country. Prospective students should note that since 1986 it is impossible to change a short tourist visa into a long-stay visa without returning to one's home country.

Second and third-year students/postgraduates

For those who have already completed a degree in their home country and who wish to follow another in France, the procedure is similar. Students entering into the *deuxième cycle* will be considered on the basis of their motivation and qualifications, and can only enrol in a subject they have already studied. Entrants into the *troisième cycle* will be accepted if their qualifications are judged equivalent to the French *maîtrise* in the same subject. Application packs must be requested between March 1 and April 30 and returned by May 15. The following should accompany each application:

1 Birth certificate
2 Secondary education final certificate
3 University degree certificate; university transcript (with list of subjects studied and grades received)
4 Certificate confirming that the diplomas attained equip the student to enrol in the chosen course

DEA students need to include an outline of a research project. All documents should be accompanied by an official translation into French.

Grandes Écoles

The *grandes* are of great interest to the French, but of limited interest to foreigners. They are competitive entry, elite public sector schools which are the Gallic equivalent to Oxford and Cambridge, or Harvard and Yale. In order to gain entry, prospective students spend two years in CPGE (Classes Préparatoires aux Grandes Écoles) cramming and preparing the entrance exam. The future, both educational and professional, is assured for those who pass. Those who fail tend to enrol in universities or less-competitive schools. Very few foreigners are accepted, since the *écoles* are seen as the training ground for the next generation of France's public and private sector elite.

CROUS: Centre Regional des Oeuvres Universitaires

The CROUS crops up across France in every university city. It is a publicly (read poorly) funded organisation which is part of the Ministry of National Education, and it is the closest approximation to British or American student associations.

THE PRIVATE SECTOR

There are two Ministry-designated categories of private schools, differentiated by the type of teaching. The *établissement privé d'enseignement supérieur libre* covers everything from language schools to art studios. Those designated under this term can have a convention with a university to offer and examine national diplomas. It is a designation to look out for when considering any type of private school. The *établissements privés d'enseignement technique* which offer professional, technical education, are legalised and regulated by national standards. They can benefit from state recognition of their diplomas.

Arriving in France

IMMIGRATION, VISAS AND CARTES DE SEJOURS

EU nationals are entitled to live and work in France without a visa although those planning to stay for over three months, whether as a student or employee, need to obtain a *carte de séjour* (resident's permit), easily the most irritating and time-consuming process new arrivals will have to face.

Take a photocopy of every original. Everything must be in French and you will need to provide officially-recognised translations of all foreign paperwork. Ask the local town hall for a list of official translators or check whether your consulate has one. The British Consul in Paris provides a limited service. Don't be shocked when two lines of French that you could have written yourself cost 80FF. Your own translation might be just as good but without the all-important *tampon*, the official rubber stamp of whichever service you are using, it will mean nothing to a French bureaucrat.

Once you have amassed all this information, find out where you are supposed to go. In Paris there is a special office at:

13 rue Miollis, 75015 Paris
Nearest Station: (Métro) Cambronne or Ségur

which is open from 8H30-16H30 Monday to Friday and 8H30-16H00

on Friday. Outside this office there is an ominous piece of paper stuck to the door, with an arrow signalling the direction of the queue...expect to wait, especially at the beginning of the academic year. Some warn of four-five hour waits and miserable staff, and although this is more likely than not, it is also possible that you will be the only person there and that you encounter someone charming. It might take six

The nearest **airports** to Paris are **Roissy Charles de Gaulle** (the main airport), and **Orly** (which also receives transatlantic flights). Both can be reached from the city in about 30mins, by bus/train/taxi.

Eurostar operate **13 trains** daily from London Waterloo to Paris Gare du Nord, and the journey takes three and a half hours. From London to Lille the journey is two hours, and there are seven trains a day. For the latest information, tel: 0990 186 186.

Travel by **hovercraft** and train between London and Paris takes six hours, while travel by **ferry** and train between these two cities takes seven to eight hours. For Continental Rail Enquiries, tel: 0990 848 848.

OBTAINING A CARTE DE SÉJOUR

EU Nationals

Take the following documents, plus a photocopy of each, to the local mairie (town hall) or *préfecture de police* (police headquarters):

1 valid passport

2 marriage certificate (if your marital status has changed in relation to your passport or your maiden name does not appear on your passport)

3 proof of residence in France (EDF/GDF bills work; a lease does not). If you are renting a room ask the landlady/lord to provide you with a copy of a bill, a letter confirming the rental of the room and a photocopy of his/her *carte d'identité* (identity card) or resident's permit, if not a French national. For those staying in university residences or foyers a letter from the director is required.

4 three black-and-white passport photos

5 proof of studies (certificate of enrolment) or contract of employment

6 E111 (document giving EU nationals the right to benefit from French social security)

Non EU nationals

All of the above, plus the following

1 a long-stay student visa (see below)

2 proof of financial resources (grant certificate; bank statement detailing regular support from a foreign source, such as parents or scholarship or documentation proving a French sponsor's support–2500FF per month is considered adequate)

3 proof of medical insurance

4 a work permit (if intending to work) obtained in the country of origin

5 either a stamped, self-addressed envelope or a *timbre fiscal* (available at post offices) – check with the police or town hall where you are living. In Paris applicants must provide a 200FF *timbre fiscal*.

Au pairs will need to provide a copy of a work contract or a letter from the family, stamped by the:

Service de la Main d'Œuvre Etrangere, 127 bd de la Villette, 75483 Paris Cedex 10

Nearest Station: (Métro) Jaurès.

Check with the local town hall outside Paris to find out where to go.

months for the permit to arrive but sometimes it takes six days. Such is the unpredictability of French bureaucracy. Expect to be confounded and you will find it much easier to negotiate; you may even be pleasantly surprised.

Non EU Visas

Students and workers from outside the EU must obtain a *visa de long séjour* before arriving in France. Apply at a French consulate in your country of origin before departure. You must apply for a resident's permit within eight days of arriving in France.

See *p33* for a list of embassy addresses, or write to the Ministère des Affaires Étrangères information centre for a list of Consular addresses:

Ministère des Affaires Étrangères 34 rue La Perouse 75116 Paris Tel: +33 140 66 60 79

TRAVEL TIPS

Before leaving home, make sure that you make a separate record of credit card and charge card numbers, as well as of your travellers cheques and airline tickets. Leave this copy at home, and in the event of having to cancel one or more of these items because of theft, this will make life a lot simpler.

It is possible to change money into French currency (francs and centimes: 1 franc=100 centimes) at the airport, although the rates might not be the most favourable available.

You may require further advice about the area you are visiting, in which case look for the 'I' sign at stations and airports, which is usually used to indicate the local tourist information office.

If you are not going to be in one place long enough to have an address, you can receive mail at the main post office

David Plevsky

in a city. It must be directed as follows: Name, Poste Restante, City, Country.

Paris is likely to be a port of call at some point during your stay, in which case you may wish to purchase a 'Paris Visite' card, which entitles you to unlimited travel in Paris by bus and Metro. It also allows for travel within the greater Paris region (such as to Versailles, Disneyland Paris, Orly/Charles de Gaulle airports) by RER express system or SNCF lines, zones one to five. There are four options as to the type of card (ie how long it is valid for):

1 Two consecutive days
2 Two consecutive days and one flexible day
3 Two consecutive days and two flexible days
4 Two consecutive days and three flexible days

The card may also entitle you to up to 40 per cent off the entrance fees to some of the museums and art galleries.

Medical and Emergencies
Emergencies
In an emergency you can call one of the following:

Police: 17
Ambulance (SAMU): 15
Fire Brigade (Sapeurs Pompiers): 18

It is worth noting that in the case of serious medical emergencies the Sapeurs Pompiers are trained paramedics and not the SAMU.

SOS Help is an English language helpline open from 3pm to 11pm every day. A team of trained listeners is available to lend an ear and advise in times of crisis.

Medical
When you're feeling under the weather, the pharmacy should be your first port of call as French pharmacists are highly

Victoria Davies/Benoît Besnard

trained and qualified to deal with many illnesses and basic first aid. They will either be able to prescribe something for you or may advise you to consult a doctor.

Visiting a doctor or obtaining prescribed drugs does not come cheap in France. If you are an EU citizen or from a Scandinavian country you are entitled to French social security health care. It is worth remembering that this may not cover repatriation. Non-EU citizens are advised to take out medical insurance. If you are going to take part in hazardous sports it is advisable to check the policy to see what it covers. Bills for helicopter mountain rescue run to thousands of pounds!

A list of doctors can either be found in the Yellow Pages (*Pages Jaunes*) or from a pharmacy. Your place of study may also be able to recommend a local doctor. For many doctors, you do not need an appointment. Patients are seen on a first come, first served basis.

To qualify for social security refunds, you should check that the doctor is a médecin conventionné. You should be a given a *Feuille de Soins*; this is necessary for claiming costs back. Prescriptions should be taken to the pharmacy and you will have to pay for them. The little stickers (vignettes) from the medicine containers and the prescription itself need to be attached to the Feuille de Soins – the pharmacist will probably do this.

Social Security refunds can be claimed either in France or back in your home country.

Addresses of French Embassies and Consulates

ALGERIA
Embassy
chem. Gadouche
16000 Alger Hydra
Algeria
Tel: +213 2 692488
Fax: +213 2 605369

ANDORA
Embassy
38-40, Carrer-les-Canals
BP 155
Andorre-la-Vieille
Tel: +628 20809
Fax: +628 60132

ARGENTINA
Embassy
Cerrito 1399
Buenos Aires
Tel: +54 01 379 2930
Fax: +54 01 393 1235

Consulate
av. Santa-Fé 846
Buenos-Aires 1059
Argentine

AUSTRALIA
Embassy
6 Perth Avenue
Yarralumia
A.C.T. 2600
Canberra
Tel: +61 6 270 5111
Fax: +61 6 273 3193

Consulate
492, St-Kilda Road
Melbourne
Victoria 3004
Tel: +61 3 982 00921
Fax: +61 3 982 09363

Level 26
St Martins Tower
31 Market Street
Sydney NSW 2000
Tel: +61 2 261 5779
Fax: +61 2 267 2467

AUSTRIA
Embassy
Technikerstrasse 2
1040 Vienna
Austria
Tel: +43 01 505 4747
Fax: +43 01 505 639268

BELGIUM
Embassy
65, rue Ducale
1000 Brussels
Belgium
Tel: +32 2 548 8711
Fax: +32 2 512 2713

BRAZIL
Embassy
Avenida das Naçoès
lot $\mathrm{n^o}$ 4
70404 Brasilia D.F.
Tel: +55 61 312 9100
Fax: +55 61 312 9108

BULGARIA
Embassy
23, rue Oborichté
1505 Sofia
Bulgaria
Tel: +359 2 441 1172
Fax: +359 2 467 068

CAMEROON
Embassy
Plateau Atémengué
BP 1631
Yaoundé
Cameroon
Tel: +237 230463
Fax: +237 235043

CANADA
Embassy
42, Promenade Sussex
Ottawa
Ontario
K1M 2C9
Canada
Tel: +1 613 789 1795
Fax: +1 513 789 0279

Consulate
300, Highfield Place
10010
106 Street
Edmonton
Alberta
T5J3L8
Canada
Tel: +1 403 428 0232
Fax: +1 403 426 1450

250 Lutz Street
C.P. 1109
Moncton N.B.
E1C 8P6
Canada
Tel: +1 506 857 4191
Fax: +1 506 858 8169

1 Place Villa-Marie
bureau 2601
Montréal
Quebec
H3B4S3
Canada
Tel: +1 514 878 4381
Fax: +1 514 878 3981

1110, avenue des Laurentides
Québec
QC G1S 3C3
Canada
Tel: +1 418 688 0430
Fax: +1 418 688 0430

130, Bloor Street West
Suite 400

Toronto
Pntario M5S 1N5
Canada
Tel: +1 416 925 8041
Fax: +1 416 925 8233

1201-736 Granville Street
Vancouver
BC V6Z 1H9
Canada
Tel: 1 604 681 4345
Fax: 1 604 681 4287

CHILE
Embassy
avenue Condell 65
Providencia
Santiago
Chile
Tel: +56 2 225 1030
Fax: +56 2 274 1353

CHINA
Embassy
3, Est San Li Tun
Chao Yang
Peking
China
Tel: +86 01 532 1331
Fax: +86 01 532 4841

CYPRUS
Embassy
6, Pourtarchou Street
Engomi
P.O. Box 1671
Nicoise
Cyprus

DENMARK
Embassy
Kongens Nytorv 4
BP 1017
1050 Copenhagen
Denmark
Tel: +45 33 155 122
Fax: +45 33 939 752

EGYPT
Embassy
29 Guizeh avenue
BP 1777, Guizeh
Cairo, Egypt
Tel: +20 2 570 3916
Fax: +20 2 728508

ENGLAND
Embassy
58 Knightsbridge, London
SW1X 7JT
Tel: +44 171 201 1000
Fax: +44 171 201 1059

Consulate
21 Cromwell Road
London
SW7 2DQ
Tel: +44 171 838 2000
Fax: +44 171 838 2001

FINLAND
Embassy
Itaïnen Puistotie 13
00140 Helsinki
Finland
Tel: +358 0 171 521
Fax: +358 0 174 440

GERMANY
Embassy
An der Marienakapelle 3
D-53179 Bonn
Germany
Tel: +49 228 955 6000
Fax: +49 228 955 6055

Consulate
Cecilienallee 10
D-40474 Düsseldorf
Germany
Tel: +49 211 499077
Fax: +49 211 491 2240

Ludolfusstrasse 13
D-69487

Frankfurt-am-Main
Germany
Tel: +49 69 795 0960
Fax: +49 69 79509646

Pöseldorferweg 32
D-20148 Hambourg
Germany
Tel: +49 40 414 1060
Fax: +49 40 414 10660

6, Springerstrasse
D-04105 Leipzig
Germany
Tel: +49 341 51516
Fax: +49 341 51326

Kaiserstrasse 39
D-55009 Mainz
Germany
Tel: +49 6131 674603
Fax: +49 6131 616897

Möhlstrasse 5
D-81675 Munich
Germany
Tel: +49 89 475016
Fax: +49 89 470 6139

Johannisstrasse 2
D-66111 Sarrebrücken
Germany
Tel: +49 681 936750
Fax: +49 681 31028

Richard Wagner Strasse 53
D-70184 Stuttgart
Germany
Tel: +49 711 235566
Fax: +49 711 640 0458

HUNGARY
Embassy
27 Lendvay utca
1062 Budapest VI
Hungary
Tel: +36 01 132 4980

IRELAND
Embassy
36 Ailesbury Road
Ballsbridge
Dublin 4
Ireland
Tel: +353 01 260 1666
Fax: +353 01 283 0178

ISRAEL
Embassy
112, promenade Herbert-Samuel
P.O. Box 3480
63572 Tel-Aviv
Israel
Tel: +972 3 524 5371
Fax: +972 3 522 6094

Consulate
5, Paul Emile Botta Street
P.O. Box 182
91001 Jerusalem
Israel
Tel: +972 2 625 9481
Fax: +972 2 625 9178

imm. 'Migdalor'
1-3 Ben Yehuda Street
BP 26126
63801 Tel-Aviv
Israel
Tel: +972 3 510 1415
Fax: +972 3 510 4370

37 Hagefen Street
P.O. Box 9539
35053 Haifa
Israel
Tel: +972 4 513111
Fax: +972 4 513931

ITALY
Embassy
67, piazza Farnese
00186 Rome
Tel: +39 6 686 011
Fax: +39 6 686 01360

Consulates
251 via Giulia
00186 Rome
Italy
Tel: +39 6 6860 6437
Fax: +39 6 6860 1260

Piazza Ognissanti 2
50123 Florence
Italy
Tel: +39 55 230 2556
Fax: +39 55 230 2551

Via della Moscova 12
20121 Milan
Italy
Tel: +39 2 655 9141
Fax: +39 2 6559 1344

2, piazza della Repubblica
80122 Naples
Italy
Tel: +39 81 761 2275
Fax: +39 81 761 4883

8, via Bogino
10123 Turin
Italy
Tel: +39 11 835 252
Fax: +39 11 839 5859

20, via Garibaldi
16124 Genoa
Italy
Tel: +39 10 200879
Fax: +39 10 299991
Palazzo Clary
Zattere 1397
30123 Venice
Italy
Tel: +39 41 522 4319
Fax: +39 41 522 1798

JAPAN
Embassy
11-44, 4 Chome
Minami-Azabu

Minato-Ku
Tokyo 106
Japan
Tel: +81 3 5420 8800
Fax: +81 3 5420 8847

LUXEMBOURG
Embassy
9 bd Prince-Henri
BP 359
L. 2013 Luxembourg
Tel: +35 2 475 5881
Fax: +35 2 475 58827

MEXICO
Embassy
Havre n. 15
Mexico 06600
Tel: +52 5 533 1360
Fax: +52 5 514 7311

NORWAY
Embassy
Drammensveien 69
0271 Oslo 2
Norway
Tel: +47 2 441820
Fax: +47 2 563221

NETHERLANDS
Embassy
Smidsplein 1
2514 BT
The Hague
Tel: +31 70 356 0606
Fax: +31 70 356 2047

NEW ZEALAND
Embassy
1 Willeston Street
PO Box 1695
Wellington
New Zealand
Tel: +64 4 472 0200
Fax: +64 4 472 5887

PERU
Embassy
avenida Arequipa
San Isidro
CC 607
Lima, Peru
Tel: +51 1 221 7837
Fax: +51 1 421 3693

POLAND
Embassy
1 Piekna Road
00477 Warsaw
Poland
Tel: +48 2 628 8400
Fax: +48 3 912 0326

PORTUGAL
Embassy
Rua Santos o Velho n.5
1293 Lisbonne codex
Portugal
Tel: +351 1 608 121
Fax: +351 1 395 2539

Consulate
123, Calçada Marques-de-Abrantes
Lisbonne 1200
Portugal
Tel: +351 1 608131
Fax: +351 1 395 3981

Rua Eugénio de Castro
352-2 ét. gauche
quart. Foco
4100 Porto, Portugal
Tel: +351 2 694 805
Fax: +351 2 694 806

RUSSIA
Embassy
43 Ulitsa Dimitrova
Moscow
Russia
Tel: +7 095 236 0003
Fax: +7 095 237 1956

Consulate
43, Ulitsa Dimitrova
Moscow
Russia
Tel: +7 095 236 0003

15 quai Moika
St Petersburg
Russia
Tel: +7 812 312 1130
Fax: +7 812 312 7283

SOUTH AFRICA
Embassy
1009 Main Tower
Cape Town Center
Heerengracht
8001 Cape Town
South Africa
Tel: +27 21 212050
Fax: +27 21 261996

807, George Avenue
Arcadia
Pretoria 0083
South Africa
Tel: +27 12 435564
Fax: +27 12 433481

Consulate
Carlton Center
35th Floor
Commissioner Street
PO Box 11278
Johannesburg 2000
Tel: +27 11 331 3460
Fax: +27 11 331 3497

SPAIN
Embassy
Calle de Salustiano Olozaga 9
28001 Madrid
Spain
Tel: +34 01 435 5560
Fax: +34 01 435 6655

Consulates

Calle Marques de la Ensenada 10
28004 Madrid
Spain
Tel: +34 01 319 7188
Fax: +34 01 308 6273

8, Calle Arquitecto Morell
BP 75
03003 Alicante, Spain
Tel: +34 65 921836
Fax: +34 65 921832

11, Paseo de Gracia
08007 Barcelona
Spain
Tel: +34 3 317 8150
Fax: +34 3 412 4282

26, calle Iparraguirre
48011 Bilbao, Spain
Tel: +34 4 424 9000
Fax: +34 4 423 8812

1, plaza de Santa-Cruz
41004 Seville
Spain
Tel: +34 5 422 2896
Fax: +34 5 422 7240

SWEDEN
Embassy
Narvavägen 28
PO Box 10241
10055 Stockholm
Sweden
Tel: +46 8 663 0270
Fax: +46 8 660 6290

SWITZERLAND
Embassy
46, Schosshaldenstrasse
BP 3000
3006 Berne
Switzerland
Tel: +41 31 432424
Fax: +41 31 352 0526

Consulate
Elisabethenstrasse 33
BP 255
4010 Bale
Switzerland
Tel: +41 61 272 6318
Fax: +41 61 272 6438

11, rue Imbert-Galloix
BP 1200
Geneva
Switzerland
Tel: +41 22 311 3441
Fax: +41 22 310 8339

Mühlebachstrasse 7
8008 Zurich
Switzerland
Tel: +41 01 251 8544
Fax: +41 01 252 9356

UNITED STATES OF AMERICA
Embassy
4101 Reservoir Road,
NW Washington DC 20007
USA
Tel: +01 202 944 6166
Fax: +01 202 944 6175

Consulate
4101 Reservoir Road,
N.W. Washington DC 20007
USA
Tel: +01 202 944 6166
Fax: +01 202 944 6175

285 Peachtree center avenue, suite
2800
Marquis TWO Atlanta,
GA 30303
USA
Tel: +01 404 522 4226
Fax: +01 404 880 9408

3 Commonwealth Avenue
Boston
MA 02116

USA
Tel: +01 617 266 1680
Fax: +01 617 437 1090

737 North Michigan avenue
Olympia Center
suite 2020
Chicago
IL 60611
USA
Tel: +01 312 787 5359
Fax: +01 312 664 4196

2777 Allen Parkway
Riviana Building
suite 650
Houston
TX 77019
USA
Tel: +01 713 528 2181
Fax: +01 713 528 1933

Lykes Center
300, Poydras
suite 2105
New Orleans
USA
Tel: +01 504 523 5772
Fax: +01 504 523 5725

10990, Wilshire boulevard
suite 300
Los Angeles
C A 90024
USA
Tel: +01 310 479 4426
Fax: +01 310 312 0704

1, Biscayne-Tower
suite 1710
2 south Biscayne Road
Miami
FL 33131,
USA
Tel: +01 305 372 9798
Fax: +01 305 372 9549

934 Fifth Avenue
New York
NY 10021
USA
Tel: +01 212 606 3689
Fax: +01 212 606 3620

540 Bush Street
San Francisco
CA 94108
USA
Tel: +01 415 397 4330
Fax: +01 415 433 8357

Living in France

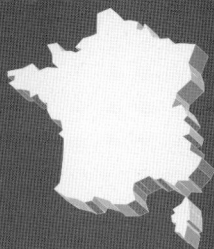

FINDING SOMEWHERE TO LIVE

In order to apply for a resident's permit you will need an address. To get one you will need:

1) lots of money (if you're lucky the owner will only request one month's rent in advance and one month's *caution* – deposit – but two month's of one or the other, or even both, is more likely)

David Pievsky

2) proof of identity

3) proof of student enrolment or employment

and, especially in Paris, lots of patience and persistence. In the provinces prices are lower and demand is less intense, but the process is still harrowing, especially for British and North American students who are used to cheap accommodation sharing with other students. In France this doesn't happen. Most students will live alone in residences and studios' or share flats with their friends from high school/sixth-form or their boyfriend/girlfriend. Students rarely live in houses, except with their parents, and the large rambling properties that Brits and North Americans are used to don't exist. Resign yourself to a studio or a small flat, a possible flat-share with an unknown person or lodging with a family.

It is likely, if you are a 'year abroad' student, that you will be arriving in September and October, when everyone is looking. Several options exist but there is no magic formula. Try CROUS *(see p28)*, the local free press (especially foreign language papers such as Fusac in Paris), agencies (although you may pay as much as one month's rent in commission) and milk any contacts you can muster. Be aware that rented accommodation is almost always unfurnished, so if you don't plan to stay long enough to acquire mugs and mattresses, look for a room in someone's house or a foyer. Check that there is a cooker (*cuisinière*) and fridge (*frigo*) since these are not standard either.

If you are renting a flat/studio, ask for a monthly *quittance de loyer* which is a receipt that serves both as a proof of payment and address. At the beginning of the lease obtain an *état des lieux* (an inventory). It will be hard enough to get your deposit back, but without an inventory it will be practically impossible. Whoever resides in a property on January 1st is liable for the *taxe d'habitation* (resident's tax, a cousin of the old UK rates system). Don't expect to get away with not paying it... the

ELECTRICITY

Remember that in France electrical equipment runs on 220-volt, 50 cycle alternating current, as compared with the United States 110-volt, 60 cycle AC.

owner will just deduct it from your *caution* if it is unpaid at the end of your lease.

The Language of Lodging

There are numerous abbreviations to look out for, when looking for somewhere to live, and numerous codes, keys and geography to master in order to get in and out of your own building (and those of your friends). When scanning advertisements it helps to know the vocabulary. A first concern will probably be the price and size. Apartments are listed in terms of square metres... don't be surprised to see ads for rooms and studios measuring as little as $10m^2$. In Paris, *chambres de bonnes* (tiny attic rooms that used to house a family's maid) are one of the cheapest lodgings available. They are also one of the most basic: expect a seventh floor narrow room with a sink and a hotplate and shared bathroom facilities on the landing. Check if the *charges*, an additional payment usually for maintenance of an apartment

building, are included (ie TTC: *toutes charges comprises*), otherwise they will be payable in addition to the rent. Different forms of accommodation include *studios* (bedsits/efficiencies), *chambres indépendantes* (room in an apartment, sometimes with separate entrance) and *appartements* (from a tiny one-bedroom to every flat you have seen in French films, lots of large, high-ceilinged rooms, wooden floors and long drifting curtains).

Other information to discover is whether the bedroom or flat is *meublé* (furnished) or *vide* (unfurnished), whether it has a *salle d'eau* (just a sink), a *w.c* (just a toilet) or a *salle de bains* (everything you'd expect plus possibly the French favourite, a *bidet*), a *coin cuisine* (kitchenette, often just a single cupboard with two rings, a tiny sink and a tiny fridge) or a *cuisine equipée* (kitchen with cooker and fridge).

Once you have found somewhere to live and you have your *coordonnées* (the term used to describe every detail of an address), learn the different parts. Many people live in *immeubles* (apartment buildings) with entry code systems and interphones. When visiting someone and when giving out your own address make sure you get all the relevant details, including (where necessary) codes for the building and the lift, staircase or building number, and floor. There is nothing more frustrating than standing in the street, without a phone box in sight, looking up at a friend's building, trying to remember the code.

MOVING IN AND OUT

If you are staying for long you will need to deal with the EDF/GDF (Electricité de France and Gaz de France) and France Télécom. Make sure you get a meter reading when you move in (this is often listed on the *droit de bail*, the lease) then take your lease to the EDF/GDF offices and ask for service. For a telephone, head to a France Télécom office, armed with a lease. Even if you don't have a socket in your new home, this can be organised within days and it is not, as might be thought, very expensive. Phones can be rented or bought. The strange brown-grey box sitting in all FT offices is a Minitel, the French forerunner to the Internet. The unit is free but you will pay for the information it accesses, such as phone directories, travel information and ubiquitous chat lines. The prefixes 3615 or 3616 that you see all over advertising hoardings /billboards throughout France refer to Minitel services.

Insurance

Whether renting a *chambre de bonne* or a *loft de grand standing* (luxury loft) the tenant is liable for fire and water

damage and thus obliged to obtain property insurance. Agents are used to this sort of request and student/short-term rates can usually be found.

BANKING

Once you have an address, you can open a bank account. Again, this process involves lots of proof of who you are, where you live, what you do and how you expect to pay for it. You will need some form of identification (it is unlikely that you will have your resident's permit if you have just arrived, so take your passport), a student card, proof of university/class enrolment or job contract and a bill with your name on it or the package from the landlord/lady listed above (EDF/GDF bills, photocopy of identity card and confirmation of your tenant status). You will want a *compte-chèques* (the UK equivalent of a current account and US equivalent of a checking account). Cheques are widely used but don't lose your book: unlike in the UK where a cheque guarantee card is a standard requirement, many shops will accept a cheque without any further ID. You may be offered a *Carte Bleue*, which is a debit card that works as a credit card in terms of flexibility, but as a cheque in terms of immediate withdrawal from your bank account. This will incur a fee (around 180FF per year) but it is extremely useful.

TELEPHONES

Whether you are going to France to study for two weeks or two years, you are likely to need a phone within the first few days. Most telephone boxes use *Télécartes* (phone cards) not coins and these are available from post offices and *tabacs*. They are

TELEPHONING ABROAD

To call France from abroad, dial 33 initially.

To call abroad from France, dial 19 initially, then the code of the country, then your number.

Cheap telephone rates operate between 9.30pm and 8.00am Monday to Friday, and 2pm until midnight on Saturdays. On Sunday there are cheap rates all day.

The phrase for a reverse charge/collect call is *téléphoner en PCV*.

cheaper to use than cash: a 50 unit card costs 40FF and a 120 unit card costs 96FF. All telephone numbers are ten digits and the first two designate the area of France called (01 numbers are Paris; 02 is North-West France; 03 is North-East; 04 is South-East; 05 is South-West). If, for any reason, a phone card is inconvenient, it is possible to phone from post offices (La Poste: look out for its big yellow signs with the blue logo). You will be allocated a booth and you pay at the end of the call. So beware going in when you feel homesick over the first few weeks. It is very easy to run up a hefty bill – France Télécom is expensive.

TRAVEL AND TRANSPORT

Metropolitan and intercity public transport, from local buses to the TGV (*Trains à Grande Vitesse*), is exceptional in France: cheap; clean and, except in winter 'strike season', reliable. The SNCF network has several different discounts for cross-country travel, available to under 25s, those travelling with children and over 60s. The timetable is divided into colour-coded days (red, blue and white) and those travelling with a discounted ticket should check if it's valid. Tickets can be bought in advance from travel agents and stations, and intercity stations have automatic touch-screen machines for reservations and purchases. Before getting on a train, and often when getting on a bus, don't forget to *'composte'* (punch) your ticket: there are orange columns in every SNCF station into which you insert the ticket, and on buses the machine is usually just beside the driver or in the middle of the bus. Unpunched tickets are not valid and you will be fined if inspected.

LOST PROPERTY

You may find that you inadvertently leave something on a bus or a train. If this happens, go to the appropriate terminal immediately; if you are unsuccessful, 48 hours later contact:

The Lost and Found Office,
Prefecture de Police,
Bureau des Objets Trouvés,
36 rue des Morillons,
75015 Paris
Tel: (1) 45 31 14 80
Nearest train: (Métro) Convention

Lost property is held here for a year and a day. If your item is there, you will be required to pay 4% of its value in

John James

order to retrieve it. The office is open weekdays, from 8.30am until 5pm (Tuesdays and Thursdays until 8pm).

INFORMATION FOR THE DISABLED

The following are two possible organisations to contact if you have special needs:

Comité National Français de Liaison pour la Readaptation des Handicapes (CNFLRH)

Point Handicap,
38, boulevard Raspail,
75007 Paris
Tel: (1) 45 48 98 90
Fax: (1) 45 48 99 21

Association des Paralyses

Delegation de Paris,
17, boulevard Auguste-Blanqui,
75013 Paris
Tel: (1) 40 78 69 00
Fax: (1) 45 89 40 57

Specially adapted taxis are available for use in Paris, but they need to be arranged the day before (tel: 0147 71 74 90/01 47 08 93 50).

OPENING HOURS

The routine hours of business in France are from 8am/9am to noon/1pm, and then 2pm/3pm to 6.30pm/7.30pm. Museums are usually open from 9am, closing for lunch at noon until 2pm, when they reopen, usually until 6pm.

Exchange Schemes and Assistantships

Anyone who wants to go to France who needs a more professional or academic structure should consider getting involved in one of the many exchanges organised in the European Economic Area. There are schemes available and organisations to administer them for students contemplating a year out, teachers considering a sabbatical, trainees and graduates.

How to Find Out

The British Council's Central Bureau for Educational Visits and Exchanges is the most useful source of information for anyone, whether a teacher, student, trainee or graduate, who is interested in working or studying abroad. It administers and provides information about assistantships, transnational work placements, teacher exchanges and European programmes. It also publishes helpful posters, such as *Ten Ways to Fill the Gap and Ten Ways to Work and Travel* (all available free of charge), and books (not free of charge!) including: *A Year Between: The Complete Guide to Taking a Year Out.*

ASSISTANTSHIPS

Many UK students will have encountered French language assistants, either at school or sixth-form college, and many modern language students will apply for an assistantship in the third year of their degree. Most universities will provide an organised programme of application and advice for their undergraduates. However, assistantships are also open to anyone who has completed at least two years of a degree course, usually in the language of the country in question but not necessarily. If you have an A-level in French, but have followed a Chemistry degree, you may still be considered. However, when applications exceed places, priority is given to 'undergraduates for whom an intercalated year abroad is a course requirement'. Eligibility is restricted to native speakers of English, aged between 20 and 30 years old, who are students at or graduates of a British University. All assistantships are administered by the Central Bureau for Educational Visits and Exchanges and graduates should contact them directly.

England and Wales

Central Bureau
10 Spring Gardens
London
SW1A 2BN
Tel: 0171 389 4004
Fax: 0171 389 4426
Email: info@centralbureau.
org.uk

Scotland

Central Bureau
3 Bruntsfield Crescent
Edinburgh
EH10 4HD
Tel: 0131 447 8024
Fax: 0131 452 8569
Email: information@ed.
centralbureau.org.uk

Northern Ireland

Central Bureau
1 Chlorine Gardens
Belfast

BT9 5DJ
Tel: 01232 664 418
Fax: 01232 661 275
British Council Website:
www.britcoun.org/cbeve/

Where to Go

Assistantships are available in metropolitan France, in French territories, in Sénégal, Québec and Belgium. Within the metropolitan departments, applicants are advised to take into account that Paris is the most expensive place to live in the country, and the allowance does not increase accordingly. Paris rents are at least a third more expensive than those in the provinces. However, it is worth noting that there is no guarantee that an applicant will be placed in a city. Applicants may end up in a rural town or village with limited transport and facilities.

Application

The application process begins in the preceding academic year. Candidates must complete two copies of a form, provide a duplicate of a recent medical certificate (not pre-dating October 1 of the year of application), confirming that they are medically fit and healthy. Undergraduates must return their forms to the relevant department for a reference to be attached, whereas graduates should request that a reference be sent directly to the Head of the Assistants Department at the Central Bureau. Completed dossiers are due in early December the exact date will be marked in the documents accompanying the application form. Candidates may have to attend an interview in the spring.

Conditions

The 1998-99 monthly allowance is 5593FF per month for a 12-hour working week. This is payable in arrears so take enough money to survive the first month

(or even two months just to be safe). Accommodation is not provided and assistants are responsible for their travel costs. Assistants who stay for less than two years are not liable for income tax.

The Work

The role of an assistant is literally to assist in the teaching of their native language. This can and will be interpreted in different ways depending on the school. Some institutions will give an assistant specific classes and independent control; others might expect the assistant to provide as much support as possible to the permanent teaching staff.

Lingua Action C

Graduates considering a teaching career should also consider the Lingua Action C programme which appoints prospective teachers as assistants in other EU/EEA countries. Contact the LINGUA Unit at the Central Bureau in London, tel: 0171 389 4004.

SOCRATES—ERASMUS

The SOCRATES-ERASMUS programmes promote student/teacher exchange and mobility within the European Economic Area (EEA). Students enrolled in a Higher Education Institution can apply to spend from three months to an academic year in another EU or EEA country, and receive formal credit from their home institution for the period spent studying abroad. Students will continue to receive grants and may be eligible for extra funding to cover additional costs incurred. Candidates should note that as a result of the introduction of tuition fees, students will now be liable for these whilst studying abroad (£500 for those spending an academic year abroad and £1000 if spending part of the year abroad). Tuition fees are waived in the 'host' institution. Applicants should be EU/EEA nationals or legally resident in the UK, registered at a UK Institution of Higher Education and ideally able to communicate in the language of the country chosen. Interested students should contact their European Office or ask in their department to find out if it is possible to take part in an ERASMUS exchange.

LEONARDO DA VINCI

If you're a British NVQ student, not an undergraduate or a graduate, why not consider Leonardo da Vinci? This is the European Union's vocational training programme and placements are available from three weeks to nine months. The time spent abroad can be integrated and accredited into the UK training programme. Students at FE colleges or any institution offering initial vocational training, young people under 28, young/recent graduates and trainees are eligible and financial assistance is available. Applications must be made through a college, not on an individual basis.

Tel: 0171 389 4389
Fax: 0171 389 4426
E-mail: leonardo@centralbureau.org.uk

Useful Publications

The European Choice: A Guide to Opportunities for Higher Education in Europe, (free)
DfEE Publications Centre
PO Box 6927
London E3 3NZ
Tel: 0171-510 0150

UK Guide to Erasmus (details of all first degree and diploma courses involved in the Socrates-Erasmus programme)
ISCO Publications
12a-18a Princess Way
Camberley, Surrey
GU15 3SP

Travelling, Studying, Working and Living within the European Union
Publications Department
The European Commission
8 Storey's Gate
London SW1T 3AT

A Year Between: The Complete Guide to Taking a Year Out
The Central Bureau
10 Spring Gardens
London SW1A 2BN

Useful Addresses

UK SOCRATES-ERASMUS
R and D Centre
The University
Canterbury
Kent CT2 7PD
Tel: 01227 762 712
Fax: 01227 762 711
Email: erasmus@ukc.ac.uk
Web: www.ukc.ac.uk/ERASMUS/erasmus

Useful Internet sites

The British Council-UK:
www.britcoun.org/

The British Council Central Bureau for Educational Visits and Exchanges:
www.britcoun.org/cbeve/

Leonardo da Vinci:
www.ece.lu/en/comm/dg22/leonardo.html

ORTELIUS – Database on higher education in Europe containing information on institutions and courses: ortelius.unifi.it/

UKCOSA – The Council for International Education web page: www.britcoun.org/web_site/ukcosa/

Art and Design Courses

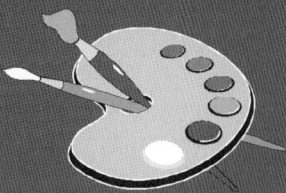

Everyone dreams of running off to France to paint, write or even just sit around in cafés watching other people painting and writing. Some go ahead and do it, but dramatic steps aren't necessary. In two weeks, a week or even a weekend, anyone can learn the rudiments of drawing and painting whilst enjoying French countryside and culture. For those who wish to pursue an artistic career, whether in graphics or *gravure*, France has an enormous choice of schools, many of which are both incredibly cheap and internationally recognised. Furthermore, the possibilities don't end with basic techniques. In an age of mass digital communication, France remains at the forefront of the art world, with inordinate numbers of schools and universities offering training in computer-aided design, multimedia techniques and digital illustration. Whether you want to learn how to use a stylus and scanner or a pencil and paper, spend a weekend, or complete a degree, France has something to offer.

Range of Schools

There are several questions to consider before choosing a school. What is your objective? How much time do you have? What is your budget? A weekend holiday course in a farmhouse or country studio will be very different to a month-long stint in a Parisian *atelier*. A year-long foundation course might be the start of an artistic education in France or a means of improving your French whilst learning a new skill. The following is a broad description of options available:

Holidays

Try out painting in the Aisne (L'Ile des Peintres), printing in Antibes (Atelier du Safranier), etching in Paris (La Taille Douce) or sculpture in Vence (Centre d'Art Vaas). Most centres organise accommodation. Teaching is by practising artists, and students generally spend half a day in a studio or working on a project and the other half visiting the area. The emphasis is on enjoyment, not expertise, and although the focus is professional, experience will generally not be necessary. Participants vary in age, background and nationality. Prices also vary enormously: check whether the fee includes accommodation and/or meals, materials and equipment and transfers to and from the airport or railway station.

The Atelier System

Winding staircases and wooden floorboards, canvasses and cigarettes, easels and eaves are all emblems of an artist's studio. In Paris the studio, or *atelier*, occupies a fundamental position in the world of art. Like learning to draw, learning to work in an *atelier* is one of

> L'art est beau quand la main, la tête et le coeur travaillent ensemble
>
> J RUSKIN

the starting points of an artistic education. Most *ateliers* run a self-service system, whereby students buy blocks of time and attend whenever it suits them, and some offer a per-trimester rate. Few run fixed classes or projects. Once at the studio, students will have access to materials, instruction and a model or still-life; they choose whether to work on a personal project or one suggested by the teacher. For the beginner or amateur this system might sound very daunting but it is, in fact, an extremely pleasant and reassuring way to learn. There are no fixed parameters or expectations, and students benefit from extremely thorough and professional instruction, whilst retaining the freedom to express themselves.

The Académie

The term *Académie* is often used to describe a school that lies somewhere between the free-form *atelier* and the hierarchical education system. Although it is not a technical term, most *Académies* seem to run on a similar basis. They are generally larger than *ateliers*, but retain the same objectives and working practices, and offer the possibility of a longer commitment to artistic instruction without the constraints of an academic institution. Some, like the Académie Port-Royal in Paris (which is recognised by the Rectorat de Paris), offer a year-long programme, which means that, once enrolled for a certain period, international students gain the right to visa privileges. One-year certificates and foundation courses are usually available.

The École

From the singular ENS-BA to the many regional and municipal schools in the public and private sectors, the French education system has a panoply of different art schools, certificates and specialisms. Art education, like the French education system in general, appears very complicated until you master the art of its acronyms and cycles. It can be loosely divided into three types of course, university, fine art and vocational. Within universities there are courses in the first, second and third cycle. In the first students follow a two-year DEUG (*Diplôme d'Études Universitaires Générales*) which is available countrywide. In the second cycle there are two one-year courses, the *licence* and the *maîtrise*. At this stage students will have an equivalent education to the US or UK BA. In the third cycle, which is roughly equivalent to Master's-level education, the DEA (*Diplôme d'Etudes Approfondies*) is a one-year course. Teaching tends to be more theoretical than practical and many students choose this option, especially the DEUG, as a stop-gap whilst preparing an entrance exam for the Beaux-Arts or the Grandes Écoles.

Joan Heath

> ### Five famous movements in the French Art World
>
> **The Renaissance** – during the 15th/16th century; artists such as Leonardo da Vinci
>
> **The Enlightenment** – during the 18th century
>
> **The Impressionists** – during the 19th century; artists such as Monet
>
> **Art Nouveau** – also during the 19th century
>
> **The avant garde**: between the two world wars

Fine Art

The Écoles des Beaux Arts provide a practical and theoretical education in Fine Arts. There are two national diplomas available country-wide. The DNAP (*Diplôme National d'Arts Plastiques*) takes three years and is roughly equivalent to a BA in Fine Arts in America or the UK. The DNSEP (*Diplôme National Supérieur d'Expression Plastique*), a two-year degree, follows on from the DNAP and is roughly equivalent to an MA or MFA. There are certain diplomas which are only available in specific schools, such as the five-year DSAP (*Diplôme Supérieur d'Arts Plastiques*) at the ENS-BA and the *Diplôme de l'ENSAD* (Ecole Nationale Supérieur des Arts Decoratifs), a four-year course which trains interior designers.

The Vocational Sector

France's education system is such that whatever profession you are interested in, there will be a relevant course or qualification. The vocational/professional sector is thus very well-established and respected. Students following this route start with a two-year CAP (*Certificat d'Aptitude Professionnel*). This is a national qualification readily available in schools specialising in photography, bookbinding and decoration. At *baccalauréat* level there are two options, a *baccalauréat professionnel* and a *baccalauréat technologique*: the former is available in subjects such as photography, graphic communication and upholstery, and the latter provides access to fine art and design schools and to the Applied Arts BTS. A BTS (*Brevet de Technicien Supérieure*) is a two or three-year course which follows on from the *baccalauréat* (generally with a technical bias). The DMA (*Diplôme des Métiers d'Art*) is the first applied arts qualification post-*baccalauréat* and is roughly equivalent to two years of university-level education. At the ENSCI (École Nationale Supérieure de Création Industrielle) there is a Diplôme de Créateur Industriel which takes two-five years depending on a student's entrance qualifications.

The Private Sector

Within the private sector there are innumerable schools. Each one will have its own diploma and many are sanctioned and recognised by the *Ministère de l'Éducation*.

Costs

Unlike most other countries in the Western world, France still has a state education system that is practically free, and every European has the right to study here. One year's study in a design school may cost as little as 1403FF, not including materials or the 1020FF annual social security fee. Private schools are, in comparison, inordinately expensive, but the prices are cheap compared to the US. An art foundation course at ATEP costs 27.750FF plus 750FF enrolment whereas one at the Paris branch of Parson's, the New York Art and Design school, costs 92.000FF plus 1600FF registration fee.

Entrance Requirements

Ateliers and holiday courses expect enthusiasm, not experience. In academic institutions entrance requirements will depend on students' objectives and plans. Students starting a course from scratch will be subject to the same requirements as French nationals. These vary. Every school will expect a qualification equivalent to the *baccalauréat*. In addition some schools will require a letter of motivation and a portfolio in order to consider a candidate; others will also expect candidates to attend an interview. All the *Écoles des Beaux Arts* and many of the private schools have *concours*, entrance exams which are fiercely contested. A foundation course, or *prépa* as it is known, is indispensable training for these exams. For those already studying art in their home countries there are two other options. An exchange is usually possible in most schools. If you really want to study at a particular school, such as the ETPA in Rennes or the ESAM in Reims, contact them directly. Transfers are a little more complicated. Candidates will need to send a portfolio of work, letter of motivation and details of previous and current artistic education and experience. The school will then send this to the Ministry of Culture where it will be considered by a *comité d'équivalences*, a jury that determines the transferability and level of foreign qualifications.

Paris versus the Provinces

Where to study will depend on what you're studying. Most holiday courses are run outside of Paris, mainly because students want to combine a painting class with trips to beaches and mountains. However, you might also want to consider what it is that inspires you. Would you be happier with an *à la carte* two weeks in the streets and studios of Paris, trying out different *ateliers*, staying in a hotel and eating meals out, or would you prefer a ready-made package in the countryside?

Paris is, of course, the capital and there are few cities that contain so much in such a small space. Hundreds of museums, art galleries and exhibitions are within reach. The buildings and monuments are unique and the whole city is an inspiration. However, it does have its downside: it is expensive and smelly. It is also more likely that you will spend time with foreigners and meet fewer French students. Living in a garret will become a necessity, not a choice, since Paris real estate and living costs are extortionate.

If you plan to take *atelier* instruction, Paris is the only real option. There are a few provincial studios in Rennes and in the South of France, but the choice is limited. Paris is the historical heart of the system and therefore has the highest concentration. For those considering a longer stay or more academic instruction the choice isn't so obvious. Several provincial towns have excellent schools and specialisms. Rennes, for example, is renowned throughout France as a

> I go into the landscape every day, the subjects are beautiful and I spend my days more pleasantly than anywhere else.
>
> CÉZANNE, September 1906

leading site of research and development in information technology and audiovisual communication. Art Nouveau buffs should consider Nancy, its birthplace. Bordeaux's fine art school pioneered a revamp of the whole sector and it has a radical and innovative approach to art education. Sepia in Nantes has a thoroughly professional course in visual communication, and the ESAM in Reims has a young, dynamic approach to design and impressive connections.

Thanks to the TGV (*Train à Grande Vitesse*), Paris is only a few hours from most large provincial cities, such as Rennes, Lyon and Bordeaux, so students can enjoy the cheapness of provincial living and the proximity of the countryside, whilst remaining close to the capital.

Level of French

On holiday courses and in the *ateliers*, a basic level of French will help, but as with all artistic instruction, a willingness to learn through practice not theory is more important. Within the academic system, students will be expected to have at least a high or secondary school qualification in French or evidence of intermediate linguistic ability. Selection is not based on this but your survival might be!

PARIS

Académie Charpentier

2, rue Jules Chaplain, 75006 Paris
Tel: +33 1 43 54 31 12
Fax: +33 1 44 07 20 55
Established: 1945
Level of French: Intermediate
Nearest Station: (Métro) Vavin
Contact: Madame Annie Pave

Académie de la Grande Chaumière

14, rue de la Grande Chaumière, 75006 Paris
Tel: +33 1 43 26 13 72
Fax: +33 1 44 07 20 55
Established: 1902
Level of French: Basic
Nearest Station: (Métro) Vavin
Contact: Monsieur Jean-Marc Lemessier

These two institutions, separate in their practice, yet joined in theory, combine the best of what Paris can offer in art schools. The Académie de la Grande Chaumière is one of the oldest and most famous *ateliers* in the city, offering the best of Parisian studio traditions – a large open space, full of light, in the centre of Montparnasse, a historically artistic quarter that has been home to Modigliani, Gauguin, Man Ray and Calder. The Académie Charpentier is part of a very modern French tradition: an art school which focuses on Visual Communication and Interior Design, plus a foundation course to prepare entrance for the '*grandes écoles*'.

At the Chaumière students are both professional artists and amateurs, of differing age and nationality, all passionate about artistic expression but not interested in learning in an institutionalised structure, and not necessarily seeking a career in art. At the Académie Charpentier students enrol for a one-year foundation or a three-year Diploma course leading to the ACCES (*Académie Charpentier Certificat d'Études Supérieures*). The three-year Visual Communication Certificate covers all aspects of art and design from sketching to storyboards, including options on Communication Codes, Image: Theory and Practice, Photography and Media. The three-four year Interior Design course trains students in the arts of spatial and product design for home and work environments, from Geometry to Computer-Aided Design.

Open six days a week, the Académie runs a Painting and Drawing *atelier* in the mornings and a Sketching *atelier* in the afternoons. Enrolment is 1500FF, but once this somewhat steep fee is paid, the classes are very cheap. A morning session (9am-12pm) costs 140FF or 1700FF for four consecutive weeks. An afternoon session (3pm-6pm or 2pm-6pm on Saturdays) costs 70FF or 650FF for 12. There are approximately two students per class.

There is no accommodation service in either Académie. To reach either one, take Metro line 6 to Vavin. There are several exits, all of which lead to Place Pablo Picasso. Rue de la Grande Chaumière is sandwiched between boulevard du Montparnasse and boulevard Raspail. The *atelier* is on the left. For rue Jules Chaplain, with the Montparnasse tower on the left walk a very short distance along boulevard Raspail until reaching rue Brea. Turn right and then right again into rue Jules Chaplain. The Académie is on the left.

Académie Julian-Del Debbio

28, boulevard St. Jacques, 75014 Paris
Tel: +33 1 43 37 80 65
Established: 1868
Level of French required: None
Nearest Station: (Métro/RER) Denfert-Rochereau
Contact: Monsieur Andre Del Debbio

The Académie and its founder and director, Monsieur Julian Del Debbio, are so unique and yet so much a part of Parisian history that they remain unforgettable. The approach to the Académie is somewhat deceptive. Arriving from boulevard St Jacques and turning into Number 28, you would be forgiven for giving up and turning back. It is a large complex full of 60s and 70s tower blocks; ugly, uninspiring, unexpected. This isn't the Montparnasse that you were looking for; full of artists, cafes and sweet little streets. But persevere. On the other side of the car park, there is a blank, plain metal door. The doorbell says Debbio. Behind this 20th-century exterior lies a piece of the past. Monsieur Del Debbio has been running the Académie for over 50 years. This is Montparnasse and Montmartre rolled into one, the last remnant of a historical *atelier*, begun in 1868 by Rodolphe Julian, once frequented by Vuillard, Bonnard, Leger, Matisse, Duchamp... the list goes on.

Easels and sculpture litter the room, paints spill from all sides, the walls are covered in paintings, the window is huge, the floor is wooden and there is a little staircase leading up to some unknown upstairs territory. Monsieur Del Debbio's *atelier* is a serious place to learn classic techniques – whether in painting, portraiture, sculpture or drawing – and to share the experience and talent of a man who has worked with and taught painters we are used to seeing as names on museum walls.

Like most ateliers, the system is *à la carte*. Students buy blocks of time and then come when they like. A booklet of ten tickets costs 1500FF and there is a 300FF enrolment fee (400FF for sculpture). Materials are not included, except for sculpture. The *atelier* is open all year round, except from mid-July to the end of August, from Monday to

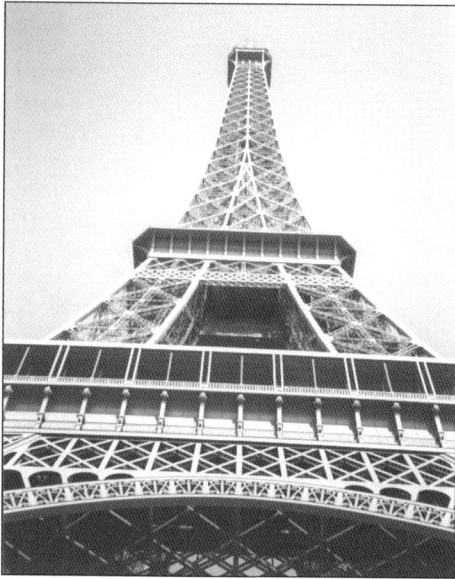

Fidelma Smith

Friday 9am to 12pm and 2pm to 5pm. You can learn as much or as little as you want, though there is no chance you will feel uninspired or lack encouragement.

Take Métro Line 4 or RER B to Denfert Rochereau. One of the large boulevards descending from the Place Denfert-Rochereau is boulevard St Jacques. Number 28 is on the left and looks like a car park. Persist!

Académie de Port Royal

2, impasse Montlouis, 75011 Paris
Tel: +33 1 43 73 90 03
Fax: +33 1 45 83 75 09
Established: 1969
Level of French required: None
Nearest Station: (Métro)
Philippe Auguste
Contact: Dina Pickard

The Académie de Port-Royal is the perfect studio for the international student who wants to study in an *atelier*

libre but who needs a visa to do so. It is one of the few that is affiliated to the Rectorat de Paris and its students are therefore eligible, where necessary, for a visa. Formalities aside, it is also engaging and encouraging, large enough to accommodate around 30 students, but small enough to retain a close, friendly atmosphere. Dina Pickard, who runs the Académie with her husband, Jean-Maxime Relange, is a veritable inspiration. She has been in France so long that her English sounds translated, although it is her native language. When not doing her own painting, writing or teaching she is helping students with their personal lives. One of her best students is a deaf and dumb Brazilian woman. Her Parisian plumber is proving a problem and she turns to Dina to sort him out. Like the other three teachers, Dina is a professional artist and her job in the *atelier* is, she says, to give advice and propose projects, whilst allowing the student the freedom to follow a set project or to work on their own ideas. One of the teacher-artists, Jean Marzelle was an *émule de Cezanne* and as he tours the room, advising and correcting, he tells stories and recounts anecdotes that better any other art history lesson.

The Académie runs a scholarship prize which is open to all the students in the preceding academic year. Each entrant presents three pieces of work and an external jury selects two or three of them who win a free year of studio instruction. These three students are then eligible for the Grand Prize: another free year of instruction and an exhibition in a Parisian gallery organised by the Académie. Students with limited resources can try for the Prix Hélène Gauvry: the winner receives a year's free instruction.

There are several course options available: a week in the studio (which is open Monday to Friday, 9am to 5pm) costs 900FF; a month costs 2500FF; three months 6300FF; one year from 11 000FF (two days attendance per week) to 16,200FF (five days attendance). 'By the day' passes, valid for three months, cost 1300FF for six days or 2300FF for twelve. A life drawing model poses twice a day and the 'still life' paintings on display are renewed every two weeks. Trips to visit galleries, in cities such as London, Leningrad and Bruges, are also organised. Dina also runs summer Landscape painting classes in her Burgundy farmhouse. Call for details.

No previous artistic experience is necessary, although those who have previously attended a studio are encouraged to bring a portfolio of work when enrolling. The Académie is open all year round Monday-Friday, 9am to to 5pm, except July and August and two weeks at Christmas and Easter.

Take Métro line 2 to Philippe Auguste. Turn into rue de Mont Louis, the first left after the exit and then take the second right into Impasse Mont Louis. The Académie is on the right.

Académie Valette Internationale
4, rue Valette, 75005 Paris
Tel: +33 1 43 29 37 99
Fax: +33 1 43 54 76 50
Nearest Station: (RER)
Luxembourg .
Contact: Madame Gazonnois
Level of French: Intermediate

Paris isn't renowned for its hills but this school is balanced on one of them, the Montagne Ste-Geneviève, right next to the Panthéon, the church which looms over the Latin Quarter. It offers an art foundation course (one year full-time or two years part-time) and a classic three-year programme in Arts Plastiques. One of its specialities is preparing students for the entrance exams to the National Landscape Schools in Blois, Bordeaux and Versailles, which train landscape designers and gardeners. Students need a DEUG and an art foundation to qualify for entry and the two-year course allows time to do both. A basic knowledge of French and art is necessary to be considered for the foundation. One year's study costs 26,100FF full-time. Single room accommodation is available (fees and half-board: 32,100FF; fees and full-board: 58,200FF).

Ateliers Anne Leduc
224, rue de Charenton, 75012 Paris
Tel: +33 1 43 40 12 85
Established: 1982
Level of French required: Basic
Nearest Station: (Métro) Dugommier
Contact: Anne Leduc

Drawing is one of those mythical skills (like singing, or dancing), that seems unearthly to the novice, with a pencil and paper but no idea how to combine the two. When I arrived at the Ateliers Anne Leduc, I wasn't aware that I was about to learn. This was an interview, a chance to see Anne at work, not a test of my own abilities. But I arrived a little late, the studio was in full swing, the life drawing class was on the go and I had no chance to explain who I was. Before I knew it the charcoal was in my hand and the large white blank was next to me and I was being encouraged to make sense of the model. It would have been easy, in retrospect, to stand up, explain my presence and merely watch the proceedings. However, I was, as it were, drawn, and when at the break I finally had the chance to talk to Anne, she asked if I was planning to continue the class. It hadn't crossed my mind to leave, despite the rather embarrassing scribbles I had produced so far. Such is the pull of this small studio. Many of the students have been coming for years and although I had just arrived, I felt comfortable, both showing off my drawings and asking for help. There is no pretension, no expectation, merely a desire to share a love of art and to encourage beginners or established artists in the development of a skill. Anne provides detailed, instructive and individual advice, and students either work on the model or on a personal project.

Classes are payable per month. A two hour session every week for four weeks costs 580FF, three hours is 840FF and four hours 900FF. Individual sessions cost 150FF (two hours), 220FF (three hours) and 900FF (four hours). It is open on Monday and Wednesday afternoon (2pm to 5pm), Thursday evening (6.30pm to 9.30pm) and Saturday morning (9.30am to 1.30pm). Anne only speaks a little English so French would be helpful. However, the class is, like most *ateliers*, based on practice not theory, so once past the enrolment stage French isn't essential as long as you are willing to get by with sign language and goodwill. All materials provided. Take Métro line 6 to Dugommier. With Square Jean Morin on the left, walk across boulevard de Reuilly/boulevard de Bercy. Number 224 is on the left. Look out for a double-fronted shop.

Atelier d'Arts Appliqués du Vesinet

28 bis Chemin du Tour des Bois, 78400 Chatou
Tel: +33 1 39 52 85 90
Fax: +33 1 39 52 28 78
Nearest Station: (RER) Le Vesinet-Le Pecq/Le Vesinet-Centre
Contact: Mme Rojy
Level of French: Conversational

Passionate book-lovers the world over come to this small, residential suburb west of Paris to spend hours learning the arts of book-binding, restoration and framing. Classes, which are aimed at professional or amateur adults rather than younger students, focus on modern methods and styles of bookbinding and decoration, and can be followed for a period of a few days, months or a school year. Teaching is by professional artisans who come into the school just for their class, and prices range from 3600FF for a year of Book Decoration to 6100FF for the second and third year of Traditional Bookbinding. It helps to speak French but many of the teachers speak English. Accommodation can be arranged on an individual basis through consultation with the school.

Ateliers du Carrousel

Palais du Louvre, 111 rue de Rivoli, 75001 Paris
Tel: +33 1 44 55 59 02
Fax: +33 1 44 55 57 65
Website: www.ucad.fr
Established:1953
Level of French required: Conversational
Nearest Station: (Métro) Tuileries/Palais Royal
Contact: Jean-Michel Correia
In terms of reaching the heart of the Parisian artistic establishment, you

cannot get much closer than the Ateliers du Carrousel. Part of the Union Centrale des Arts Decoratifs, the *ateliers* offer painting, drawing and sculpture classes in one of the most dramatic settings in the city. The studios are all sited at one end of the Palais du Louvre, with the sort of incredible views across the Jardin des Tuileries that most tourists don't ever see. Established over 40 years ago, the objective of the *ateliers* remains the same: the encouragement of creative ability, whatever a student's chosen domain. Unlike most *ateliers*, students enrol for a whole year in September. Each class lasts approximately two-three hours and all are taught by professional artists. Options include Clay Pottery (quite rare in Paris), Watercolour, Trompe-l'oeil and Art History. Prices range from 3390FF for Life Drawing to 6170FF for Oil Painting. Students (enrolled elsewhere) receive reductions.

International students who wish to follow a basic art education, especially those considering further study in a French art school, should consider the summer *ateliers*. Students on this course spend time learning artistic techniques and attending seminars but also using the famous museums that surround and incorporate their classes (the Louvre, Jeu de Paume, Museum of Decorative Arts, Orsay Museum and the Museum of Fashion and Textiles). Mornings are devoted to studio work and in the afternoons students attend conferences and guided tours to monuments and museums. The course is open to everyone and includes two half-day sessions devoted to preparing a portfolio for art school entrance exams. The six-week course costs 8400FF and enrolment begins in March. Shorter courses are also available throughout the year. In 1997 these included Scenery – Painting (four days full-time: 2350FF) and Floral Art (one day: 750FF).

To reach the *ateliers*, take Métro line 1 to Palais Royal/Musée du Louvre or Tuileries. On exiting either of these stations walk along rue de Rivoli towards the Jardin des Tuileries end of the Musée du Louvre where you will find the Union Centrale (and Musée) des Arts Decoratifs.

Ateliers du Chat

5, rue Dautancourt,
75017 Paris
Tel: +33 1 42 28 94 96
Established: 1960
Nearest Station: La Fourche
Level of French: None
Contact: Christian Houdaille

One of the only Pottery studios in Paris, the Ateliers du Chat offers classes working with clay, in ceramics, earthenware and porcelain and in decoration and enamelling. The workshop is taught by Christian Houdaille, who is a ceramicist and potter, in a ground-floor studio looking out onto a garden. The two-hour classes take place in the evenings and a trimester costs 1400FF. The first session is free. To find out further information, try writing or turning up at the door. The *atelier* is quite difficult to reach by telephone and they never return calls.

To reach the Ateliers du Chat, take Métro line 13 to La Fourche. At the exit take the left-hand street. Rue Dautancourt is the second on the right. Number 5 is on the left.

Atelier National d'Art Textile

48, rue Saint-Sabin, 75011

Paris
Tel: +33 1 49 23 12 80
Fax: +33 1 43 38 51 36
E-mail: tournay@ensci-les-
ateliers.culture.fr
Established: 1976
Level of French required: Intermediate
Nearest Station: (Métro)
Bastille
Contact: Chantal Tournay/Jane
Landau/Clotilde Ancellin

In Paris don't expect to be able to see anyone in a school in the summer, at midday or after 6pm. Unless it is the ANAT. Open 24 hours a day, seven days a week, all year round, this *atelier* of textile design is an aberration of all that defines Parisian living and working patterns. Such accessibility defines its approach to its teaching and students. It is an open studio, attached to the École Nationale Supérieure de Creation Industrielle, which offers a two-year research programme providing students with the skills, experience and portfolio necessary to work in varying design sectors, whether fashion, fabrics or furniture. Students learn the art of designing an image, designing and producing fabrics, understanding the use of textiles and creating a fabric col-

lection. Classes are full-time over two years, and students are expected to work in their own time. The first-year project focuses on working with fabrics for a clothes collection and the second-year project focuses on upholstery materials.

The large studio has a workstation for each student, equipped with looms and knitting machines. There are also Apple Mac computers and PCs, loaded with software such as Haute Tension and 'nfo Design, on which students learn pattern-drafting, fabric simulations and print designs.

No previous textile experience is necessary, although students are expected to have some artistic experience (namely being able to draw and work with colour) and they must have some proof of their commitment and interest in textiles. The course is aimed at those with a first degree, preferably in an artistic subject, although the *atelier* will consider everyone in terms of their experience and interests. The course costs 2090FF per year plus 200FF enrolment fee. A maximum of 20 students is admitted per year, most in their twenties, and classes are taught in French. The *atelier* is seeking to validate its course and establish a three-year diploma.

To enrol, send a letter in January requesting the application details. This must be returned with a dossier of personal work by the end of May. A first selection then takes place and students who reach the second stage will be expected to attend an interview

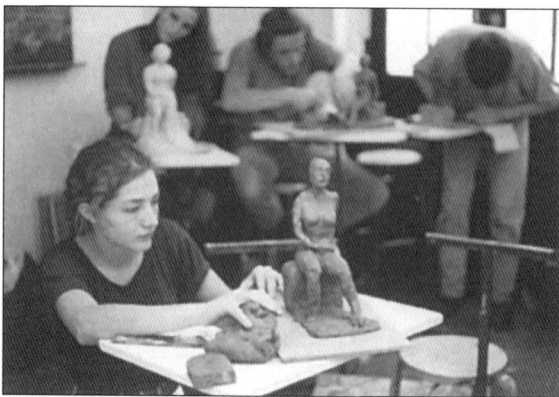

(the interview is obligatory, regardless of a student's location).

Take Métro line 5 to Breguet-Sabin. Walk away from the park and along rue Saint-Sabin, crossing rue du Chemin Vert. Number 48 is the École Nationale Supérieure de la Creation Industrielle. The ANAT is on the fifth floor. Ask at the Accueil if you get stuck.

Atelier de Sèvres

47, rue de Sèvres, 75006 Paris
Tel: +33 1 42 22 59 73
Fax: +33 1 45 44 01 93
Email: atelier@pair.com
Website: www/pair.com/atelier
Nearest Station: Montparnasse
Level of French: Conversational

Situated in the heart of St Germain-des-Prés, surrounded by museums and galleries, the Atelier de Sèvres is one of the few schools in France that offers only a foundation course. Such specialisation leads to a much more focused teaching objective, concentrating on giving the best training and information for that particular course. The one-year course, (which prepares for the entrance exams to any École Supérieure d'Art) is multidisciplinary, and covers all aspects of artistic representation, including life-drawing, painting, graphics, art history and sculpture. The lively and diverse teaching takes place in a friendly studio atmosphere in historic Parisian buildings. The price is high by French standards (28,000FF plus 1200FF enrolment), but so is the success rate. International students are welcome, even if they don't plan to compete

in the exams. Some art education is required.

BJO Formation

58, rue du Louvre, 75002 Paris
Tel: +33 1 40 26 28 45
Fax: +33 1 40 26 28 69
Established: 1972
Level of French required:
Intermediate
Nearest Station: (Métro)
Sentier
Contact: Sylvie Ballivet

Picture courtesy of BFO Formation

ART ADN DESIGN

BJO Formation is widely recognised throughout France as the best school of jewellery conception, design and fabrication. It is in the same building as the Parisian Syndicate of Jewellery and Orfèvrerie, and students work in *ateliers* under the eaves with views across the slate rooftops of the city. It is very much a professional school but courses are open to everyone. Most students are already working in the industry and come to study one or two days per week but many are international students who speak only a little French and want to learn how to design and make jewellery. All of the teachers are professionals, who either run their own businesses or work for the most illustrious jewellery houses in the world, such as Cartier, and they come to the Centre specifically to give their classes. Groups are small, the classes are very practical and the atmosphere is very relaxed.

Courses include Design, Modelling in Wax and Plastic, Engraving, Pearl Stringing, Polishing and Computer-Aided Design. There are three levels of expertise and each one takes three months to complete (with one day of training per week). Prices range from 5600FF (35 hours of classes) for Level 1 of Jewellery Design to 12,800FF (80 hours of classes) for Level 1 of Precious Jewellery Manufacturing. A certificate of attendance is delivered on the completion of a course. BJO will also organise intensive classes on request for groups of eight students or more. There are two sessions per year, one in September and one in January. Take Métro line 3 to Sentier. Walk along rue d'Aboukir, against the traffic and you will reach a large junction. Rue du Louvre is the second on the left and BJO is in the large, elegant building on the left.

Picture courtesy of Christie's Education

Centre des Arts du Livre et de l'Estampe
Hotel Nissim de Camondo, 63 rue de Monceau, 75008 Paris
Tel: +33 1 45 63 54 10
Fax: +33 1 54 75 19 40
Website: www.ucad.fr
Established: 1894
Level of French: Intermediate
Nearest Station: (Métro) Villiers or Monceau
Contact: François Somme

Located in the grand environment of the Hotel Nissim de Camondo, the Centre is one of three schools associated with the Union Centrale des Arts Decoratif. It is a private applied arts school, offering courses in the professional skills of book binding, restoration and decoration, gilding and framing. Its objective is to focus on the technical mastery of these professions, whilst encouraging an increased understanding of the creativity and history of decorative arts. The Centre offers a one-year professional course in Bookbinding (36 hours per week: 38,400FF) and a one-year non-professional course in the techniques and history of Bookbinding, Decoration and Literature (from nine to 21 hours per week: 14 600FF). The professional Framing course takes two years with approximately 18 hours of classes per week (22,800FF in the first year and 21 800FF in the second). There are also evening classes in Binding (6500FF per year for a two and a half hour weekly class) and Framing (6840FF per year for a two and a half hour class). There are no upper age limits or admission requirements, although students must be at least 17 with the educational equivalent of a *baccalauréat*. Enrolments for the academic year begin in April.

To reach the Centre, take line 2 to Monceau or Villiers. From Monceau cross the Parc and continue to Place de Rio de Janeiro. Rue de Monceau is on the left. Number 63 is on the left-hand side. Look for an imposing archway leading into a courtyard with the UCAD and Musée Nissim de Camondo insignia over the door.

Christie's Education

**Hotel Salomon Rothschild, 11 rue Berryer, 75008 Paris
Tel: +33 1 42 25 10 90
Fax: +33 1 42 25 10 91
Established: 1996
Level of French required:
Intermediate to Advanced
Nearest Station: (Métro)
Charles de Gaulle Étoile
Contact: Marie-Laure de Cazotte**

Two hundred years after its foundation, Christie's holds auctions on three continents. It also offers programmes in the fine and decorative arts in London, Paris, New York, Sydney and Glasgow; all cities renowned for their artistic collections and connections. The Paris school, which was opened in 1996, is based at the Hotel Salomon de Rothschild, a grand 19th-century house donated to the French state in 1922 by the Rothschild family. Christie's is in charge of the restoration of the Rothschild collection and students have access to this. The school is in a perfect location for both learning about and living with French art history. Museums and monuments such as the Arc de Triomphe, the Louvre, the Grand and Petit Palais and the Musée d'Orsay are minutes away.

The school offers three different one-year art history courses, with an emphasis on preservation and restoration. The focus of the programme is on French art from the Renaissance to the mid-20th century. The *Cours Classique* is for those seeking a professional qualification. It is a full-time diploma in French, with written and oral exams and a research project and costs 57,000FF. *The Cycle Art et Langage* is designed for students for whom French is a second language but who wish to follow the same programme as the Cours Classique. It costs 50,000FF. The Lecture Course is a non-diploma programme. Students follow the same lectures as those on the Cours Classiques but have the choice of joining an English or French speaking group for the weekly museum visits. It costs 20,000FF (lectures only) or 30,000FF. Teaching takes place over three ten-week terms in small groups of approximately 20 students. Enrolment begins in February for the following year and students are encouraged to enrol as early as possible. Many of the applicants are graduates or mature students, some on sabbatical, some seeking a career, others furthering a passion. There is a wide mix of age, nationalities, backgrounds and skills. Candidates need to be motivated, with a reasonable knowledge of art history and a great visual sensibility. It is also possible to audit a course, attending the classes but not studying for a diploma.

Take Métro lines 1/2/6 to Charles de Gaulle Étoile. From the Étoile take Avenue de Friedland. Rue Berryer is the third left.

Cours International Jeoffrin Byrs

28, rue Paul Valéry, 75116 Paris
Tel: +33 1 45 01 83 84
Fax: +33 1 45 01 64 87
E-mail: ism@club-internet.fr.
Established: 1959
Level of French required: Basic
Nearest Station: (Métro) Victor Hugo
Contact: Patricia Du Matz

I wonder if fashion students at Jeoffrin Byrs ever see the irony in their location. In the cutting rooms and in front of the computers, they design clothes that suit only the very thin, whilst just across the street at Lenotre, one of the best patisseries in Paris, they design cakes that make you very fat. In a tall and impressive building, steps away from the Arc de Triomphe and the Place Victor Hugo, students learn all they need to know to enter fashion, especially *haute couture*, as a designer. Short and long courses are available (from one month to two years) in design, computer-aided design, pattern-cutting and tailoring. The focus is on practical, visual teaching methods which enable students to gain technical independence so that they can focus on designing. They also learn about the business side of the fashion world, including rights and marketing. Students have access to extensive computer facilities as well as large, light cutting rooms and studios.

For an international student the visual focus and practical course basis,

"Christie's Education provides a unique opportunity to study French fine and decorative arts (from renaissance to mid 20th century) in the heart of Paris. From painting to porcelain all tuition is in French, even though you find yourself in an international environment. You are taught by leading experts and art historians and you will visit national museums as well as private galleries, collections and workshops. The choice is yours as to whether you do one, two or all three terms and a diploma awaits those who follow the course on a more serious note. All in all "a must" for those wishing to have their eyes opened to the beauty of French art."

Mary Boehm

learning from the shape of the human body, makes it possible to learn with a minimum amount of French. Courses available include the following: a one-year Fashion Design course (40,000FF, payable in four instalments) which comprises an apprenticeship at the end of the academic year in a company; a one or six month Design course (6500 FF or 20,000FF) and a two-week Computer-Aided Design course (16,000 FF). No experience is necessary because the school will teach all the necessary techniques.

Enrolment takes place all year round, but since the intake is limited to 50 students, don't leave it to the last minute. The school has addresses and information to help with finding accommodation.

Take Métro line 2 to Victor Hugo. Walk up Avenue Victor Hugo and turn left into rue Paul Valéry. Jeoffrin Byrs is immediately on the right.

École Art et Avenir
20, rue Eugene Manuel, 75016 Paris
Tel: +33 1 45 03 46 71
Established: 1969
Level of French required: Intermediate
Nearest Station: (Métro) Passy
Contact: Mme de Lombares

The École Art et Avenir is one of the few art schools situated in the chichi 16th *arrondissement*, but it is not full of the small-dog touting ladies you see walking along the rue de Passy. Started as an *école du quartier* by the current director's mother, this school is also one of the few places in France which teaches the arts of paper, painting and ceramic restoration, gilding and decorative paint techniques. The students come from all over Paris, all over the world and from very different backgrounds. It is very much a school, in terms of its programmes, enrolments and prices, but it is run as an *atelier* with small groups and a convivial atmosphere. The teachers are all professionals who are well-established, both in their fields and at the school. International students are welcome, both on the long courses and for short-term sessions in the drawing and painting studio. It helps to speak French but Madame de Lombares stresses that many of their students, whether from Russia or Korea, come to the school to learn a technique whilst learning or practising their linguistic skills.

The École offers a four-year programme in Picture Restoration and one-year programmes in Decorative Painting Techniques, China Restoration, Paper Works Restoration, Gilding, Painting and Drawing. The one-year courses in Gilding, China and Paper Restoration and Decorative Paint Effects cost 2900FF per trimester for approximately three hours of classes per week. Picture restoration costs 4900FF per trimester for nine hours of classes per week. Drawing classes cost 1490FF for ten two-hour classes. There is a special five-day summer course in Ceramics Restoration for 4600FF for 30 hours of classes. The enrolment fee is 200FF and materials cost 100FF. The four-year restoration course involves two years of practical work followed by two years writing a thesis on a picture of the student's choice. All of the short courses are examined by continuous assessment. Interested students should write to Mme de Lombares as early as possible before the start of the academic year to request documentation. Interviews (which are obligatory) take place in June. All other enrolments can take place by correspondence. No expertise is necessary. There are approximately 180 students at the school but only ten per group. Mme de Lombares will help with the necessary enrolment papers for those who need to obtain a visa or a *carte de séjour*.

Take Metro line 6 to Passy. Go up the escalator and along rue de l'Alboni. Take the second left at Place de Costa Rica, rue de Passy. Turn right at rue C. Chahu which becomes rue Eugene Manuel. The École is on the right.

École d'Arts Plastiques

10 bis rue de Seine, 75006 Paris
Tel: +33 1 43 54 23 14
Fax: +33 1 43 26 85 75
Established: 1803
Level of French required: Intermediate
Contact: Mme Chot-Plassot
Nearest Station: (Métro) Mabillon

The École d'Arts Plastiques is in illustrious company. It can claim the Louvre, the Musée d'Orsay and the ENSBA as neighbours, whilst enjoying the lively streets of St Germain des Prés and views across the Seine. It is situated in a palace that was originally commissioned by la Reine Margot and then turned into a luxury hotel in the 17th-century. Since 1803 the school has been directed by three families, including Raymond and Rosa Bonheur, Suzanne and Gigi Coutant and, since 1978, by the Chot-Plassots. The character of its teaching is very much a mix of such a historical position and the future possibilities of art. The school has two different programmes: a foundation year and a one-year Professional Computer-Aided Design course. The foundation prepares students for the Grandes Écoles entrance exams covering fine art techniques such as sculpture and life drawing, but also contemporary artistic practice, such as 3D design and illustration. The one-year CAD course trains students in the use of graphic design packages such as Quark, Photoshop and Adobe Illustrator on Macintosh computers (one per student) whilst also giving them a solid grounding in the basics of drawing and perspective. The course leads to careers in advertising, publishing and computer imaging and at the end of the year students work in a relevant business as part of the training.

The school's environment enjoys a sense of family since, with only 60 students, the teachers can remain in close contact with them. The foundation costs 27,500FF per year and the CAD course costs 35,000FF. It is possible to follow one course from either section for 4500FF (or 1600FF per trimester). Foundation students need a *baccalauréat* equivalent and can start enrolling from January. The CAD course requires a *baccalauréat* equivalent and one-year of drawing experience. Enrolments begin in January.

To reach the École, take Métro line 10 to Mabillon. At the exit cross over rue Dufour and then boulevard St Germain. Walk up rue de Buci and turn left on rue de Seine. Walk right to the end of the street. The École is on the right.

École de Dessin de Mode-Ateliers Fleuri-Delaporte

1 bis Impasse de l'Astrolabe, 75015 Paris
Tel: +33 1 45 67 09 80
Fax: +33 1 47 34 93 91

Level of French: Intermediate
Nearest Station: (Métro)
Falguiere
Contact: Mme Fleuri/
Marie-Jo Marechal

Madame Fleuri has been running the Ateliers Fleuri for almost fifty years, but she is still enthusiastic about her school and her students. The *atelier* is a large, light studio, very much in the style of the Montparnasse district where it is situated. Its objective is to turn passionate fashion aficionados into designers and illustrators. Originally a fashion illustration school, it was one of the first to focus on teaching the art of design and it now offers full-time and summer courses. Students follow classes in Art History and Painting, as well as Pattern-Cutting and Design. A maximum intake of 50 per year ensures a family atmosphere. "We do not want our students to become a number" insists Madame Fleuri, "we want to be able to share and encourage each person's vision and to follow them both through the school and in their careers."

There are several options available: a two-year designer programme (either full-time or part-time), summer courses, and two-six month enrolment. The two-year programme costs 23 400FF in the first year and 25 200FF in the second plus 1000FF enrolment fee. (14 400FF and 18 000FF part-time). Students spend mornings in the studio (approximately 21 hours per week) and afternoons are kept free for concentrating on personal work and, for international students, French lessons. In the second year, apprenticeships in fashion houses are available for all students.

Enrolment for this course begins in January and students need to send a CV, a letter of motivation and proof of experience, if relevant. They will then be expected to attend an interview (although this can be waived for international students). There is also an intensive session in January for anyone who has missed the first semester but wants to enrol in the long programme. The four-week intensive summer courses cost 2500FF for one month and 5000FF for two, plus 500FF enrolment fee. Finally, during the academic year, the *atelier* offers short *stages* from two-six months long (3000FF a month full-time). Summer course students receive a certificate and the two-year programme is examined by a jury of designers. Successful students receive a Certificate of Textile Design. Accommodation lists are available.

To reach the *atelier*, take Metro line 12 to Falguiere. Exit on to rue de Vaugirard. Walk in the direction of the traffic. Impasse de l'Astrolabe is the third on the right.

EFET

110, rue de Picpus, 75012 Paris
Tel: +33 1 43 46 86 96
Fax: +33 1 43 41 03 93
E-mail: efet@photographie.com
Website: www.photographie.
com/efet
Established: 1970
Level of French required:
Intermediate/A-level
Nearest Station: (Métro)
Michel Bizot
Contact: Jean-Charles Dreux

Nathalie Simonet, the EFET Course Administrator, is remarkably ebullient for a woman who is still at work at 7pm on a wet Thursday evening. Her enthusiasm and commitment is infectious and it is, she says, something that both staff and students share in

ART AND DESIGN

67

this private school. Situated in the 12th *arrondissement*, and thus in the trendy East of the city, EFET, established almost 30 years ago in Paris, is a Visual Communication School specialising in photography, audiovisual media, graphic design and interior design. In an educational sector that is somewhat overcrowded, EFET is very confident of its hold on the market. Courses offered include diplomas in the four specialities and a myriad of different short classes. Facilities include photography laboratories, a television studio, video, computer and sound equipment. There are approximately 450 students, either hoping to work in visual media or refreshing their professional skills. Previous students have gone on to work on films (including Germinal, La Reine Margot and Les Visiteurs), in television (TF1, F2, la 5, la 7, Canal +), in advertising, in architecture and in marketing.

Prices for short *stages* in Multimedia Design, Photography, Post-Production and Video vary. A three-day Web-page Design course costs 3000FF, five-day Photography, Video and Sound courses cost from 4400FF to 6000FF for 40 hours of classes, and longer courses (to train, for example, as an Audiovisual Technician or a Photographer) cost between 20,000FF and 40,000FF for 900 hours of classes over nine months. Week-long courses take place all year round. Enrolments for diploma courses start in January and finish in June and students need the equivalent of a *baccalauréat* and are expected to attend an interview.

Take Métro line 8 to Michel Bizot. Rue de Picpus leads off Avenue de Daumesnil and EFET is on the left.

EICAR: Ecole Internationale de Creation Audiovisuelle et Reportage

93, avenue d'Italie, 75013 Paris
Tel: +33 1 53 79 10 00
Fax: +33 1 53 79 16 26
Website: www.inforoute.cgs.fr/ actorat/eicar
Established: 1973
Level of French required: Advanced
Nearest Station: (Métro) Tolbiac
Contact: Monsieur George Touati

The EICAR occupies a unique position in the world of Parisian audiovisual education. It was established 25 years ago with the objective of reuniting all the different branches of visual communication and representation and encouraging exchange between them. It offers a complete programme in acting, screen-writing, directing, editing, sound, camera reportage and actor-directing. The school is one of the rare institutions that runs a foundation course to prepare for entrance to one of the audiovisual Grandes Écoles Nationale d'Image et de Son, such as FEMIS and Louis Lumière. It is also the only private school offering an official state diploma (a BTS) in production, editing, sound and camera work. Other courses include a two-year Camera Reportage course and three-year programmes in Multimedia and Film Directing. The school is professional, incredibly well-equipped and well-connected for professional placements. The Director is English and she helps to establish links with Universities in Cambridge, England and Boston, USA.

There are 300 students, divided into groups of 20. International students need the equivalent to a *baccalauréat*, or professional experience, and must attend an interview. There are two sessions of entrance exams, in July and September, and enrolment begins in January. Prices range from 25 000FF for a Foundation course to 38 500FF per year for the Directors course. The school is planning to set up a bilingual programme in the near future. Take line 7 to Tolbiac. Walk down Avenue d'Italie in the Porte d'Italie direction. The EICAR is on the left.

École du Louvre

34 quai du Louvre, 75038 Paris Cedex 01
Tel: +33 1 40 20 56 14
Fax: +33 1 40 20 58 24
Website: www.louvre.fr/
Established: 1882
Level of French Required: Advanced
Nearest Station: (Métro) Louvre-Rivoli
Contact: Accueil Visconti

If you want to learn about the history of art and have access to the most incredible collections in the world, there is only one place to do it: the École du Louvre. The school was established in 1882, over 700 years after the first royal fortress was built on the site by Philippe Auguste, with the twin objectives of teaching museum professionals and making the collections more accessible to the public. Classes are available on the history of art, history of civilisations and museology. Teachers are mostly conservationists and history of art professionals. There are over 2000 students per year. There are three different cycles of study which roughly correspond to those in the French university system: the *premier cycle* is a three-year course, the *deuxième cycle* is a one-year course in Museology, aimed at those continuing in the École or transfer students, and the *troisième cycle* is a three-year research degree. Prices start at 1339FF for 1 year plus 1020FF social security. The École also runs several workshops and art classes for those who want less vocational training. Subjects include Drawing, Sculpture and Pastels and prices start at 43FF per session. You will need to speak French, because there is no provision for translation or classes taught in English. Students need the equivalent of a *baccalauréat* and must pass an entrance exam. International students must start the admission process in December of the year preceding application. You must be able to prove your level of French, usually through sitting a language test at the École or at an Embassy in your home country.

École Nationale Supérieure des Beaux-Arts

14, rue Bonaparte, 75006 Paris
Tel: +33 1 47 03 50 00
Fax: +33 1 47 03 50 80
Email: rabinlegall@ensba.fr
Web: www.ensba.fr
Nearest Station: (Métro) Saint-Germain-des-Pres
Contact: Veronique Rabin Le Gall

In amongst the minefield of the different École des Beaux Arts scattered across France, know one thing…this is the only École Nationale Supérieure. Situated in St Germain des Prés, it is spread out over more than two hectares in various buildings dating from the 17th century, including the church of the Petits-Augustins convent, the former Museum of French Monuments and the 18th-century townhouse, the Hôtel de Chimay. Its permanent collections include part of the archives and inventories of The Royal Academy of Painting and Sculpture, founded in

1648 and abolished in 1793.

The ENSBA tuition is based on a studio system which divides students according to the subject not the year. Students from all years choose the studios they will attend and are allotted working space in each one. The studios are organised into three main departments, which span both ancient and modern: painting, sculpture and multimedia. There is also a strong focus on additional theoretical tuition. Finally, the tuition is complemented by technical workshops where students have access to traditional and highly technological equipment. Independence and initiative are encouraged when choosing *ateliers* and projects.

There are three (equally difficult) ways to join the school: by entrance exam as a first-year student; by portfolio for transfer students and by admission to the fifth year for those with a DNSEP. First years must be between 18-24 and must submit a portfolio containing 20 samples of the applicant's creative work in order to gain a place on the short list. Once onto the list, there are three three-hour exams, an assessment of the portfolio and an interview. If unsuccessful, applicants can only reapply once. Application forms are available from the Bureau de Scolarité and should be returned to the school, with a portfolio and 150FF. Check with the school for dates.

Transfer students (aged between 18-26) must have completed at least two years in a post-*bac* art school or have equivalent professional experience to be considered for pre-admission (the short list). A portfolio of twenty pieces of work must then be submitted in order to get onto the list. The final stage is an interview and successful applicants are

admitted to the second, third, fourth and fifth years depending on ability.

Admission to the fifth year is via interview and the period of study is limited to one year. At the end of the year students are eligible to sit the DNSAP.

Foreign students follow the same procedures. The *École's* documentation is extremely helpful, well-organised and written in French and English, so there is no chance of failing to understand the proceedings. All official documents (birth certificates and qualifications) must be translated into French. Exchanges exist with numerous North American and European art schools.

The school is superbly equipped for photography, computer graphics, sound engineering, video, wood- and metalwork.

Information about accommodation is laid out in great detail inside the prospectus.

To reach the school, take Metro line 4 to St Germain des Prés. Cross boulevard St Germain. Walk past the church. This is rue Bonaparte. Keep going across rue Jacob and the ENSBA's main entrance is on the left.

École Supérieure Artistique ATEP

16 bis Avenue Parmentier, 75011 Paris
Tel: +33 1 40 09 14 10
Fax: +33 1 40 09 12 59
Established: 1974 (Prep studio); 1984 (École Supérieure)
Level of French required: A Level
Nearest Station: (Métro) Voltaire

Contact: Sylvina Pratt

In the midst of the grey skies of a Parisian winter, ATEP's bright yellow doors are unmissable. Beyond them lie gargoyles, huge polystyrene heads, painted and shaped into fantastic expressions, sitting atop a series of pillars in the lobby, dominating it. This is not a classic and elitist institution but a young and friendly school, with a sense of humour. Established and run by two artists, a husband and wife partnership, ATEP is a private art and design school which is small enough to retain a cosy atmosphere but large enough to be aware of the most recent developments. The school offers a one-year Foundation course, for students preparing for art school entrance exams and a four-year course leading to the ATEP Diploma in Visual Communication Design. The emphasis is on pluridisciplinarity: students cover all aspects of art and design: from sculpture to 3D computer models, from sketch to screen, from drawing board to story-board.

Downstairs there are computers, upstairs easels. On one side is the prep class, full of young artists practising their drawing and painting skills. On the other is the packaging class where students on the diploma course learn to design and produce the words and pictures that will launch a new product. It's obvious, from her conversations with the students stepping into her office and with those wandering in late, why Sylvina (the administrator) says it is 'a real family'. The intake is small (around 45 in the Foundation year and 10-15 in the Diploma classes) and the teachers closely follow students' progress. The directors are not simply figureheads, both teach and work with the

students. The school alumni return frequently to talk to the students about possible careers, in such diverse domains as multimedia, advertising, animation and scenography.

In a country where education is free, ATEP isn't cheap. However, it isn't state-run either, which means that the welcome is real and so is the dedication. Those who work and study do so for the love of it, not for an externally imposed agenda. The Foundation course and Probationary years cost 27 750FF plus 750FF enrolment fee (payable in two instalments or 10% discount for those paying before 15th September: 24 975FF). The Diploma costs 32 250FF plus 750FF enrolment fee per year (1997 prices). Fees are payable in two instalments and there is a 10% discount for full payment by 15th September. Students with the *baccalauréat* or its equivalent must have an interview before being admitted to the Foundation course. For the Diploma course, students must pass a foundation course and then present a dossier (for the Probationary year) or pass the Art School entrance exam.

Take Métro line 9 to Voltaire. In front of you, on exiting, will be Place Leon Blum. Cross this to Avenue Parmentier and walk on the right-hand side about 100 metres. 16bis is through the double doors across the courtyard.

École Supérieure d'Études Cinématographiques
21, rue de Citeaux,
75012 Paris
Tel: +33 1 43 42 43 22
Fax: +33 1 43 41 95 21
Email: esec@esec.edu
Website: www.esec.edu
Established: 1973
Level of French required:

Advanced
Nearest Station: (Métro)
Reuilly-Diderot
Contact: Kostia Milhakiev

Rue de Citeaux is in Paris's newest artistic and social centre, in the 12th *arrondissement*, close to the extraordinary Viaduc des Arts, which is a 4.5km long promenade with artists' studios under its arches. It is a fitting location for the ESEC, a school specialising in cinema, an art that France has made its own. ESEC has recently become one of only three Film schools in France whose Diploma is recognised by the Minister of Culture. Offering a two-year Diplôme d'Études Supérieures de Cinématographie et de Techniques Audiovisuelles, and from 1998, 'Cycle 3', a postgraduate, professional programme in Digital Post-Production, the school is well-equipped, well-known and well-established in both the world of education and film.

In the undergraduate programme, first-year students follow a general course in all aspects of cinematography including production, direction, screen-writing, history of cinema, sound and image and the role of information technology. In the second year, students choose between two departments, Cinema Production and Direction, and Electronic Arts and Media. Each of these branches offers different options and students work both in the schools' studio and on professional placements. There is also an additional third year for those who wish to further their professional and technical skills in Virtual and Electronic Editing. Students in Cycle 3, which runs from July to October, follow different technical andtheoretical workshops taught by industry professionals.

Students at ESEC come from over 70 countries. They are expected to be motivated, with a good general knowledge of the world of arts and communication. Direct admission requires one of the following qualifications: the equivalent of the baccalauréat plus two years; an Art School Diploma; a pass in the Grandes Écoles entrance exam; professional experience. Cycle 3 students should have basic multimedia and computer experience as well as thorough knowledge of the film and video production process. International students must seek to have their diplomas and/or experience validated. Selective admission requires the *baccalauréat* or its equivalent, plus the presentation of a portfolio and a subsequent interview. The first year costs 39 125FF. The second year costs 39 125FF for the Production option, 40 650FF for the Direction option, 41 650FF for the Electronic Arts and Media Studio and 44 800FF for the Editing Studio. For information about Cycle 3 fees, contact ESEC. These fees include all necessary materials. There is an additional enrolment fee of 2050FF per year and enrolment begins in March for undergraduates and in February for postgraduates. There are no provisions for accommodation.

Take Métro line 1 to Reuilly-Diderot. Exit onto boulevard Diderot and walk away from Place de la Nation. Turn right on rue Crozatier. ESEC is at the next junction on the left next to a *tabac*.

European Institute of Multimedia

28, rue Paul Valéry,
75116 Paris
Tel: +33 1 45 01 83 84
Fax: +33 1 45 01 64 87
E-mail: ism@club-internet.fr

ART AND DESIGN

Established: 1987
Level of French required: None
Nearest Station: (Métro)
Victor Hugo
Contact: Laurens Byrs

Descending into the bowels of number 28 you would be forgiven for feeling slightly schizophrenic. Upstairs are the mannequins and models of the Jeoffrin Byrs Fashion Design School. Downstairs is the ISM where budding Digital Imaging students crouch over their workstations designing the images for future generations of film and cartoon viewers, computer games fanatics and architects. Very much a professional school, offering courses from one week to a year, its links with Digital and other IT specialists enables it to be very up-to-date in terms of teaching, equipment and connections. There is a computer for each student's use, all equipped with several different software programmes and other equipment includes scanners, printers, art pads and cameras.

Options range from two-week programmes in Photoshop and CAD (12,000FF and 15,,000FF respectively) to nine-month courses to train as a Multimedia Expert or Project Designer (75,000FF). There is a non-refundable enrolment fee of 3000FF and, since this is a professional training centre, the courses continue all year. Students are accepted on the basis of their artistic abilities and computer experience is not obligatory. The one proviso about this school is that its documentation is not very user-friendly. See for yourself when you receive the pack of cheap pink and white printed pages. Take Métro line 2 to Victor Hugo. At place Victor Hugo take Avenue Victor Hugo in the direction of the Arc de Triomphe. Rue Paul Valery is the second on the left. ISM is in the basement of the Jeoffrin Byrs building on the right.

Parson's School of Art and Design
14, rue Letellier, 75015
Tel: +33 1 45 77 39 66
Fax: +33 1 45 77 10 44

Fidelma Smith

E-mail: 106001.237@
COMPUSERVE.COM
Website: www.parsons.edu
Established: 1981
Level of French required:
None: good level of English
is necessary.
Nearest Station: (Métro)
Avenue Emile Zola
Contact: Heather Sacco

If you want North American efficiency and qualifications, combined with Parisian style, Parson's would be a good school to consider. It is a branch of the famous Parson's School of Art and Design in New York, the oldest college of art and design in the US, which has been running programmes in Paris since 1920. This separate school was founded in 1981. Situated close to the Eiffel Tower, the school is in an old building filled with modern equipment. The entrance gallery shows students' work, making sure that the school objective of transforming talented students into highly successful artists is obvious from the moment you walk through the front door.

Parsons Paris offers four-year Bachelor of Fine Arts and Bachelor of Business Administration programmes and a one-year Foundation Course. The foundation year emphasises drawing and features Design Studios which introduce the disciplines available as majors. These include Communication Design, Fine Arts, Fashion Design and Design Marketing. If following a four-year programme, most students will spend a second year in Paris and the third and fourth in New York. In true American style the education is very good and very expensive. One year's tuition costs FF92 000 plus 1600FF registration fee. A limited number of scholarships are available and

American citizens are eligible for certain federal grants.

There is also an intensive five-week summer school for US college and high school students (contact Parsons in New York), a continuing education programme and a semester/year abroad programme which is open to students from other colleges.

There are no fixed admissions criteria. Students are reviewed individually on the basis of a portfolio (12-20 pieces of work) and a home exam. Anyone living within 200 miles of Paris is expected to attend a personal interview. Transfers of credit are possible. Non-native speakers of English will need to submit TOEFL results.

To reach Parsons, take Métro line 10 to Emile Zola. At the junction of Avenue Emile Zola and rue du Commerce turn left. The first left is rue Letellier. Number 14 is not very obvious. Look out for a big blue metal door.

La Taille Douce

9, rue Ernestine, 75018 Paris
Tel: +33 1 42 52 66 76
Level of French: None/Basic
(Françoise speaks English).
Contact: Françoise Bricaut
Nearest Station: (Métro)
Marcadet-Poissoniers/
Château Rouge

After a *stage* at La Taille Douce, the phrase "Come up and see my etchings" would lose all its power of double-entendre. In a light and airy studio, ten minutes away from Sacre-Coeur, Françoise Bricaut offers classic *atelier* instruction in etching and engraving, teaching the intricacies of an art practised since the sixteenth century by, amongst others, Goya, Durer and

Rembrandt. The techniques involve creating a design with acid on copper and zinc plates, filling it with ink, then, using a *presse taille douce* to print the design onto paper. Françoise describes it as both manual and creative, a passion more than a pastime. It takes between 25 and 30 hours of tuition to learn all the techniques and subsequently students work on their own projects, with constant support from Françoise and the other artists in the *atelier*. Enthusiasm and a sense of humour are more important than previous experience and linguistic ability. Enrolment is by the month (650FF for 16 hours or 870FF for 32) or the semester (1800FF for four hours per week or 2450FF for eight). Week-long sessions are available on request (1200FF for 24 hours tuition or 1700FF for 32 hours). Basic materials are provided by the *atelier*.

La Villa Bastille

74, rue de Charenton, 75012 Paris
Tel: +33 1 43 44 23 15
Established: 1992
Level of French required: Conversational
Nearest Station: (Métro) Ledru-Rollin
Contact: Patrick Fouilhoux

The Villa Bastille is a painter's studio in the east of Paris. It is full of light, has a great atmosphere, and in the winter, there's a fireplace to keep everyone cosy. Students come to learn life drawing, painting (watercolour, oil painting, acrylics) and sculpture with clay and the motivations for doing so vary. Some attend to relax after work, others are aiming to become professional artists.

Students usually commit themselves for a weekly session for one "term" (ie 12 weeks from the first day). It is possible to start at any time in the year). Missed sessions can be replaced. A "term" costs 1650FF. It is also possible to come for shorter/longer periods or to attend the *atelier* more frequently. Around 60 to 70 students attend the studio on a regular basis though there are only eight-ten per class. Tuition is in French but the teacher can speak English, Swedish, German and Italian.

To reach La Villa Bastille, take Métro line 8 to Ledru-Rollin. Walk along Avenue Ledru Rollin against the traffic. Rue de Charenton is the first junction. Turn left. Number 74 is on the right.

NORTH-EAST

École Nationale des Beaux Arts

3, rue Michelet,
21000 Dijon
Tel: +33 3 80 30 21 27
Fax: +33 3 80 58 90 65
Email: ENBANET@infonie.fr
Nearest Station: (SNCF) Dijon
Contact: Monsieur Gerard Prevot
Level of French: Intermediate to Advanced

One of eight national fine art schools in France, the École Nationale des Beaux Arts melds a contemporary present with a historic past. Located in an eighteenth-century building, which previously housed the Bishop of Dijon, it offers up-to-date courses in 'Fine Art' (five years) and 'Design' (three years). Although traditional *ateliers* are available in painting, sculpture and ceramics, the school specialises in contemporary art and design, offering classes in photography, computer graphics and video. There are approxi-

ART AND DESIGN

mately 30 different *ateliers*, 200 students and 40 teachers. International students are accepted, either for the whole course, or, if they have already studied art in their home countries, for one or two years' study, on presentation of a portfolio. Fees are 1200FF per year. Students, once enrolled, are entitled to apply for University accommodation and the school will provide the necessary addresses. An understanding of French is required but linguistic ability is not used as a selection criteria. Facilities include a large library and a cafeteria.

École Nationale des Beaux-Arts
1 avenue Boffrand,
54000 Nancy
Tel: +33 3 41 61 61
Nearest Station: (SNCF) Nancy
Level of French: Intermediate

Nancy gave birth to Art Nouveau and the city's architecture reflects this, with decorated windows and houses and an Art Nouveau museum. The city's École des Beaux Arts continues the tradition of engagement with modern style, offering three specialisations in Contemporary Art, Design, Art and Communication. The school's 19th-century building used to be a hospital during the war, but now houses large classrooms and modern audiovisual equipment. In collaboration with the Centre Dramatique de Nancy and the Centre Culturel André Malraux the school organises seminars with film-makers and artists. Fees per year are 1200FF not including materials.

École Supérieure d'Art et de Design de Reims
12, rue Libergier, 51100 Reims
Tel: +33 3 26 84 69 90
Fax: +33 3 26 84 69 98
Email/Web: None
Contact: Madame Chantal Macadre
Level of French: Intermediate

Young, dynamic and international: three adjectives that could be applied to every aspect of ESAM, whether the teachers, the courses or the school itself. Even the brochures and prospectuses are brightly coloured and trendy. Formed in 1992 by Gervais Jassaud, ESAM aims to form creators and designers for the 21st century. The staff are all professionals and their collaborators read like a Who's Who of modern design. They include Philippe Starck, Pedro Almodovar and Alessi. The school prides itself on its international connections and is very open to students from all over the world, whether for short exchanges, or a transfer for the whole three-five years. Diplomas offered include the DNAP and the DNSEP, with different specialisations after year one, including Photo/Video, Product Design and Graphic Design. The school has studios for work in video, photography, computer graphics, model and prototype-building and sculpture. It is one of the rare art schools in France that offers a Research Masters degree.

Reims is also a great place to study, not least because it is the home of Champagne. It is well-located for several artistically dynamic European cities: Paris, (45 mins), Strasbourg (three hours), London and Brussels via Eurostar (two hours).

Entrance for the programme is via portfolio and interview. There are 220 students in total and only two or three places in each year open to transfer students. Enrolment costs 1403 FF per

Picture courtesy of Ecole Regionale des Beaux-Arts de Rennes

Both artist and business-man, he exhibits his work in galleries, but also lays mosaic floors and decorates bathrooms and fireplaces. At present he offers classes that run on an *atelier* system. Students attend two-hour sessions twice a week on Wednesdays and Saturdays, working on their own projects, such as vases, mirrors and photo frames, with instruction and help from Monsieur Yvon. No expertise is necessary but a love of detailed, hands-on work helps. On demand he will also organise tailor-made weekend or week-long courses throughout the year (except August) for groups of five-six people.

Atelier du Thabor
3E place Saint Melaine,
35000 Rennes
Tel: +33 2 99 63 73 97
Contact: The Atelier
Level of French: Conversational
Nearest Station: (SNCF) Rennes

A Parisian-style *atelier* in the provinces, the Atelier du Thabor is right in the middle of Rennes, next to the Jardins du Thabor. Founded in 1979 by a group of professional artists, the atelier is open to anyone with an interest in Drawing, Painting or Engraving. For a yearly fee (1800FF, 1300FF for students) the student has unlimited access to the *atelier* six days a week and four evenings. The system is very flexible. Students are free to learn with one of the

year in the first two years and 2335FF per year in the next three.

NORTH-WEST

Art et Feu
26, boulevard de Verdun,
35000 Rennes
Tel: +33 2 99 59 12 57
Contact: Alix Yvon
Nearest Station: (SNCF) Rennes
Level of French: Conversational

Fashionable since Roman times, mosaic-making is once again *a la mode*, both in interior design and as a fine art technique. For the past three years, in a small studio at the back of his shop in central Rennes, Alix Yvon has been sharing his expertise in this ancient art.

three teachers or to work on their own projects. Beginners or professionals are welcome.

École Regionale des Beaux-Arts, Angers

72, rue Bressigny, 49100 Angers
Tel: +33 2 41 24 13 50
Fax: +33 2 41 87 26 49
Email/Web: None
Nearest Station: (SNCF) Angers
Contact: Mlle Ariel Portaz
Level of French: Intermediate to Advanced

If you are looking for a small fine arts school with a strong local connection, look no further. The school, situated in an 18th-century townhouse with a park behind it, prides itself on its connections with the region and the city. Out of 240 students at the École Regionale in Angers, only 5% are international. In addition to the two national diplomas, the DNAP (three years) and the DNSEP (five years), the school offers a two-year diploma in Tapestry, validated by the City of Angers, which is a recognised centre for this craft. This course can lead to a restoration or crafts career. It is also renowned for its Interior Design option, which is taught over three years by professional designers. Students can enrol for the whole course from year one or present a portfolio and enter directly at a later stage. Inscription fees are 2540FF per year (plus secu) and accommodation information can be obtained through CROUS.

École Regionale des Beaux-Arts de Rennes

3-4, rue Hoche, 35000 Rennes
Tel: +33 2 99 28 55 78
Fax: +33 2 99 28 58 24
Email: erbar@wanadoo.fr./ erbar. etudiant@wanadoo.fr
Web: www.erba - rennes.fr
Nearest Station: (SNCF) Rennes
Contact: Isabelle Gascard
Level of French: Conversational to Advanced

Smack in the middle of Rennes, one of the liveliest student cities in France (students make up a quarter of the population), sits a beautiful 18th-century building, looking out onto a cobbled courtyard. This former convent is home to the École des Beaux Arts. Established over 200 years ago, the school offers not only three options, Art, Design and Communication leading to the DNSEP and the DNAP, but also a Masters in New Technology and a DNAT in Digital Imaging and Graphic Design (*Diplôme National d'Arts et Techniques*). Since Rennes is renowned for its expertise in information technology (this is, after all, where the Internet's predecessor, the Minitel, was created), the Beaux Arts offers a valuable compromise: a school with a history looking to the future. With 410 students in total (over five years), this is one of the larger provincial art schools. Information about enrolment and the entrance exam is available from January and the exam takes place in May.

There is an annual fee of 1960FF (+1020FF Social Security). Information about accommodation is available through CROUS.

ETPA Rennes

1, rue Xavier Grall, 35700 Rennes
Tel: +33 2 99 36 64 64
Fax: +33 2 99 36 26 40
Email: ETPA@etpa_galeode.fr
Nearest Station: (SNCF) Rennes
Contact: Monsieur Andre Ferre
Level of French: Intermediate

Rennes is renowned in France as a centre for audiovisual research and innovation. The Minitel, a close relative of the Internet, was designed here and it is home to the CCETP, a centre for television and telecommunications research. Jean Levy, founder of the ETPA in Toulouse took such a reputation into account when he chose to found his second school in this busy student city. The ETPA's objective is to give students the knowledge and ability to adapt and work with any multimedia or audiovisual equipment, without focussing on a particular career. The Website for the ETPA was designed by the students, and they would be equally adept at filming promotional videos or working in a recording studio. It offers a three-year multidisciplinary course, which covers all aspects of media production. In 1997 the school began a new one-year course in 'Make-Up'. For 32,000FF it is possible to learn all aspects of film and TV make-up, special effects and fashion make-up. Students gain a *Certificat de Compétence Professionelle* after three years and fees are 39,000FF per year (including all material and laboratory costs). There is limited help with accommodation.

Le Moulinot
Le Port, 89660 Mailly le Chateau, France
Tel/Fax: +33 3 86 8110 83
Contact: Stan Rose
Nearest Station: (SNCF) Mailly la Ville
Nearest Airport: Orly

The 'Moulinot' is an 18th century water mill set in its own grounds on the river Cure. The village in which it is situated, Vermenton, is located near to the cathedral town of Auscerre, in the heart of Burgundy. Stan and Avril Rose are professional painters who have been running workshops in France for the past ten years; they exhibit regularly in Europe.

Each course runs for seven days; students can work in any medium. They are encouraged to personally respond to their own choice of subject matter, such as a village scene or a still life. In the evening relaxed group discussions take place, enabling an exchange of ideas over a glass of wine. Students of all abilities are welcome, as well as their non-painting partners. It is expected that students will provide their own materials, according to their preferred medium, although additional stocks of paper and paints may be purchased as required.

Sepia
15, rue Lamoriciere,
44100 Nantes
Tel: +33 2 40 69 27 54
Fax: +33 2 40 69 05 77
Email/Web: None
Nearest Station: (SNCF) Nantes
Contact: Michel Martin/ Eric Lamour
Level of French: Intermediate

On the edge of the Loire, close to the port of Nantes, sits Sepia, an art school with a professional mission: training art directors and designers with an awareness of the commercial needs of advertising. Its three-year *Certificat des Carrières Creatives en Arts Graphiques* is not only developed in collaboration with advertising and communication agencies, but also examined by them. Students follow classic art courses such as Drawing and Still Life, as well as Computer Design and Storyboards, spending 20 per cent of their time on placements. For their final exam, which constitutes 70 per cent of the total

Picture courtesy of Centre d'Art Vaas

mark, students produce an advertising campaign from the conception of the product, to its packaging and publicity. The school's buildings are as modern as its objectives, with classrooms looking out onto a leafy patio. Admission is by interview and presentation of a portfolio. Matriculation fees are 19,300FF per year, plus 1,050FF for supplies, 750FF for enrolment and 250FF for the exam. The school can help to find accommodation in the locality.

SOUTH-WEST

Atelier Arts Plastiques

2 Montee du Serret, 06380
Sospel, France
Tel: +33 4 93 75 04 97
Established: 1992
Level of French: None (Iris speaks English and Dutch)
Contact: Iris Blancardi de Jong
Nearest Station: (SNCF) Sospel

In the hinterland of the Côte d'Azur sits the small town of Sospel. Here, in a rural foyer, Iris Blancardi de Jong teaches two week-long holiday courses in contemporary art. A teacher and artist by profession, she offers classes in drawing, graphics, painting, observation and volume. Her approach is very open and international, using different materials and working with the specificities of each student. The workshop is very much a learning environment but Iris stresses that it is also a place where people from different countries can engage and make friends. It is also a bargain...there are very few places to receive artistic instruction for 45FF an hour, and certainly hardly any in such a beautiful part of the country.

A two-week *stage* with a two hour class every weekday costs 450FF. No previous experience is necessary but it helps to have an open mind and a willingness to learn about art. Enrolment needs to be made by telephone with final payment due 15 days before the start of the workshop. The *atelier* does not organise accommodation but can provide information about local hotels, *gîtes* or campsites. Alternatively call the Sospel Tourist Office on: +33 4 93 04 15 80.

Trains to Sospel are available from Nice station.

Les Ateliers Virgulin – Art et Style

18, rue Joseph Serlin,
69001
Lyon
Tel: +33 4 78 30 56 99
Fax: +33 4 72 00 93 64
Established: 1982
Level of French:
Conversational
Nearest Station: (SNCF) Lyon Perrache and Lyon Part-Dieu
Contact: Francoise Virgulin

Have you ever wanted to change jobs and launch yourself into an artistic career? If so, the Ateliers Virgulin's preparatory year might be an option. Open both to school-leavers planning an art education, and those who have changed their minds about their career or their course of study, this programme is specifically designed to give students a thorough grounding in art, with options available in applied art, contemporary art and textiles. For those determined to make a career in Interior Design, Restoration or Costume design the Ateliers runs a three-year programme in each subject.

Ateliers Virgulin is in the centre of Lyon, next to the Opera House. It is very small, with 50 students and only ten per class, and this ensures that it retains both the scale and spirit of an *atelier*. The price of one's year study is 26 000FF. An interview is obligatory as part of the selection procedure.

Centre d'Art Vaas

14 Traverse des Moulins,
06140
Vence
Tel: +33 4 93 58 29 42
Fax: +33 4 93 58 30 83
Contact: Mme Patricia Lossel
Level of French: Basic/
Conversational

Jean Dubuffet's work does not belie its geographical origins. A Vence studio in the Nice hinterland (with views of the Mediterranean and the mountains) seems an unlikely place to find inspiration for his "dirty-style blues" painting, strong on line, colour and texture, but not big on representation and landscape – yet this is where he painted. Having bought this studio, the Centre d'Art Vaas is now continuing this artistic tradition, offering classes in painting, drawing, sculpture and ceramics. Its objective, says Patricia, is to promote art for everyone, not for an elite, and it has worked closely with many local artists, especially the disabled, to encourage the promotion/distribution of their art. At a second site, close to the Place Godot, there is a gallery where artists connected to the Centre show their work. The atmosphere is warm and engaging, and for those who are staying a little longer, rooms are available to rent in one of the two buildings (from 2100FF to 3500FF a month sharing a bathroom and kitchen). Prices range from 80F per hour to 1000FF or 3000FF for eight hours over a month. Classes are small (maximum of 10) and during the winter they are even smaller. Many of the teachers speak English.

École des Beaux Arts Appliqués

Rue Emile Tavan, 13100
Aix-en-Provence
Tel: +33 4 42 27 57 35
Fax: +33 4 42 27 63 99
Email: cypres@aix.ensam.fr
Web: www.aix.ensam.fr/cypres
Level of French: Advanced
Contact: Ysabel de
Roquette/Marie-Paule Jouve
Nearest Station: (SNCF)
Marseille/Aix-en-Provence

Most French language students will have struggled with their pronunciation of "l'oeil" ("eye") but few will know that in Aix-en-Provence it has become a technological acronym. The Laboratoire Objet Espaces Intelligents Langages, at the École d'Art in Aix-en-Provence, is an *atelier* where students build robots and animated sculptures using electronical and mechanical technology. It is, states Ysabel de Roquette, emblematic of the transdisciplinary nature of the École d'Art, which aims to focus on the links between fine art and new technology. There are DNAP and DNSEP programmes and the school is equipped to teach all aspects of multimedia, including 2D and 3D, digital imaging, web design and video. The small number of students enrolled in this school (approximately 130 per year) enables a friendly atmosphere whereas the other 18,000 or so enrolled in Aix ensure a lively social life. Fees: 1,450FF per year for Europeans; 2,170FF per year for non-Europeans.

École de Conde

40 bis rue Vaubecour, 69002
Lyon
Tel: +33 4 78 42 92 39
Fax: +33 4 78 42 80 91
Email: +conde@infonie.fr
Web: www.infonie.fr
Nearest Station: (SNCF)
Lyon-Perrache
Contact: Pierre Guenegan
Level of French:
Intermediate

If you're looking for a big city lifestyle but can't quite face Paris, then try Lyon. An hour away from the ski slopes, three hours from the sea and two hours from Paris (on the TGV), France's second city is also home to the École de Conde, the biggest art school in the Rhône-Alpes region and one that is renowned for its good results. Situated on five sites along one street in the centre of Lyon, students follow courses in several domains: art, fashion and tourism. It is a very professional school and much in demand (enrolments begin in January for the following September). Only 16 students are accepted onto the two-year BTS in Fashion Design (26,000FF per year). International students need to send details of their qualifications and a covering letter.

École Regionale d'Art et d'Artisanat

488 Avenue Amiral de
Grasse, 06620
Le Bar-sur-Loup
Tel/Fax: +33 4 93 09 40 62
Email: ERAA@alpes-azur.com
Web: www.alpes-azur.
com/eraa
Nearest Station:
(SNCF) Nice
Contact:
Francois Raymond

In the hinterland of Nice and the Côte d'Azur, with a view of the mountains, sits this small school which offers classes in all areas of Arts Plastiques:

art history, drawing, painting, decoration, photography, computer graphics and sculpture. There are two methods of study, either signing up for an *atelier* on a termly basis (400FF per month per studio; 900FF for computer design), or enrolling for 30 hours per week over nine months (2,000FF per month; 335FF extra for computer design). The school is very new and is, at the time of writing, seeking recognition from the Minister of Culture. Many of the teachers speak English. Prospective students can either go to the school and try out the classes for a few days before enrolling or send a letter, explaining their motivation and objectives. Information about accommodation can be provided. The best way to reach the school is by car or bus: contact the school for more precise details.

Studio Mode

18, rue Anterrieu,
34000 Montpellier
Tel: +33 4 67 92 57 77
Fax: +33 4 67 58 59 45
Contact: Mme Gijouchet
Level of French: A-Level-
Intermediate
Nearest Station: (SNCF)
Montpellier

Montpellier is renowned for its student population and its sunny position. Two hours from the Pyrénées and 15 minutes from the sea, it is one of the liveliest and loveliest places to study in France. Studio Mode, in the centre of the city, is one of the few audiovisual schools on the Côte d'Azur, offering two-year BTS courses in photography, multimedia, camera and sound techniques, fashion design and graphic art. At present the school has approximately 180 students but in 1998 the school will be moving to larger premises in order to increase enrolment to 400. Classes are small (15 students maximum) and the teaching style is both professional and comprehensive. Enrolment takes place in February/March and interested applicants must send a letter of motivation and details of their qualifications.

Villa Arson- École Pilote Internationale d'Art et de Recherche

20 avenue Stephen Liegeard,
06000 Nice
Tel: +33 4 92 07 73 70
Fax: +33 4 93 84 41 55
Email: villa.arson@mail.azur.fr
Nearest station: (SNCF) Nice
Contact: Mme Muriel Virieu
Level of French: *Baccalauréat*
equivalent.

Nice beaches are not nice. Stones, rather than sand, greet the traveller, and getting in and out of the sea verges on the hazardous. But these "galets", as they are known, can be put to good use elsewhere. The École Pilote, a contemporary art school and centre in the north of the city, is in an old villa with walls made of the stones set in concrete. It prides itself on being an "école cool" where students feel at home. One of its great advantages is its artists in residence system. Professionals are always on site, setting up exhibitions with the students, giving advice and working on their own projects. Specialising in contemporary art, students follow the DNSEP or the DNAP but, unlike many other schools, the first year is probationary, and students are interviewed to determine their artistic suitability for the rest of the programme. The school is very international and modern, but, with approximately 160 students per year, will appeal to those looking for a friendly approachable place to study. Fees are 1200FF per year. There is a limited amount of accommodation on site.

SOUTH-WEST

La Boissière

F 19310 Ayen
Tel: +33 5 55 25 15 69
Fax: +33 5 55 25 23 87
Website/Email:
www.pageszoom.com/la-boissiere
Level of French: Variable
Established: 1974
Contact: Gerard Veillet
Nearest station: (SNCF) Brive

La Boissière, a big house in the Correze, bordered by Limousin, Quercy and Perigord, has, says its director Monsieur Veillet, 'a soul, the sort of atmosphere that encourages creativity'. For an art centre this is rather a trump card, and during the summer months holidaymakers and artists, beginners and professionals of every age and nationality come to learn how to paint, photograph and pot in this rural idyll. Two artists, a ceramicist and painter, work here all year round in studios and in July and August, joined by teachers of music, dance, photography, mime, theatre and sculpture, they run week-long sessions in their various specialisms.

Participants work in small groups (maximum six in photography, 15 in theatre), attending the studio and class in the mornings and having free afternoons either to work on a particular project or to visit the area. Prices range from 1,400FF for a sculpture class to 1,850FF for black and white photography. No previous experience is required and within mixed ability groups teachers direct instruction according to

an individual's needs. Although most of the classes are in French a lack of linguistic ability is not an obstacle to artistic expression. Some of the teachers speak other languages, and everyone is willing to help, where necessary. Anyone aged 15 and over can attend classes and there is a babysitting service for younger children.

Not every visitor has to take part in a course. If one member of a group wants to paint, but every one else wants to pot or just potter, this is perfectly acceptable. Accommodation is available in the house. There are six double bedrooms, plus a dormitory that sleeps twelve and six further bedrooms in the village. Prices include half-board and students can eat lunch in La Boissière's bar. Possibilities range from 1,944FF for seven nights in a single room with private bathroom, to 936FF for seven nights in a dormitory. Children up to the age of two stay free, from three-six years a third of the tariff is payable, from seven to 10 years half-tariff, and from 11 to 14 at 15 per cent.

Enrolments begin in January.

École des Beaux-Arts de Bordeaux

7, rue des Beaux-Arts,
33800 Bordeaux
Tel: +33 5 56 33 49 10
Fax: +33 5 56 31 46 23
Established: 1584
Level of French: Advanced
Nearest Station: (SNCF)
Bordeaux
Contact: Brigitte Beau-Poncie

Established by Michel de Montaigne (the Mayor of Bordeaux) in 1584, the École des Beaux Arts in Bordeaux is the oldest fine art school in provincial France. It is also at the forefront of a modern revolution. In 1997 a new teaching system was put in place across the whole state sector of art schools, modelled on the independent reforms carried out five years ago in Bordeaux. Rather than simply teaching students particular techniques, students centre their learning around personal projects. They are thus liberated from the usual educational pattern of years of compulsory classes followed by a brief period of individual responsibility and input. From year one the students are implicated and involved in what they are creating and what they are learning.

This open attitude towards study is part of the school's overall vision. Learning is neither static nor centralised. If it is necessary to set up a studio in Seville or LA, for one month or a year, in order to study Nomadic Thought, then students travel to take part in it. In the past students have worked in Africa, Mexico and Dakar. The school organises study voyages, at greatly subsidised prices (an all inclusive ten-day trip to New York for 1000FF!) in order to enable students to see and engage with as much of the international art world as possible.

The school specialises in Contemporary and Modern Art and Design, although the courses cover everything from drawing and painting to digital imaging. Approximately 450 students take the school entrance exam, and 60 pass every year. Registration (for the exam) begins in January, ends in March, and the tests take place in the first two weeks in May. Foreign students can apply through a portfolio and credit transfer but should realise that it is a state (not school) policy to interview every foreign transfer student, usually in May. Accommodation for students enrolling for the whole programme is available through CROUS. Rooms can be reserved in a student residence for those staying for short periods. Fees are the usual: incredibly cheap for the Bordelaise resident (595FF per year) or almost as incredibly cheap for the non-Bordelaise (1525FF per year).

The School is so close to the Gare SNCF Bordeaux that taxi drivers will refuse the fare. So walk!

École Nationale des Arts et Techniques de l'Image

26, rue Jean Alexandre,
86000 Poitiers
Tel: +33 5 49 88 96 53
Fax: +33 5 49 88 24 46
Nearest Station:
Poitiers/Angouleme
Level of French: Advanced
Contact: Francois Pelletier

The old Jesuits' college in the centre of Poitiers is now home to the ENAT, a modern art school which offers instruction in three academic cycles: creation-design; authoring; production. The Poitiers site focuses on Televisual Creation and Virtual Reality, whereas in Angouleme, the focus is on Multimedia Creation and Publishing. Students learn about Animation as well as Art History, Volume and Video. The school's equipment was recently updated to include a 3D studio and a large TV studio. The site is shared with the École des Beaux Arts which runs classic *ateliers* for part-timers, so on Wednesday afternoons children and adults swell the otherwise small population (approximately 100 students). There is a family atmosphere, but the city itself welcomes over 30 000 students per year (a third of the whole population) so there is plenty of student life. Enrolment begins in January for the following October. The entrance exam is in four stages: take-away paper; written paper; interview; tests on site. Fees for

ART AND DESIGN

Joan Heath

years one to four are 2350FF (plus Social Security) and year five costs 6500FF (plus Social Security). Accommodation information can be obtained through CROUS.

L'Île aux Peintres/Societé Hôtel Racine

Place du Port au Ble, 02460 La Ferte Milon
Tel: +33 3 23 96 72 02
Fax: +33 3 23 96 72 37
Established: 1987
Level of French:
Conversational
Nearest Station: (SNCF)
La Ferte-Milon
Nearest Airport: Roissy Charles de Gaulle
Contact: Mme Waterlot

Visitors to the Île aux Peintres will be forgiven for thinking that they have arrived in a painters' idyll. Situated in the Hôtel Racine, a 400-year old house with a leafy garden next to the River Ourcq, this painting school will encourage the most latent of talents. For a weekend or a week, amateur artists do nothing but paint... no cooking, cleaning, bed-making or washing-up. Most of the students are from Northern Europe and the atmosphere is both international and intimate... everyone feels at home.

The instruction is professional and flexible. Small groups (minimum four, maximum ten) are taught by artists and teachers from the École des Beaux Arts in Paris, and once the brushes are downed glasses are raised as students and teachers all eat together in a group.

No previous experience is necessary so beginners will feel as comfortable as the amateur who has already spent time in front of an easel. The *atelier* runs weekend or week-long courses and accommodation is included in private hotel bedrooms. A week's course from Monday to Saturday morning costs around 4,200FF or 4,500FF in July and August (this includes accommodation and full-board, classes, materials (not brushes) and, if necessary, the return trip from Paris). A weekend costs 1,200FF. To enrol, write or fax to ask for the documentation (in English or French). La Ferte-Milon is one hour from Paris by train and 45 minutes from Roissy airport by car.

Food
and Wine
Courses

Every English-speaker knows the words 'restaurant', 'gourmet' and 'café', and many will have said 'bon appetit' before a meal. The proliferation of French words in the English language is a sign of the importance of Gallic gastronomy in our lives. Whether you come from New Zealand or New York, it is likely that you have come across boeuf bourguignon or mousse au chocolat. Rather than just eating the dishes that symbolise this historic gastronomic tradition, why not learn how to make them? France is full of cookery schools, and whether you're planning a weekend in Provence or a year in Paris, there will be an option to suit you.

Food

The course or school you choose will depend on your personal objectives. If you're planning to start a business or work in a restaurant, a nine-month course is the obvious option. In Paris there are three schools offering year-long professional courses: the Ritz, Le Cordon Bleu and the École Supérieure de Cuisine Ferrandi. The Ritz and the Cordon Bleu also offer shorter courses ranging from a half-day to six weeks. If you're interested in food as an amateur, not a professional, several shorter and less formidable options are available. The residential and holiday courses, and the shorter half-day classes are not academically structured in terms of hours and expectations but their

Victoria Davies/Benoît Besnard

classes are just as professional and comprehensive.

École Lenotre, part of the famous Lenotre patisserie and caterer, has a one classroom school offering half-day or full-day courses which teach a lot more than the art of the croissant. Catering professionals like Sue Young, Francoise Meunier and, in the royal category, Princesse Marie-Blanche de Broglie, run friendly, tourist-oriented courses in homely yet professional environments. Beyond Paris short, holiday courses predominate. These take place in restaurants and hotels, at chefs' homes, or sometimes in chateaux.

Demonstration/Practical Classes

Every course lasting more than a day will be a taught practical to a small group. Participants are involved at every stage. In Paris there is also the option of demonstration classes. These are taught in larger groups and although recipes and information are provided, it is the chefs not the classes who get their hands dirty. This is very much a tourist option, since the large groups make it a rather passive experience. Sitting at the back, with 40 other foreigners between you and the chef, is nowhere near as much fun as standing at the front, with the ingredients and knife in your hand.

Wine

For wine aficionados the breakdown is similar. Professional wine experts, either established or aspiring, will find oenology degrees available at Universities in most wine-producing regions, such as Reims and Bordeaux, as well as wine-marketing Masters degrees at the Université des Eaux de Vie et Boissons Spiritueuses near Cognac. The Université des Eaux de Vie et Boissons

Spiritueuses also organises wine-tastings and presentations, both scheduled and on demand. Short courses for the amateur can be followed country-wide, at the Institut Vatel in Paris, for example, or at the Université du Vin in Suze-la-Rousse. There are also several more personality-led options, with characters like Ylan Schwartz and Jacques Vivet, and with focused and friendly centres like the CIDD. Tourist offices across France, especially Bordeaux, Champagne and Burgundy, organise weekend and week-long tours of their regions for individuals and groups. A typical package will include wine-tastings, vineyard tours and oenology lessons, as well as accommodation and meals.

Costs

The cost of the course will depend on both content and cachet. The Ritz and Cordon Bleu Grand Diplôme courses are expensive but they have international reputations and certificates (nine months at the Cordon Bleu costs 170,900FF and at the Ritz 170,150FF). A similar and equally professional course is available at the École de Cuisine Supérieure Ferrandi for 90,000FF. A half-day course costs from 750FF to 950FF at the Cordon Bleu and from 600FF to 1,300FF at the Ritz. At Lenotre, a much smaller but equally professional school, a similar half-day will cost 420FF. Amongst the smaller schools prices vary. Marie-Blanche de Broglie charges 5,500FF for a week-long course in Cuisine and Art de Vivre. Sue Young charges 275FF for a demonstration and 450FF for a practical class; Françoise Meunier's practical classes cost 450FF for one class, 2,000FF for five classes and 3,800FF for ten classes. In the wine world Ylan Schwartz's five-session initiation, which can be taught over a weekend, costs 1,600FF.

Jacques Vivet's five-session evening class costs 1,100FF, and a one-off at the Institut Vatel, which organises wine-tastings throughout the year, costs 260FF (this is taught in French).

Prices change dramatically outside the capital because many of the schools listed offer packages combining accommodation and classes. Cuisine en Provence is one of the most expensive at 8,500FF, per week but the price includes everything from tuition to airport transfers. Visit Bourgogne's four-day gastronomic discovery of Burgundy costs 5,000FF but prospective participants should consider that an extra two nights accommodation are recommended, which adds another 600FF to the price. Sylvie Lallemand's residential week in Provence costs 3,400FF (and she has a swimming pool) and Olga Manguin's Provençal cooking classes cost 1,000FF per day, including full board (the seventh day is free when booking six).

Levels of French

Language skills are unnecessary in most of the established schools, which all offer classes in English or simultaneous translation. Many of the schools run by individuals also operate bilingually. Exceptions include the École Lenotre, the Institut Vatel and the full-time oenology courses. The classes and trips organised by tourist boards and associations like Les Toques Nivernaises are more likely to be taught in French. However, translations and interpretations are generally available on demand.

Levels of Expertise

Whether you want professional training or a pleasurable trip, enthusiasm and motivation are more important than experience and mastery.

Even the year-long courses (which demand a large commitment in terms of time and money) do not necessarily assume any prior knowledge of wine and food. Shorter holiday packages, which are more relaxed in structure but just as professional in teaching terms, will teach participants everything from shopping and chopping to sauces and courses.

PARIS VS THE PROVINCES

Paris offers more choice in terms of schools and types of classes, but there are no organised holiday options available. Enterprising learners could book themselves into a hotel and try out several half-day classes in wine and food. Those seeking an all-in-one package will need to look beyond the capital. The other important factor to consider is whether you are interested in food and wine in general, or in a particular speciality. France is a very centralised country in some respects, but when it comes to gastronomy the different regions come into their own. Whether discovering the bright tastes and colours of Provençal cooking or the *foie gras* of the Perigord, the local produce and knowledge will be unsurpassed. When it comes to wine, nothing can quite rival the experience of touring local vineyards before descending into a cellar to taste the latest vintage.

PARIS

Centre de Dégustation Jacques Vivet
48, rue de Vaugirard, 75006 Paris
Tel: +33 1 43 25 96 30
Fax: +33 1 46 33 20 33
Established: 1982
Level of French required: Intermediate

Nearest Station: (Métro)
Rennes. (RER) Luxembourg.
Contact: Jacques Vivet

Jacques Vivet's Centre de Dégustation is next to the sort of courtyard that Francophiles dream of – heavy wooden doors, cobblestones underfoot and tall, white buildings. From here Monsieur Vivet runs various courses and, in his opinion, everyone has the necessary basic equipment for tasting and appreciating wine: a nose. The style of classes is both informative and informal. French, British and American amateurs, of all ages and from all backgrounds, find a common connection in contemplating mouthfuls of Sauvignon and Sancerre.

Wine-tasting, for Monsieur Vivet, is an art and, as such, once students have a basic knowledge, they will be able to use their skills and continually improve. The initiation course which lasts ten hours (in five two-hour blocks) costs 1,100FF, and takes place on Tuesdays at 8.30pm. More advanced classes, concentrating on particular regions, appelations and vintages, last one-two hours and prices vary. Monsieur Vivet also teaches an evening class for the Mairie du Paris. Since class size is very limited, both at the Mairie and at the Centre, book early. Payment is made at the time of enrolment.

The Centre is at 48, rue de Vaugirard, in the 6th *arrondissement*. Rennes and Luxembourg stations are on either side of the Jardin du Luxembourg. From Rennes follow either the rue de Rennes or boulevard Raspail, and you will hit rue de Vaugirard. Turn left and 48 is on the left just before the Senate on the right. If you pass the Senate you have gone too far. From Luxembourg take

the rue Gay Lussac exit. When you surface, keep the Jardin du Luxembourg on your left and follow the rue de Medicis which will become rue de Vaugirard. The Centre is on your right just past the Senate. Press the "Vivet-Vins" buzzer.

CIDD: Centre d'Information, de Documentation et de Dégustation

30 rue de la Sablière, 75014 Paris.
Tel: +33 1 45 45 32 20/ +33 1 45 45 44 20
Fax: +33 1 45 42 78 20
Established: 1982
Level of French required: Basic to Advanced depending on course. Courses also available in English, Japanese and Korean.
Nearest Station: (Métro) Pernety/Alesia
Contact: Alain Segelle

Do not be misled by the name. This is not a haughty, grandiose institution but a small, cosy centre which aims to educate amateurs and professionals alike about all aspects of wine appreciation. Once a month the Centre runs an open house when wine-makers from a specific region of France bring their products along for a tasting. On one of these particular evenings I discovered a wine region I'd never heard of (Côtes du Toul) and tasted old favourites (Vouvray and Montlouis). Amateur through and through, I was a little nervous about tasting the wine (did I have to spit it out? Should I make intelligent comments?) but the relaxed and amicable atmosphere made it easy to try, compare and ask questions. Such an evening suggests that the comprehensive, professional courses, taught by the

FOOD AND WINE

90

founder Alain Segelle, are also worth following. These are for the serious wine buff, who wishes to make a love of wine into a career.

There are so many courses available that it would be impossible to describe them all. In English, sessions include three hour classes on the Principles and Procedures of Wine-Making, Harmony of Food and Wines and the Alsace Wine Region. Prices range from one session for 390FF, 950FF for three, to an Amateur Cycle including twelve different classes for 3,360FF. To enrol, contact Alain Segelle.

Take métro line 13 to Pernety. Cross over rue Raymond Losserand, and with the métro behind you, walk along rue Pernety. The road forks at the junction with rue Didot. Take the left-hand street. CIDD is on a left-hand corner a few minutes away from the junction.

Le Cordon Bleu

8 rue Delhomme, 75015 Paris
Tel: +33 1 53 68 22 50
Fax: +33 1 48 56 03 96
Website: cordonbleu.net
Established: 1895
Level of French required: None: all classes translated into English.
Nearest Station: (Métro) Vaugirard
Contact: Mlle Sabine Bailly

The Cordon Bleu is renowned worldwide for a culinary tradition of excellence. The name derives from the sixteenth century when King Henry III created the "Order of the Holy Spirit". Members were awarded a cross which hung from a blue ribbon, the *cordon bleu*. By the eighteenth century the term was used to describe anyone who

excelled in a chosen field, particularly the culinary arts. The School was established in 1895 and in the 20th century students from all over the world, especially North America, Korea and Japan, come to learn the secrets of French cuisine. The school is quite unnoticeable at first, situated in a small, unprepossessing street. As you approach, the familiar logo looms in blue and white on the side of an otherwise grey building. Inside the school, a large, leafy cafeteria takes up much of the ground floor and classes take place in ultra-modern practice kitchens upstairs.

The school makes much of its international renown, both in Paris and in its publicity. What it is not renowned for is friendliness. Teachers in language schools all over the city mentioned that their students had complained about the Cordon Bleu's elitism, snobbery and coldness. On a visit to the school, I experienced all three.

Options range in level and price, from the nine-month Grand Diplôme (170 900FF), to three-hour demonstrations (220FF). Courses include a month's Introduction to French Patisserie (10,250FF), a week-long session on Regional Cooking (4,590FF) or a day-long Paris Market Tour (645 FF). There is a Sabrina cooking and pastry demonstration which pays homage to the film of the same name, in which Audrey Hepburn followed cordon bleu classes (220FF), and an Easter Egg workshop (750FF). For full-time courses, uniforms and equipment must either be purchased or provided by the student. For workshops a uniform and equipment will be lent to you. Classes are limited to 40 students per demonstration, eight to 10 for practical sessions.

Contact Mlle Sabine Bailly for an application form and further details. The certificate and diploma classes start four times a year and applications must be made three months prior to the start of the desired course. Studies can be broken up by semester if necessary. The school can help to find accommodation.

Exit Métro Vaugirard and you will see a small square, place Adolphe Cherioux. Keep this on your right and head down rue de Vaugirard. Take the first left into rue Dalleray. Turn immediately right into rue Francois Villon then left into rue Delhomme. The school is on the right.

Cours de Cuisine Marie-Blanche de Broglie

18 avenue de la Motte-Picquet, 75007 Paris
Tel: +33 1 45 51 36 34
Fax: +33 1 45 51 90 19
Established: 1975
Level of French required: None – on request classes can be taught in English, French and Spanish; a Japanese interpreter can be provided if necessary
Nearest Station: (Métro) La Tour Maubourg
Contact: Princesse Marie-Blanche de Broglie

If you don't want to make a faux pas when organising a dinner party in France, come to one of Marie-Blanche de Broglie's classes. A real Princess, she can teach you all there is to know about social etiquette and French *haute cuisine*. For example, did you know that the guest of honour at a dinner sits in the middle of the table in France, not at the end? In a land that prides itself on social formality, this detail of social etiquette might prove invaluable to any

expatriate brave enough to invite their new patron to dinner. In the seventh *arrondissement*, in a large, elegant apartment, Princesse de Broglie runs the veritable aristocracy of small non-professional schools. Established for over two decades, she offers practical classes and courses in the Art of Entertaining. Classes take place every morning from 10.30 to 1.30 and students then eat what they have prepared. The emphasis is on reacting to students' needs and wants whilst teaching them cooking skills from scratch. In the Art of Entertaining classes, the Princess can draw on her own family background and experience to teach her students the formalities and details that separate a casual meal from an elegant dinner.

Marie-Blanche offers a veritable panoply of courses. A block of Classic Cooking classes costs from 3,010FF for 5 to 10,260FF for 20 (1997 prices). The programme of dishes and recipes depends on the students. At the end of each class the next is planned in terms of seasonal availability and student requests. An introductory Art de Vivre class costs 780FF and one week costs 3,500FF. The week-long course (four afternoons from Monday to Thursday) includes the following classes: A History of French Gastronomy; French Traditions; How to Receive Guests; How to Serve Drinks and three different table layouts (traditional, contemporary and disposable). A combined week of cooking and Art de Vivre costs 5,500FF (all day Monday to Thursday) and there is a third weekly course A la Française (all day Monday to Friday). This includes four cooking classes followed by lunch, one evening class with candlelit dinner, one dessert and pastry class, three Art de Vivre classes and one Introduction to French

Cheeses. Groups are small (maximum six) and students come from all over the world. Prices include a free apron! No expertise is required. Classes run all year round except in August and during Christmas and Easter holidays. A 10 per cent deposit is required to secure a place and all payments must be made by the first day of classes.

Sandwiched between the École Militaire and the Hôtel des Invalides, the formality of the location matches the formality of the school. Take line 8 to La Tour-Maubourg and head away from Les Invalides along avenue de La Motte-Picquet. CMB is on the right. Be prepared for the butler...

École de Cuisine Supérieure Ferrandi

28, rue de l'Abbé Gregoire,
75006 Paris
Tel: +33 1 49 55 29 19
Fax: +33 1 49 54 29 78
Established: 1983
Level of French required: None
Nearest Station: (Métro) St Placide/Rennes
Contact: Mme Auffret

The École de Cuisine Supérieure Ferrandi is a veritable labyrinth of a school; a huge building, which from the ground up is devoted to the art of the table, from slicing an onion to serving a soufflé. Part of the Chamber of Commerce, the ECSF is one of the few professional catering colleges that offers a state programme suitable for international students. Like the Ritz and the Cordon Bleu, it offers a nine-month bilingual programme, but unlike both those schools, the ECSF course, established 15 years ago, leads to a C.A.P (Certificat d'Aptitude Professionnel) in French Cuisine, which is the first qualification gained by any French

chef. Every year 14 students, from all over the world, spend nine months learning about French cooking and culture. The school prides itself on its technical and on-the-job training. From day one students prepare dishes which will be served to the public and staff in the school restaurant. ECSF students mingle with French students, not just with other foreigners. They are focused from the start on cooking as a career and a business, not on cooking for pleasure or leisure. The style of cooking is classic and traditional French. Demonstrations by Maîtres Ouvriers de France (Master Craftspeople who are the leaders in a profession) take place on a regular basis.

The nine-month course costs 90,000 FF. The price includes a three-day trip to Bordeaux and a gastronomic wine weekend in Burgundy. Classes are taught in English and French five days a week with French language lessons on Friday afternoon. Accommodation is the student's responsibility.

To enrol, contact Mme Auffret for a brochure and application form. No previous experience is necessary. US students should note that the ECSF is an institution eligible for Guaranteed Student Loans.

Take métro line 4 to St Placide or 12 to Rennes. From either station head to rue de Vaugirard. From Rennes turn right on Vaugirard then right again into rue de l'Abbé Gregoire. From St Placide turn left onto Vaugirard then right onto rue de l'Abbé Gregoire. ECSF is on the left.

École de Paris des Métiers de la Table

17 rue Jacques Ibert, B.P. 14407, 75816 Paris, Cedex 17
Tel: +33 1 44 09 12 00
Fax: +33 1 44 09 12 34
Established: 1978
Level of French: Intermediate
Nearest Station: (Métro) Louise Michel; (RER) Pereire-Levallois
Contact: Myriam Fiasca

It would be worth learning some French to study here since it is the only school to offer a month-long course in Chocolate. The École is a professional school aimed at 14- to 25-year-olds planning a catering career but it also runs short non-professional modules for the gourmands who like the idea of catering but not the reality. You can test the quality of the teaching and end result by booking into the restaurant for lunch or dinner. A four-course meal costs 80FF (or 100FF for the extra-special Tuesday evening dinner with more up-market ingredients such as scallops and trout in Chablis). The school is small, as are the classes (15 students maximum) and unpretentious, with dedicated staff and excellent facilities. Don't expect the fuss of the tourist market schools.

There are several modules available, in Cuisine and Patisserie. From September to December you could complete modules in Starters and Soups, Fish, Classic Pastry and Cake Pastry. Each Cuisine module takes 21 hours, over three weeks, with a four-hour practical and a three-hour theoretical class. They cost 1,890FF and there is a 10 per cent discount for those following more than four modules (20 per cent for more than six). Each Patisserie module lasts an average of 24 hours with three-hour classes on Monday and Tuesday. They cost from 1,890FF for Decoration to 2430FF for Ice-creams and Meringues (Chocolate comes in at 2,160FF). For those following all six modules there is a 50 per cent discount on Module 6 (Decoration). All students receive a certificate of attendance. It is possible (though probably a little exhausting) to complete both sets over the space of a year. No previous experience is necessary.

Take line 3 (direction Levallois-Perret) to Louise Michel. Walk along rue Louise Michel to rue Carnot which is the second on the right. At the junction with rue Jacques Ibert, turn left and the École is on the right.

L'École du Vin

17 passage Foubert, 75013 Paris
Tel: +33 1 45 89 77 39
Fax: +33 1 45 80 72 80
Established: 1988
Level of French required: Basic (though Monsieur Schwartz speaks English)
Nearest Station: (Métro) Tolbiac
Contact: Ylan Schwartz

Bored with teaching and determined to make something of his love of wine, Ylan Schwartz took a camper van around France and learnt about every vineyard and vintage in the country. He brought his knowledge back to Paris a year later and set up his own school to teach amateurs how to taste and enjoy wine. He is the sort of person that every wine amateur needs to help them understand the complicated art of oenology. He is knowledgeable and passionate about wine and the food that accompanies it, but he is neither a snob nor a scientist. Working either as a roving expert or teaching sessions in his flat, he aims to encourage the enjoyment and love of wine rather than blind the amateur with the science and jargon of wine-tasting.

Ylan's courses are truly individual, a little like the man himself. He teaches five different wine discovery courses: five sessions (three-four hours each) for 1,600FF. There is a maximum of eight students per group since only eight can taste from a bottle! During the first session Ylan devises the programme for the next three in consultation with the students and for the last session, which takes place in a restaurant, he plans a specific menu to match the wines to be tasted.

Avid wine-buffs already living in Paris can book themselves onto one of the evening courses. Those from further afield can either book Ylan for a whole weekend in the capital or arrange to spend a week discovering one or two of the vineyards of France (you will need a group to make it viable). Send a fax for further details and to enrol.

Ylan's Paris-based classes take place in 17 passage Foubert in the 13th *arrondissement*. Take métro line 7 to Tolbiac. Walk along rue Tolbiac (increasing numbers direction). Passage Foubert is third on the left. Ylan's apartment building is on the left-hand side.

École Lenotre

48 avenue Victor Hugo,
75116 Paris
Tel: +33 1 45 02 21 19
Fax: +33 1 45 00 34 64
Established: 1995
Level of French required:
Advanced (the chef is French)
Nearest Station: (Métro)
Victor Hugo
Contact: Linda Hrmo

The École Lenotre is the youngest cooking school in Paris. It is small in size yet grand in reputation, since it is part of Lenotre, one of the most famous patisseries and caterers in Paris. Situated in the rather select sixteenth *arrondissement*, just along the street from the Arc de Triomphe, the school is literally a large, practical kitchen inside the Lenotre boutique. A huge marble island, seating a maximum of eight students, is flanked by cupboards, ovens, and the patisserie. The window, looking out onto the street, makes the classroom light and provides ample opportunity (for nosy souls who like to see before they buy) to gauge the quality of the work in progress.

The École's objective is to give passionate amateurs the chance to share professional experience. It offers short, practical courses covering all areas of cuisine, not just, as its origins might imply, patisserie. Sessions last four hours and subjects covered include Game Terrines, Croissants and Pains au Chocolat and Cooking with Wine. Day-long sessions, covering five-course menus, are also periodically available. Alain the chef, begins with a short theoretical introduction, followed by a practical class which aims to provide each student with the skills and information to reproduce the recipes at home. The limited number of students ensures unlimited involvement, both from the chef and from the class. All materials are provided, including ingredients, aprons and details of recipes and, at the end of the session, the amateurs take home their creations. Most of the students are Parisians such that this is probably one of the best places to get an idea of what interests the French, rather than other foreigners, in the world of cuisine. The chef is French which suggests that this isn't an option for those with basic linguistic ability. However, on the day I visited there were at least two students (one who had flown all the way from Portugal) who were far from fluent yet still enjoyed the class. Numbers are limited to eight per half-day session and no previous experience is necessary. A half-day costs 420FF whereas a full day, including lunch, costs 1150FF.

Contact the École directly for a programme and reservation form in order to enrol. Sessions are payable in advance and cancellations must be received at least two days before the class date to qualify for a refund. To reach École Lenotre take métro line 2 to Victor Hugo. In the Square head down avenue Victor Hugo towards place Charles de Gaulle (between avenue Leonardo de Vinci and rue Copernic). École Lenotre is on the left-hand side, on the corner of rue Paul Valéry.

Françoise Meunier

7, rue Paul Lelong, (Esc. A bis, 2nd Floor), 75002 Paris
Tel/Fax: +33 1 40 26 14 00
E-mail: fmeunier@easynet.fr
Website: www.intiweb.com/fmeunier
Established: 1997
Level of French required: None
Nearest Station: (Métro) Sentier
Contact: Françoise Meunier

On the day I visited Françoise Meunier she wasn't running a class but participating in a photo shoot for a food magazine. Fresh salmon and white wine were proferred as I stood and watched the supermodel of terrines being dressed up for its big moment. Somehow, amongst all the

activity, she found time to tell me about her classes. The school, in a lovely, light apartment with a large cooking island flanked by ovens and equipment, is the result of much research. Françoise had talked about starting it for 25 years. The day after leaving her job as Director of Human Resources at Moulinex, she enrolled for a class at Lenotre. Over the next few months she tried every cooking school in Paris and, once she had seen what was already on offer, she designed her own. The result is modern, no-nonsense cooking courses which draw on her vast professional experience in the food industry and a large repertoire of recipes. Her objective is to start with basic techniques and simple ingredients in order to show her students what they can achieve in their own kitchens without any fuss or ceremony. Aiming to teach whatever her students want to know, whether it's how to cook from scratch (one Japanese woman comes every day for a class) or how to prepare a celebratory dinner, her approach is personal and welcoming.

Classes are all practical and there is a maximum of six students per group. One class costs 450FF and blocks of five, ten and fifteen classes cost 2000FF, 3800FF and 7200FF respectively. Wine courses, taught by region, cost 750FF for three or 1250FF for five. Weekend packages or group occasions (how about a birthday present of a cooking class followed by dinner?) can be organised on demand. Françoise teaches in English, Spanish and French. Contact Francoise directly to discuss availability and cost. Take métro line 3 to Sentier. Walk along rue Reaumur to the junction with rue Montmartre. Turn left. Rue Paul Lelong is the first on the right.

IMHI: Institut de Management Hôtelier International

Avenue Bernard Hirsch, B.P. 105, 95021 Cergy-Pontoise Cedex, France
Tel: +33 1 34 43 32 55
Fax: +33 1 34 43 17 01
E-mail: infoimhi@edu.essec.fr
Website: www.hotelschool. cornell.edu/imhi
Established: 1981
Level of French required: Intermediate
Nearest Station: Cergy-Préfecture

IMHI, a private postgraduate hospitality management school, is the product of a Franco-American partnership between ESSEC, one of Europe's most prestigious business schools, and Cornell University's School of Hotel Administration. Situated in Cergy, a new town on the outskirts of Paris, IMHI's objective is to educate managers with an international outlook, capable of leading the globalization of the hospitality industry.' What differentiates it from many similar schools is that both Cornell and ESSEC are fully involved in the programme and not just in name only.

IMHI offers a 21-month Masters-level study programme for professionals and graduates. Applicants must have a good Bachelor's degree, at least one year's experience in the hospitality business and be fluent in English. There is no age limit, most students are in their late 20s and all classes are taught in English. In order to graduate students must complete 34 units (68 credits): 13 core courses and 21 electives covering eight different disciplines, including accountancy, properties management and business policy. The six full-time trimesters (18 months) can be followed in succession or over a longer period (up to four years). The 18 months of study are complemented by a three-month management internship in the summer of the first year. About 55 candidates are admitted from approximately 180 pre-selected applicants and the annual tuition fee is 56 000FF ($10 200). 85 per cent of students find jobs within three months of graduating and the remaining 15 per cent within six months. Accommodation is available in university residences on the ESSEC campus or in ESSEC apartments shared with other students.

Initial enrolment, including completing an application form, forwarding references and academic documentation, finishes on May 15th. Selected students are then invited for interviews and, where necessary, an English language test. International candidates unable to travel to Europe may be interviewed at Cornell in New York, IMHI's Japan office or at a French embassy with an IMHI representative.

"I am from Argentina. I came here because I wanted a good professional training, which is not really available in South America. I knew of several other people who had studied at IMHI. Also the Institut have good publicity around the world and a high profile."

Elinora TarzibachiInstitut

To reach IMHI, take the RER A for Cergy and stop at Cergy Préfecture. From the station walk towards the Préfecture which is a modern, pyramid-shaped building. There is a BNP and cinemas on the left. Walk around the left-hand side of the Préfecture. The ESSEC campus is in front of you, to the left.

Ritz Escoffier École de la Gastronomie Française

Hotel Ritz, 15 place Vendôme, 75041 Paris Cedex 01
Tel: +33 1 43 16 30 50
Fax: +33 1 43 16 31 50
Established: 1988
Level of French required: None
Nearest Station: (Métro)
Concorde; Opéra; Madeleine
Contact: Mademoiselle Beaufils

The Ritz Escoffier School is situated in one of the finest hotels in the world. The school was established in 1988, almost a hundred years after the hotel, and aims to teach French gastronomy and related services to professionals and enthusiastic amateurs. The name itself would be enough to tempt many but it is also extremely well-run and friendly. The cadre is grand but the clientele and the chefs are very approachable. Classes are bilingual, taught in French with English translations and the students are international. Practical classes are limited to 10 students.

Amateur and professional courses are available. The Grand Diplôme, (170 150FF) a comprehensive culinary degree lasting 30 weeks, is composed of three levels: the Cesar Ritz, a six-week initiation and intermediate level course; the Ritz Escoffier, a 12-week advanced level course; the Art of French Pastry, a twelve-week course covering basic to advanced pastry techniques and practice. Students may enrol for one to six weeks of the Cesar Ritz and the Art of French Pastry and no previous experience is necessary. For the Ritz Escoffier previous experience, or completion of the Cesar Ritz, is required and students must enrol for the full twelve weeks. The Ritz diplomas are the only French culinary degrees recognised in America. Courses can be taken consecutively or in weekly increments over an extended period. For amateurs and those with less time and/or money to spare there are various week-long courses, such as Bread-making, The A to Z of sauces and A Taste of Perigord; one-day and afternoon workshops focusing on a particular menu or ingredient; evening classes and wine-tasting classes.

One of the most tempting options available involves one of the most ubiquitous French symbols, the croissant. By completing a week-long baking course in Bread Making and a week-long course in Breakfast Pastry Making (5,600FF each), students are entitled to ask for an apprenticeship in the hotel bakery. Imagine, two weeks and 11,000FF later, you could be making croissants for the customers at the Ritz.

Students attending courses for one week or more are provided with a complete chef's uniform with complimentary laundry, and those attending one-day practical classes are provided with an apron and kitchen towels. Students must wear appropriate shoes. All other kitchen equipment is provided by the school. To enrol, contact the school for a brochure. Classes at all levels start throughout the year.

The School entrance is at the back of the hotel, 38 rue Cambon, 75001 Paris. Exit métro Madeleine onto boulevard de la Madeleine. Turn right into rue Cambon. The School is on the left halfway down.

La Toque d'Or

55, rue de Varenne,
75007 Paris
Tel: +33 1 45 44 86 51
Fax: +33 1 45 44 63 81
E-mail: parisgourmet@mfn.com
Established: 1994
Level of French required: None
Nearest Station: (Métro)
Solferino
Contact: Sue Young

Nestled in the heart of the bourgeois and residential seventh *arrondissement*, home to the French establishment, is this very non-establishment cooking school. Having trained at Le Cordon Bleu and worked in a Michelin-starred restaurant in Brittany, Sue Young established La Toque d'Or in 1994. An English woman who has always had a passion for cooking, Sue teaches half-day demonstrations and full-day master classes, runs wine weekends in Burgundy and Alsace, wine appreciation courses and 'French for a day' trips. Most of her students are women, often expatriate Americans, who want to learn about French cuisine but can face neither the crowds or the costs of the bigger schools. The large and luminous room where she teaches in her flat perfectly symbolises the character of her work. It is both professional, thanks to the sleek demonstration equipment and facilities, and personal, thanks to the china and cookery books that line the walls.

A demonstration class (9am to 1pm: 275FF including a *dégustation* of the prepared menu) is a good starting point for a novice. Up to 16 students sit close enough to the action to see, taste and smell, but far enough away to avoid getting dirty. In a practical class (9am to 1pm: 450FF including lunch) a maximum of eight students take a step closer to the gleaming marble island and make the dishes themselves, with Sue's help. During a 'French for a day' class (all day 600FF) Sue and Irene and a group of eight to 10 gastronomes, spend the morning in the city's markets, discussing the products on display. Having stocked up on whatever looks interesting, they return to rue de Varenne to make lunch. In the afternoon, Irene leads a tour around antique shops, galleries and furniture dealers. The content of the day can be tailor-made depending on a particular group's interests. David Cobbold, an English wine writer and lecturer, teaches the wine appreciation class (1,200FF for four weekly sessions) and, again, these can be organised according to a group's timetable and level. For a real treat, enrol on a wine weekend. Two days in the Loire or Champagne region, with tastings, meals, 1st class TGV, accommodation and champagne breakfast costs 3,200FF (from Paris).

To reach La Toque d'Or, take métro Line 12 (direction Mairie d'Issy) to Solferino. Use the rue Villersexel exit. Rue de Bellechasse will be to your right. Head along this street with boulevard Saint Germain behind you. Rue de Varenne is the second cross street. Turn left and 55 is on your right. Go through the first courtyard, under the second arch and enter the building through the double glass doors on the left. La Toque d'Or is on the fourth floor. The door is on the right as you exit the lift.

FOOD AND WINE

Union des Oenologues de France: anatomy of a wine-tasting

(For enrolment) 2 Avenue Gallieni, 91710 Vert le Petit
(For classes) Institut Vatel, 107 rue Nollet, 75017 Paris; Office International de la Vigne et du Vin, 18 rue d'Aguesseau, 75008 Paris
Tel: 33 1 64 93 23 38
Fax: +33 1 64 93 28 32
Established: 1899
Level of French required: Advanced
Nearest Station: (Métro) Brochant/Madeleine
Contact: Arnaud Didier

To reach the Union des Oenologues wine-tasting class you pass in front of some of the most chic shops in Paris, steps away from the Élysées Palace, home of the President of the Republique. The sense of grandeur continues once you reach the Office International du Vin. After crossing a darkened courtyard you must ring the doorbell on a big red door. An old man comes to answer and ushers you across the high-ceilinged lobby and down a red-carpeted stairway. There the grandeur ends when you find yourself in a stone-walled room full of the paraphernalia of teaching: formica tables, horseshoe layout, overhead projector. However, although the sweeping staircases and red carpets may be over, the fun is just beginning.

There are 18 of us, sitting close together, with a folder each and a wine bucket on every table. For the next two and a half hours we work our way through a rather slow history of wine and its production, then into an extremely detailed and comprehensive elaboration of seven different wines, from a Blanc de Touraine to a Bordeaux. Since it happens to be the third Thursday in November, and this being France not the States, we also test this year's Beaujolais Nouveau (what dedication to the art of wine and tasting... we are missing Paris's biggest party night in order to discover how to turn vine into wine). The room started off quiet and tentative, with few offering a judgement on each bottle but our tongues are soon loosened by the convivial atmosphere, not the wine (seven bottles between 18 bottles results in about one glass, most of which, alas, ends up in the bucket). Tastes and opinions are shared and by 10.30pm everyone is confident enough to pass comment on some aspect of each bottle, whether its colour or character.

One session costs 260FF. A series of seven, four on technique and three focusing on different regions, costs 1,400FF; the whole series, 14 *séances* covering technique and ten regions, costs 2,200FF. Classes take place in the evenings throughout the year, except during the summer. There is a maximum of 18 students per group.

To enrol, contact:
Union des Oenologues, 2 Avenue Gallieni, 91710 Vert le Petit.

Check where the class is taking place. To reach the Institut Vatel, take métro line 13 (direction Gabriel Peri-Asnieres) to Brochant. Follow rue Brochant to the junction with rue Nollet. Turn right. The Institut is on the left.

To reach the OIV, take métro lines 12 or 8 to Madeleine. Place de la Madeleine is large and somewhat confusing. The simplest and most attractive route is to walk down rue

Royale (which, at night, allows a wonderful vista onto the Place de la Concorde), turn right onto rue du Faubourg St Honoré. Rue d'Aguesseau is the fourth on the right. Number 18 is on the right.

NORTH-EAST

Le Cellier du Gout

Tel: +33 3 86 70 36 21
Fax: +33 3 86 70 35 76
Email: daniel.descamps@hol.fr
Level of French: Basic (interpreter available)
Nearest Station: (SNCF) La Charite-sur-Loire

La Charite-sur-Loire is on the route of St Jacques de Compostelle's pilgrimage and is home to the first church built by the Benedictine monks of Cluny. Monsieur Daniel Descamps, one of the members of the association of Le Cellier du Gout, is justifiably proud of the town and of its history. He is equally proud of the classes and courses run by Le Cellier in all aspects of gastronomy. For example, there is a three-day chocolate course with Monsieur Stret, who is, in Monsieur Descamps opinion, the best *chocolatier* in France. Or three days on honey or a week of cooking classes in a local restaurant...

Any combination of subjects and programmes is possible since the association responds to customers' demands rather than offering a fixed schedule. There are no more than 15 students per group and beginners are welcome. Prices vary in terms of subject, duration and numbers. Call, fax or email Monsieur Descamps. He is not only friendly, amenable but also very knowledgeable.

École du Vin du Bureau Interprofessionnel des Vins de Bourgogne

12, boulevard Bretonnière, BP 150, 21200 Beaune
Tel: +33 3 80 25 04 95
Fax: +33 3 80 25 04 90
Established: 1974
Level of French: Advanced
Nearest Station: (SNCF) Beaune
Contact: Damien Delattre

Even without its fabulous vineyards, Burgundy has plenty to offer, not least the towns of Beaune (with its famous Hospice) and Dijon, the fairy-tale village of Vézelay and the Abbaye de Fontenay, famous for the filming of Cyrano de Bergerac. Those who follow the wine programmes at the Bureau Interprofessionel des Vins de Bourgogne will have plenty to occupy their time, if and when they tire of Chablis and Nuits-Saints-Georges.

From a large, classically French house in Beaune, the BIVB runs several different wine-tasting programmes, from short half-day tastings to five-day courses in Advanced Knowledge of the Wines of Burgundy. The half-day, one-day and weekend (Saturday/Sunday) programmes (120FF; 350FF and 1,300FF) are aimed at groups of at least ten participants. The weekend course includes lunch and dinner on Saturday, Sunday lunch, a visit to the Hospices de Beaune, four vineyard and wine-merchant visits and one night's accommodation in a three-star hotel. Three- and five-day Beginners and Advanced courses (1,950FF for three days and 3,250FF for five days) include lessons on wine-tasting technique, presentation of the region (covering its geography and geology as well as the different *appellations*), vineyard, cellar and wine house visits, two to three tastings per day and a lunch-tasting every day. There are also three-day Discovering Vintage (1,750FF) and Discovering Grands Crus courses (2,250FF). Prices do not include accommodation (except for the weekend course) or evening meals. Multiple bookings (from two) benefit from a 20 per cent reduction, and students benefit from a per cent reduction.

The BIVB can organise accommodation where necessary. Enrolments must be completed at least ten days before the course begins. A 500FF deposit must accompany the application form. This is refundable in the event of cancellation by BIVB but is non-refundable in the case of a cancellation less than five days before the start date (an administration fee of 200FF will be charged for cancellations received ten days before the start date).

Institut des Vins de Champagne

15, rue Jeanson, 51160 Ay
Tel: +33 3 26 55 78 78
Fax: +33 3 26 54 84 76
Established: 1998
Level of French: None to Advanced (depending on the class)
Nearest Station: (SNCF) Ay/Épernay
Contact: Yves Richardot

At the time of writing, the Institut de Champagne was in the process of setting up its programmes for the first time. Prices are thus liable to change and this description is an indication of what will be on offer rather than a comment on established courses.

Like the CIVB in Burgundy and Bordeaux, the CIVC aims to promote its products, both to professionals and amateurs. In conjunction with Reims university, the Institut runs an academic course for oenologists and it also offers weekend and evening class for the budding oenophile.

Les Toques Nivernaises

Le Grand Monarque, 33 Quai Clemenceau, 58400 La Charite-sur-Loire
Tel: +33 3 86 70 21 73
Level of French: Conversational [translations possible on demand]
Contact: James Grennerat
Nearest Station: La Charite-sur-Loire

Cooking in France is both a national and regional obsession. In every *département* devoted cooks will find dishes which concentrate on making the most of seasonal and local produce. The speciality of the Nevers, which is to the north-west of Burgundy, is traditional French country cooking. The Toques Nivernaises, an association based in La Charite-sur-Loire (one of the oldest towns in France) offers cooking classes which acknowledge these local traditions and ingredients, whilst updating them for modern tastes. Three-hour practical classes (350F) take place every Friday afternoon in the kitchen at Le Grand Monarque, a three-star hotel, and weekend packages (including two classes, a tasting in a wine cellar, food and accommodation) are available for groups (call for prices). Students make either a starter and main course, or main course and dessert, and after each session they taste their work along with appropriate wines chosen by the two chefs. Classes are small (maximum ten) and take place from September to June.

Visit Bourgogne

**Visit Bourgogne, 71510
Charrecey
Tel: +33 3 85 45 38 97
Fax: +33 3 85 45 38 98
Email: visitb@cleb-internet.fr
Contact: Monsieur Gerard
Carpentier
Nearest Station: (SNCF) Le
Creusot-Monchanin**

Visit Bourgogne offers a complete package of cooking classes, wine tastings, hotel accommodation and sight-seeing in Burgundy. Over four days groups of six to twelve students learn the secrets of Bourguignon cuisine, making sauces, terrines, pastry and tarts, whilst visiting wine cellars, vineyards and local markets. Taught in the kitchens of a village hotel, the classes are very technical and comprehensive and students work within a real restaurant environment. On the final evening there is a *répas gastronomique* and wine-tasting. Vintage Burgundy wines and Champagne accompany the dishes prepared in class. Monsieur Carpentier stresses that no previous expertise is necessary and teaching is in French and English. The package including three nights' accommodation in a three-star hotel (no supplement for single rooms), four days of classes and activities, all food and drink costs 5,000FF. Prospective applicants should consider booking an extra room (approximately 300FF) for Sunday and Thursday since the classes begin at 8am on Monday and the dinner ends at who knows when... The programmes are established according to demand, thus groups and individuals should call/fax to check availability and schedule a programme.

NORTH-WEST

La Crêpière

**3, rue des Deux Ponts, 56920
St Gonnery
Tel: +33 2 97 38 43 74
Fax: +33 2 97 38 43 89
Contact: Maryse Digue
Level of French: Advanced**

Picture courtesy of La Crêpière

Nearest Station: (SNCF) Rennes (1 hr) and Vannes; St Malo port Roscoff port. A car will be necessary to reach La Crêpière.

In five days, with some manual dexterity and linguistic ability, you could gain a new career. Situated in the heart of Brittany (home of the *galette* and the *crêpe*) is La Crêpière where Maryse Digue, who ran her own restaurant for 15 years, has spent the last five teaching complete amateur pancake-makers how to become professional chefs and restaurant owners. Cooking classes in the morning, with, of course, crêpes for lunch, are followed by business training in the afternoon, and out of 300 past students 150 have started their own crêperies. Students stay in Maryse's lovely old house (in which she also offers bed and breakfast throughout the year), sharing meals with the family. Classes are limited to three people and take place three times a month all year round (except July and August). The

course costs 4,800FF and half-board accommodation is 1,475FF extra.

Other Possibilities

Auberge de la Cognette
26 rue des Minimes, 36100 Issoudun
Tel: +33 2 54 21 21 83
Fax: +33 2 54 03 13 03

Castel de Bray et Monts
37130 Brehemont
Tel: +33 2 47 96 70 47
Fax: +33 2 47 96 57 36

Cours de Cuisine au Château
Hôtel La Chenevière, Escures-Commes, 14520 Port en Bessin Huppain
Tel: +33 2 31 21 25 25
Fax: +33 2 31 21 25 20

Cours de Cuisine au Château Country Cooking

Picture courtesy of Auberge La Fontaine

FOOD AND WINE

Course

**Domaine de la Tortinière,
37250 Montbazon
Tel: +33 2 47 34 35 00
Fax: +33 2 47 65 95 70**

L'École Maître-crêpier

**66, rue de Guer, 35330 Maure
de Bretagne
Tel: +33 2 99 34 86 76
Fax: +33 2 99 59 81 01**

SOUTH-EAST

Auberge La Fontaine

**Place de la Fontaine,
84210 Venasque
Tel: +33 4 90 66 02 96
Fax: +33 4 90 66 13 14
E-mail: None
Website: None
Established: 1988
Level of French: None
(Classes taught in French,
English or German)
Nearest Station: (SNCF)
Avignon or Carpentras
Contact: Ingrid and
Christian Soehlke**

Auberge La Fontaine is one of those rare places that lives up to its brochure. A large stone house looking out onto the fountain of its name, it has been converted by Ingrid and Christian Soehlke into a veritable inn, with a restaurant and five suites. Suite, in fact, is hardly adequate to describe the mini-apartments, each with a bedroom, bathroom, dining room, fully equipped kitchen, living room with fireplace, terrace, guest bed, television, telephone, stereo system and air conditioning. The accommodation itself would be tempting enough but the Auberge also runs cookery classes, taught in the restaurant kitchen. Christian Soehlke,

chef and teacher, aims to offer a philosophy of cooking, not simply a series of recipes and menus. His students are encouraged to learn techniques and ideas – everything from basic principles to how to adapt recipes to the season or ingredients available.

Classes run according to demand, not a programme, so it is perfectly possible to be the only person in the kitchen with Christian, helping him prepare for the evening service in the restaurant, or one of a small group (maximum four to five). The price remains the same and each session lasts from 10pm to 3pm. In high season (from Easter to October) courses cost 500FF per day including lunch. Accommodation is an additional 800FF per day (for one or two people). From October to December and January to March there are tuition and accommodation packages available. A three-day course including lunches, lessons and four nights' accommodation costs 2,000FF for one person, or 3,200FF for two people sharing the same room (ie the courses are free). A special Truffle option is available in January and February (supplement payable depending on how much of a pig you are and how many you use/cook with/eat...!) Contact the Auberge for availability.

Venasque is 10km from Carpentras and 30km from Avignon and Orange. There are train stations in all three towns. The nearest international airport is Marseille.

Les Casseroles de Provence

**L'Anastasie, Île de la Barthe-
lasse, 84000 Avignon
Tel: +33 4 90 85 55 94
Fax: +33 4 90 82 59 40
Contact: Olga Manguin**

Level of French: None
Nearest Station: (SNCF)
Avignon (but a car is
indispensable).

The name says it all. Les Casseroles de Provence perfectly describes the unpretentious nature of Olga Manguin's classes. She believes in making the most of good ingredients and this principle underlies her cooking classes. For those gastronomes who love cooking but hate the intellectualisation of it, Les Casseroles would be a good choice. No theorising, just simple French country cuisine which anyone can learn. Although only six minutes drive away from Avignon, her farmhouse is in the middle of the countryside situated on one of the few river islands in the Rhône. She runs courses for up to eight people and up to six days. Beginners are very welcome and Olga speaks English, German and Italian. Classes can be booked at any time of the year. Full board and class costs 1,000FF per day with a seventh day free when booking six. Couples booking together pay 1,700FF per day. Call or fax the above numbers to receive further information.

Cuisine en Provence
21 Ellerslie Road, London W12
7BN/38 Cours P.Puget,
13006 Marseille
Tel: +44 181 740 9193; +33 4
91 54 24 19
Fax: +44 181 740 9193; +33 4
91 33 65 30
Level of French: None
Contact: Jean-Marie
Carret (London)
Charleric Gensollen (Marseille)
Nearest Airport: Marseille (cost
of transfer from this airport is
included in the price).

Air-conditioning wasn't necessary in the 16th-century. Not, that is, for the chateau dwellers. Thick stone walls ensured a perfect temperature, even in the summer, and Jean-Marie Carret and Charleric Gensollen are now using this architectural advantage to keep their cooking students cool. Half an hour away from the sea sits the beautiful 16th-century Château de Vins sur Caramy, where these two young chefs run Cuisine en Provence, offering complete culinary holidays throughout the year. Small groups (maximum 12) stay in the Château and spend their days visiting markets and vineyards, swimming in the nearby lake and, once the day cools off slightly, following courses in Provençale cuisine, learning the secrets of *bouillabaisse* and *tian de courgettes*. No experience is necessary and classes are taught in French and English. This is certainly not the cheapest cooking holiday available (8,500FF for a week; 4,500FF for four days/three nights). Yet it is definitely one of the most comprehensive in terms of what is included in the price and what it offers: tuition, six or seven nights' accommodation; full board with wine; organised excursions; two restaurant outings; transfer from recommended flight.

Hôtel de la Mirande
4 place de la Mirande, 84000
Avignon, France
Tel: +33 4 90 85 93 93
Fax: +33 4 90 86 26 85
Established: 1994
Level of French: Conversational
Nearest Station: (SNCF)
Avignon
Contact: Martin Stein or
Michael Hanhardt

In the heart of Avignon, sharing a square with the Palais des Papes, is the

Hôtel de la Mirande. Not content with offering four-star accommodation in a gorgeous and elegant 19th-century townhouse, the hotel also runs a cookery class programme. The house's original kitchen was too small to be used for the hotel and it has now been restored for use as a cookery workshop, along with its wood-fired cast-iron stove. Once a month there is a week of four day-time sessions and one Friday evening class. Taught by chefs in a marble-countered kitchen, the options available change according to the seasons and the skills of the particular chef. Menus cover everything from pressed lobster to pigeon hot pot with truffles, chocolate charlotte to chestnut soufflé. Students prepare three dishes and at the end of the session they eat everything they have created, washed down with a few glasses of wine. Participants in the Friday class prepare dinner for themselves and for their guests (250FF per non-student). Classes are small (maximum of 12), taught in English and French, and students receive copies/translations of the recipes. No experience is necessary and participants come from all over the world as well as locally.

La Mirande offers all-inclusive holiday packages as well as tuition-only options. One morning or evening class with one night's accommodation in a double room with continental breakfast costs from 1,345FF to 1,915FF per person. A six-night stay with breakfast, four morning classes and one evening class costs from 7,670FF to 10,300FF. Since a night in the hotel alone costs at least 1,700FF, these prices are bargains. One cooking class costs from 400FF to 600FF; a block of four morning classes costs from 2000FF to 2,500FF; a block of four morning and one evening class costs from 2400FF to 2500FF; 12

classes (which can be taken over a year) cost 3,600FF. The price of each class includes a meal and drinks. A 25 per cent deposit is required (refundable in the event of a cancellation as long as notification is received at least three weeks in advance). The hotel can organise classes for groups of eight or more on demand.

The nearest international airport to Avignon is Marseille (one hour away) and there are regular internal flights to Avignon from Charles de Gaulle and Orly in Paris. The train station is a ten minute walk from the hotel.

Le Jardin de la Tour

9, rue de la Tour, 84000 Avignon
Tel: +33 4 90 85 66 50
Fax: +33 4 90 27 90 72
Level of French: None (English, Japanese,German spoken).
Contact: Jean-Marc LarRue
Nearest Station: (SNCF) Avignon

Jean-Marc Lar Rue, the chef who teaches cooking classes at Le Jardin de la Tour, also runs the gastronomic restaurant and a catering company. Despite being so busy, he still finds time to discuss the finer points of olive oil harvesting and production over the phone and his enthusiasm for the Cuisine Meridionale that he champions in all areas of his business is evident. His objective is to increase awareness of the diversity of Provençale cooking and ingredients and he does this in the classes and in special sessions on a particular local delicacy. You could choose to spend an afternoon on a truffle hunt, for example, or visiting an olive grove.

Classes also include advice on matching wines with food and Jean-Marc stresses that the classes are about learning something, not just having fun. Groups are 15 students maximum. All classes include a theoretical demonstration, practical application, aperitif and meal. Full day sessions also include a trip to the city market and a second meal. Courses last from a half-day up to a month and take place from Tuesday to Saturday all year round (except the last two weeks in August). Prices range from 550FF for a half-day. Accommodation can be organised in the town where a hotel room with breakfast costs approximately 250F. Call/fax for further details...the brochure in itself is a work of art.

Provence 3D

Château de la Roseraie, 84000 Carpentras
Tel: +33 4 90 67 02 90/+1 303 494 7988
Fax: +33 4 90 67 02 91/+1 303 494 7999
Email: mdepar@avignon. pacwan.net
Level of French: None
Contact: Michel Depardon (France)/Robert Reynolds (USA)
Nearest Station: (SNCF) Avignon

Carpentras is the truffle capital of France, has the biggest vegetable market in the whole country and is home to the Provence 3D cooking school, where you can learn to prepare all the wonderful products you've discovered. Situated in a baroque, fairy-tale chateau in Carpentras, the school offers five-day sessions to teach basic and classic cuisine, with a strong emphasis on local produce and delicacies, especially truffles, strawberries and melons. The content of the classes are determined by what is found in the morning market visit. Four types of strawberries might

form the basis of discussion and dishes on Thursday, whereas Friday's class might consider the flavour and uses of different olive oils. Trips to local markets are complemented by visits to cheese-makers and vineyards and meals out in local bistros.

Michel stresses the professional and serious nature of the teaching but emphasises that amateurs are welcome. Courses are in English, available from October to June, and groups are small (12 maximum). Master classes on Mediterranean cuisine (for professionals) are also available, and the school also works in association with the University of Wine in nearby Suze la Rousse. A five day session, including tuition, first-class hotel accommodation, tours, meals and guided visits costs $2,250 per person.

Stages de Cuisine Erick Vedel

30, rue Pierre Euzeby, 13200 Arles
Tel/Fax: +33 4 90 49 69 20
Email: ACTVEDEL@provnet.fr
Level of French: None
Contact: Erick Vedel
Nearest Station: (SNCF) Arles
Nearest Airport: Nimes

Arles is home to the largest market in Provence and it is here that Erick Vedel begins his cooking classes. Not only a chef, but also an author whose thorough research on the history of Provençale cuisine can be found in his book 'L'Archéologie de la Cuisine', Monsieur Vedel is well-positioned to teach every aspect of the culinary traditions of the region. In the hands-on classes students may find themselves learning how to make quails stuffed with mushrooms and ginger, nut bread or aubergine caviar. Half-day classes (9am to 2pm: 500FF), day classes (9am to 2pm, 5pm to 10pm: 700FF), weekends and week-long sessions are available. Erick prefers to respond to demand rather than plan a fixed schedule, so groups or individuals need to call and discuss availability. Groups are a minimum of two and a maximum of eight. There are several hotels close to the house and Erick will make reservations.

Sylvie Lallemand

Les Megalithes, 84220 Gordes
Tel: +33 4 90 72 23 41
Level of French: None
Contact: Sylvie Lallemand
Nearest Station: (SNCF)
Avignon (but, from here, a car
is indispensable).

When you can't stand the heat in Sylvie Lallemand's kitchen, you can get into the swimming pool. However, since the kitchen is open-air, and on a terrace in Provence, the heat might be more bearable than usual. For 18 years Sylvie has been running week-long courses in the art of Provençale cuisine at her country home and gastronomes the world over come to enjoy the combined pleasures of the local countryside and cooking. The mornings are spent either visiting local markets in preparation for the afternoon class, or sightseeing, then at 3pm the class begins. The students (up to five or six per week) learn every-thing about the region's specialities and prepare the evening meal using their new expertise. Courses run from March to June inclusive and from September to November. Early booking is advised and Sylvie recommends renting a car to make the most of one's stay. Accommo-dation, all meals, and classes are included in the price of 3,400FF. Classes are given in English or French.

Université du Vin

Tel: +33 4 75 97 21 30
Fax: +33 4 75 98 24 20
Contact: Mme Payan
Level of French: Conversational
to Intermediate

Suze-la-Rousse isn't the easiest place to find but it's worth the journey. North of Orange, south of Montelimar and just off the 'Motorway to the Sun' (Autoroute du Soleil) this small village is only accessible by train and car. However, it is home to the only University of Wine in France. Established 20 years ago as a centre for continuing education, it now offers long-term professional courses in all aspects of the wine trade: marketing and sales; becoming a *sommelier*; consultancy. For the gastronomic amateurs, Suzy offers week-long conference series, which cover the history of wine production, how to taste wine and how to match wine and food. These weeks are organised on demand and interested parties should contact the University directly to discuss availability and a programme. One conference is approximately 6,000FF and five over a week will cost around 25,000FF. These prices are per group and thus it is advisable to plan a trip with friends. Planning is also essential if you want to stay in the village, since accommodation is limited and needs to be booked in advance.

Other Possibilities

Cuisine autour d'un thème chez Régis Marcon

'Le Clos des Cîmes', 43290
Saint-Bonnet-Le-Froid
Tel: +33 4 71 59 93 72
Fax: +33 4 71 59 93 40

Hostellerie de Crillon le Brave ****

84110 Crillon le brave
Tel: +33 4 90 65 61 61
Fax: +33 4 90 65 62 86
E-mail: crillonbrave@
relaischateaux.fr
Website: www.integra.fr/
relaischateaux/crillonbrave

École de cuisine du soleil

Restaurant l'Amandier, Place
du Commandant Lamy,
06250 Mougins
Tel: +33 4 93 75 35 70
Fax: +33 4 93 90 18 55

École Nationale des Arts Culinaires

Château du Vivier, BP 25,
69131 Ecully Cedex
Tel: +33 4 78 43 36 10
Fax: +33 4 78 43 33 51
La Tour Rose
Philippe Chavent, 22 rue du
Boeuf, 69005 Lyon
Tel: +33 4 78 37 25 90
Fax: +33 4 78 42 26 02

SOUTH-WEST

Château Loudenne École du Vin

33340 Saint-Yzans-De-Médoc
Tel: +33 5 56 73 17 80
Fax: +33 5 56 09 02 87
Established: 1982
Level of French: None
Nearest Station: (SNCF)
Bordeaux
Contact: Corinne Delaveyne

Bordeaux is renowned for its Anglo-French connections and Château Loudenne continues the tradition. In 1875 Walter and Alfred Gilbey, founders of a wine and spirit company in London (now known as International Distillers and Vintners) bought this 17th-century pink château overlooking the Gironde river, seduced by its position and vineyards. It is now both a successful vineyard and a wine school, offering short courses on the theory of wine-tasting and the practice of wine-making.

The five-day course is designed for both amateurs and professionals and groups are limited to 12 participants. It includes talks and presentations about the Bordeaux region and its wines, including Saint-Emilion, Pomerol and Médoc, workshops on tasting techniques; visits and tastings to several local vineyards including the Château's own and lunches; and dinners in local restaurants, wine houses and the Château. Charles Eve, the Master of Wine and Director, also organises tailor-made options on demand. When sated with wines and vineyards, participants can visit the English rose gardens or play croquet.

The courses are taught in English and it helps to have some knowledge of wine. A five-day course costs 12 500FF, for one person including accommodation or 11,150FF per person for two people sharing a room. The two day course costs 5,800FF for one person or 5,250FF per person for two people sharing. All meals and excursions are included. There are only a few courses per year with enrolment limited to 12 so it is advisable to enrol early.

The Château has a very comprehensive brochure, with details about the vineyards and a course programme. Bookings should be made on the form provided and accompanied by a 1,500FF deposit. The balance must be paid at least six weeks in advance of the start date.

Participants can be met from Bordeaux airport or railway station if they arrive at certain times. Those in cars will find a small map inside the brochure with directions.

L'École du Vin du CIVB (Conseil Interprofessionnel du Vin de Bordeaux)

1 Cours du XXX Juillet, 33075 Bordeaux Cedex
Tel: +33 5 56 00 22 66
Fax: +33 5 56 00 22 82
E-mail: CIVB@vins-bordeaux.fr
Website: www.vins-bordeaux.fr
Established: 1990
Level of French: Intermediate (courses also available in English, German, Japanese, Chinese)
Nearest Station: (SNCF/TGV) Bordeaux/Bordeaux-Mérignac airport
Contact: Florence Raffard/François Capdemourlin

The 18th-century Maison du Vin de Bordeaux is in the centre of the city but after a few hours on one of its courses participants will have sipped their way across the whole region. The Maison houses the CIVB, a professional council that promotes the wines of Bordeaux, and it runs classes for amateur and professional wine-lovers. It aims to provide practical and enjoyable introductions to wine-tasting, combined with visits to local vineyards and/or cookery classes.

Over a thousand wine aficionados a year follow a class at the CIVB. The Level One Discovery course takes beginners from tasting exercises to advice on building up a wine cellar. Six half-day sessions are programmed over three days and participants can also opt for a fourth day, visiting several local châteaux for tastings and tours. The course costs 2,000FF (reductions for groups of four or more) plus 570FF for the extra day (no reductions). An Advanced course is also available and costs 1,200FF including two days' courses and lunches. There are approximately 15

students in a class and the CIVB will also run custom-made programmes for groups of eight or more.

In conjunction with a local travel agency, the CIVB also organises weekend packages. Short two to three-day courses include Discovery of Bordeaux wine and wine-tasting, an Oenology weekend in Bordeaux and A Food and Wine Experience. The latter course is for true gastronomes who want to discover the region's wine and its cuisine. Participants follow presentations on the basics of wine-tasting with cookery classes at Le Chapon Fin, the oldest and most famous restaurant in Bordeaux (previous diners include Toulouse-Lautrec, Sarah Bernhardt and Edward VII). This costs 3,680FF and includes two nights three-star accommodation from Thursday to Saturday, two cooking lessons, a full day-tour of a wine-producing region including lunch, two wine school lessons and lunch and a guided tour with an oenologist. The Oenology Weekend (with one night's accommodation, two lunches, dinner, visits and tastings) costs 1,600FF per person. Prices based on two people sharing. Contact:

Mauriac Voyages-Bordeaux Label, 27 rue du Temple, 33000 Bordeaux
Tel: +33 5 56 81 94 00
Fax: +33 5 56 52 46 13.

Application forms (inside the CIVB brochure) should be returned with a 50 per cent deposit. This is refundable up to two weeks before the start of the course. Accommodation is not included (except where stated) but the CIVB can provide information about local hotels and help to organise your trip.

The CIVB is in the centre of Bordeaux, just opposite the Tourist Information Office close to several car parks and easily accessible from the train station.

Université Internationale des Eaux-de-Vie et Boissons Spiritueuses

BP 37, rue Gaston Briand, 16130 Segonzac
Tel: +33 5 45 83 35 35
Fax: +33 5 45 83 31 72
Web: le-cognac.com
Nearest Station: (SNCF) Angouleme; (TGV) Cognac
Level of French required: Intermediate to Advanced
Established: 1987
Contact: Simon Palmer

Victoria Davies/Benoît Besnard

New Zealand, unlike France, is renowned for its friendliness. So when it's a New Zealander who asserts that this is the "smallest and friendliest university in France" I would imagine he knows what he's talking about. This university is the only one of its kind in the world and only accepts 15 students per year. The postgraduate Diploma in Law, Management and Marketing applied to the spirits industry takes a full academic year. From October to April there are two weeks of lectures per month, covering product and sector familiarisation, practical legal aspects of the spirits industry, taxation, management and marketing. After exams in the summer, students follow an industry placement and write a research essay. The two weeks per calendar month allows those already in the profession to continue working. The course can also be followed over two years. For those who love wine and spirits but as amateurs, the university organises tasting days covering a range of spirits from Armagnac to Whisky (900FF per person). Individual and group trips can be organised on request. Simon Palmer, the director, will help to organise a holiday for those interested in combining a visit to the region with a discovery of its wines and brandies. The schedule and subject matter is planned in terms of the group, and prices depend on the length of the session and the product. A minimal presentation and tasting, for a group of 15 people, will cost approximately 1,500FF (thus 100FF per person) and a more elaborate half-day focusing on one spirit will cost 3,000FF.

Enrolment begins in January for the one-year postgraduate course. This costs 6,500FF for individuals including an all-expenses paid trip around France in November (80 per cent of the students are French). International students will need to have their qualifications validated. Minimum qualification is a Masters Degree. Accommodation advice is available. The nearest station is Cognac (15km) and prospective visitors should be aware that a car is indispensable.

Other Possibilities

Cuisine de la Mer à la Rochelle

Étoile Bleu Marine, 33 rue Thiers, 17000 La Rochelle
Tel: +33 5 46 41 62 23
Fax: +33 5 46 41 10 76

Stages culinaires et créatifs en Périgord Noir

Auberge 'Lou Peyrol', Le Speroutal, 24 480 Paleyrac-Urval
Tel: +33 5 53 22 97 28
Fax: +33 5 53 23 40 90
E-mail: elswyt@isp.fr
Website:www.finest.tm.fr/fr/dordogne/lou_peyrol

Cours de Cuisine au Domaine d'Espérance

École de cuisine, Mauvezin d'Armagnac, 40240 La Bastide d'Armagnac
Tel: +33 5 58 44 85 93

Weekend Cuisine et Traditions à Orthez

Hôtel la Reine Jeanne, Monsieur Didier Couture, 44 rue du Bourg Couture, 64300 OrthezTel: +33 5 59 67 00 76
Fax: +33 5 59 69 09 63

FOOD AND WINE

Language Schools

Many people remember learning French in terms of an experience never to be repeated. Grappling with participles and verbs, nouns and objects, before rushing off to double history and a miserable lunch. No wonder so few potential linguists make it beyond '*Je m'appelle*' and the present tense; but forget Madame Brown, the annoying boy behind you, and rote verb tables. Imagine a whole other world, where a class is animated by international learners, a native teacher and the prospect of a wonderful *bistro* for lunch where you can practise your skills. How about a morning spent discussing how to shop, then an afternoon spent doing it? Or an afternoon seminar on Godard, before an evening session at the Gaumont? Exposure to a language is half the battle and there's no better place to win the war than in the cities and regions of this diverse and beautiful country.

Range of courses and schools

Whether you want to spend a weekend refreshing your memory or a year learning the basics, there is a class to suit you. Consider the following factors: What are your objectives? What is your price range? What is your time scale? Are you learning French for professional or personal reasons? Do you need to gain a qualification, earn credit at college, or are you learning just to learn?

Once you have determined why you are taking a class decide how much time you have available. One week won't equip you for the Chamber of Commerce exams, but it is still long enough to cover the basics, working intensively. Berlitz, for example, offers nine-hour immersion days. One month, whether full-time or part-time, combined with daily language practice, can provide most beginners with a more than adequate grasp of the language and how to use it on a daily basis. A trimester or semester of study, or a year's enrolment at a university centre like the CCF at the Sorbonne, can move a beginner from stumbling to walking. For those who aspire to that holy grail of language learning, fluency, there is no predictable time scale. It is almost impossible to gauge how long it will take to achieve near-native competence in a foreign language. This depends on the learner's ear, application and experience, the amount of time spent in the classroom as well as the amount spent beyond it, practising.

With an objective and timetable decided upon, the final determining factors will be price and place. You may or may not want the cheapest possible rate per hour. Perhaps you prefer just language classes, or you may require a whole social programme. Be prepared to pay extra for schools with frills, social programmes, audio-visual and computer facilities, and accommodation services. Consider whether you learn best in a large or small group. Price is no indicator of quality or of class-size. Some of the most expensive schools teach groups of 20 students whereas some of the cheapest limit size to five per class.

Where do you want to learn? Beside the Louvre or the Loire? Paris is, of course, full of diversions and distractions, not least of which is the large number of foreigners that live and work there. In the capital it is easy to speak English. This is also true of resorts like Nice and La Rochelle. Heading into the country-side will take you away from some of the bright lights but there will be more opportunity to practice your new linguistic skills. Once your objective, time scale and price range are established, it becomes much easier to select where and how to study.

French teaching falls into five broad categories: the holiday/summer course; the small, independent school; the large independent school; the national or international association with several branches; the University institute. Holiday courses will combine language-learning with a social programme, generally splitting days into a morning class followed by an afternoon excursion. Summer courses, run by almost every type of school, except the small independents, are the ideal combination of comprehensive language instruction and tourism. Students can study from one week to three months, part-time or full-time and schools cater for every ability from the beginner to the French teacher in need of a refresher. Generally the school will organise accommodation and teaching packages, so that all you have to do is pay and turn up.

Small independent schools often offer the best deals in terms of price, but a minimal infrastructure. CFILC in Paris, for example, is very cheap at approximately 25FF per hour, but there is no social programme, no language lab and no accommodation service. This type of school is ideal for self-motivated students who need little administrative or social support, and for those with a limited budget. They are unlikely to offer exam preparation classes or to have nationally or internationally recognised qualifications. Teaching focuses on conversation and aural comprehension more than literature and grammar. Small groups (five to 10 students maximum) enable everyone to practice.

Larger independent schools tend to offer a good balance between social programme and structure and academic instruction. Their big advantage is combining friendliness with facilities. With a reasonably small number of students, they manage to remain approachable and welcoming whilst still offering many academic and social benefits, such as regular accommodation services and exam preparation, social events and accredited courses. Teaching is a mixture of grammar and oral expression and medium-sized groups (10-15) encourage participation. Those associated with SOUFFLE and ADCUEFE also offer an externally sanctioned guarantee of quality.

National and international associations, such as the Alliance Française and Eurocentre, have the advantages of well-known reputations, extensive facilities and wide networks of schools. Their Paris branches are huge, with lots of students and a large choice of classes, but the regional ones offer the same teaching system on a smaller scale.

Offering short and long courses, myriad options and certificates, such large centres provide choice and comprehensive instruction. They are suitable for the student planning either a short summer course or a long stay. They have institutional benefits, such as recognised qualifications, accommodation services and libraries and institutional disadvantages such as large classes (15-25 students per group) and long corridors. Teaching combines the study of grammar and textual comprehension with oral expression.

Nearly every provincial university and at least two Paris universities have language institutes for international students. Most of these are separate from the university, in price and practice. They generally run semester-based teaching years, which are ideal for anyone following a US or modular-style degree, who wants to attend for six months to a year, and for summer courses. The teaching techniques and class content tend to be traditional and academic, not trendy or alternative. Classes are large (20-25 students per group) and the focus is on grammar, literature and civilisation, more than oral practice. Students have the same access to university facilities (libraries, sports centres) as French undergraduates. It may be possible to enrol in university courses. Such centres do not offer the services or social programmes found in private language schools. Accommodation help is usually available through CROUS (although this is unreliable).

Typical students

There are very few schools with a predictable student population. Semester structures tend to attract university students on year abroad programmes. Smaller, cheaper schools, especially those in cities with limited social facilites, such as CFILC and Langue Onze, appeal to a maturer population, more interested in learning French than in excursions. In general, the more pastoral and protective the social structure, the more likely it is that the school will attract a young population. Whatever your level, most schools will be able to accommodate you. On arrival, all schools (whatever their size), will make you take a test to determine which class will be suitable.

PRACTICAL INFORMATION

Accommodation

Accommodation will usually be organised by most language schools. The options include host families, university residences (often summer only) and rented studios/flats. University centres generally provide accommodation for students on summer courses but not those in academic year programmes. Enrolment in a university course usually gives the student access to all services, including cheap meals at the Resto U, or *restaurant universitaire* where a three-course meal (basic but bearable and extremely variable from one city to another) costs around 14FF.

Payment

Language schools all have quite fixed methods of payment. Most request french franc cheques, bankers' drafts or international money orders. Some accept eurocheques and travellers' cheques and a few take credit cards. Nearly all will request a deposit and full payment at least two weeks before the course start date.

Cancellation

Before signing up for a class check the cancellation procedure. Many schools will not refund the full amount of a deposit in the event of a cancellation, whatever the reason.

Custom classes

If a particular school or place looks interesting but doesn't seem to offer a suitable course, call and ask. Nearly every institution will customise courses for individuals and groups.

PARIS

Accord École de Langues

14, bvd Poissonnière,
75009 Paris
Tel: +33 1 55 33 52 33
Fax: +33 1 55 33 52 34
E-mail: accordel@easynet.fr
Established: 1988
Level of French required: None
Contact: Christine Mestre

Accord is at the heart of one of the liveliest districts of Paris, the Quartier Montorgueil. Full of food shops and markets, bars and cafes, this is an area that continually reminds the visitor that they are in Paris *profond*. The school is a member of SOUFFLE, an organisation which regroups language institutes in terms of their quality. It is difficult to become a member and difficult to stay one: there are only 18 in the country and only two in Paris. Schools are checked biannually to ensure that their standards have not dropped. Students at Accord have an external guarantee of quality, which is unusual amongst the smaller, independent schools. Another distinguishing feature is Accord's theatre course run by an actress (included in the cost of the intensive class) where students are encouraged to learn French through structured role play and acting. No theatrical experience is necessary.

Semi-intensive and intensive courses are available throughout the year and in the summer. A 24-week full-time course (20 hours per week) costs 20,900FF, a three-week summer intensive course costs 3,800FF (25 hours per week) and a part-time course (three hours per week) costs 900FF for four weeks,

Picture courtesy of Accord École de Langues

Student Story

"I had come prepared: four years of 30 year-old, high school French, at least 20 solid hours of listening to "Learn French in Your Car" cassettes, and a once-a-week-for-six-weeks course in "French for Travellers" at the local high school under my belt. With this, a half-dozen books on culture shock, and a really good dictionary, I hit the streets of Paris. I loved walking the cobblestone streets, listening to the language; it is truly a magical place and I wanted to be a part of that magic. So without knowing a soul in Paris, I rented an apartment on the left bank, bought a few scarves, enrolled in a language school and set off on my adventure.

My French didn't get me through the airport! It's one thing talking to a cassette in your car and quite another talking with a real live taxi driver; you can't rewind the driver! Living in a country and not knowing the language is a truly humbling experience. Communication is the very essence of humanity and when it's compromised, even for a short time, it can be depressing and disheartening. I had arrived in Paris a few days before school was to begin to allow myself time to settle in. After four days of settling, my confidence was shattered. My "failures" as I came to call them, were piling up. And so on the fifth day I arrived at school humbled, ready to acknowledge my lack of knowledge and anxious to begin learning. I anticipated a nice juicy textbook that I could sink my teeth into. And so, I was absolutely horrified when my professor walked in "sans textbook" and began speaking French and nothing but French! Immediately I thought to myself, "Good God! They've made a terrible mistake and put me in the wrong class! I wrote beginners on the application, didn't they see that! How can I possibly learn the language if I can't understand a word the professor is saying!" I thought about slipping quietly out the door, but the professor was making eye contact with alarming frequency. I considered bolting, but he struck me as the type to give pursuit so I sat it out. And what I came to know, although I didn't think so at the time, was that I had been blessed with Bruno for a professor. He was that rare breed of person who clearly enjoys what he does for a living.

Every morning Bruno would collect our dictionaries and "store" them in a wastebasket. His philosophy was a simple one: "Look it up in a dictionary and it's forgotten a moment later; experience it and it is yours forever." And experience we did. One day I was a waiter in a restaurant, the next a TV newscaster. When we came across an unfamiliar word he would explain it by acting it out and then look around the class to see if we had understood. He had a sixth sense when it came to this and before my eyes could glaze over completely, he would zero in ... "

Ça va Barbara?" (Got it?

Understand?) I would nod and mumble "Oui. Ça va" (Sure, no problem. I understand you perfectly, now leave me alone). "Bien!" he would shout "Tu expliques à la classe" (Oh Yeah! Then explain it to everyone else). And I would have to explain it to the class using mime, gesture or whatever was available; but then, that word became mine forever because I had lived it. I'm still a long way from "speaking French" but I now have more "successes" than "failures". I can drop my shoes off at the shoemaker and pick them up on the right day. I've gotten my eyebrows waxed, my hair cut, had the plumber in twice, and spent three very long hours at the Préfecture de Police attempting to get my carte de séjour, all without uttering one word in English! In my book that's progress. And who knows what Bruno has in store for the next six weeks; I may get to be Marie Antoinette!

Barbara Hartigan

1,400FF for eight weeks and 1,800FF for 12 weeks. The theatre course is included in the intensive course but can also act as an option if studying part-time (three hours per week for 12 weeks: 1,800FF). DELF and DALF preparation is additional (three hours per week, 2,000FF for 12 weeks and 900FF for four weeks). Preparation for the CCIP (Chambre de Commerce et d'Industrie de Paris) exams takes place all year round (4,000FF or 4,500FF in July and August).

Various accommodation options are offered: in a family (1,200FF six nights for a single room with breakfast, 1,000FF for an extra week or 4,000FF for four weeks; half-board prices: 1,500FF, 13,50FF and 5,000FF respectively); a student residence (single room with half board 8,50FF, females only), in a residential hotel (1,300FF, single room with breakfast, for six nights, 1,400FF extra week, 4,300FF for four weeks; half-board 15,50FF, 1,800FF and 5,400FF respectively) and a tourist hotel (prices vary).

Alliance Française

101, boulevard Raspail, 75270 Paris Cedex 06
Tel: + 33 1 45 44 38 28
Fax: +33 1 45 44 89 42
E-mail: info@paris.alliancefrancaise.fr
Website: www.Paris.alliance-francaise.fr
Established: 1883
Level of French required: None
Nearest Station: (Métro) Notre Dame des Champs

The oldest and the best, declares Joseph Commets, the Alliance's director. Oldest cannot be argued with, but best is a very relative term. If you like large classes, large institutions and a large student population this could be the place for you. If you are looking for a more personal, cosy atmosphere try elsewhere. The Alliance Française is the cattle-market of language schools: shovelling in *débutants* and shovelling out speakers at the rate of around 2000 per month. However, for those in need of an international reputation, combined with the only diploma recognised across Europe, this is the place. It isn't, it has to be said, the most inviting of places. Huge buildings filled with echoing

Picture courtesy of Alliance Française

or those who want to train in the profession (the latter qualification is also available by correspondence). The Alliance is notably the only school in Paris that is a founding member of ALTE. Schools that are part of this European committee have certificates that are recognised and transferable across Europe; thus an ALTE qualification is more mobile and more relevant on a CV than most language diplomas. It is also a centre for the DELF, DALF and Chambre de Commerce et d'Industrie de Paris exams.

Facilities include language labs and *médiathèque* as well as a bureau de change, bookshop, restaurant and café, library, film club, and an accommodation and job service. Enrolment and placement tests take place all year round.

staircases, an enormous café, and crammed classrooms do nothing to help its PR. Yet it is, undeniably, a force to be reckoned with. The students I met, who had no notion of who I was and were certainly not feeds from the establishment, were not only an advertisement for the school in terms of their comments, but also in terms of their linguistic competence.

The range of courses is mind-boggling: from one month full-time (four hours per day) at 2,960FF to one month part-time (two hours per day) at 1,480FF. Classes cover oral comprehension, grammar, translation and prose. There are courses for au pairs, as well as for French as a Foreign Language teachers, whether those who want to brush up their skills

The Alliance Française's main building is set back from the boulevard Raspail. Take Metro line 12 to Notre Dame des Champs. Walk a short distance along boulevard Raspail and the Alliance is across the street at number 101, between rue Huysmans and rue de Fleurus. Look for a large LCD display. Unmissable.

If you want the reputation of the Alliance but can't face the numbers, try one of the regional branches:

Alliance Française de Bourgogne

29 rue Sambin, 21000 Dijon
Tel: +33 3 80 72 59 92
Fax: +33 3 80 72 59 93
Contact: Mme Françoise Berenguer
Established: 1993

20 students per month with an average of ten students per class; situated in new buildings in the centre of Dijon, the capital of Burgundy; preparation of DELF, DALF, CCIP and Alliance Française exams. Enrol any time of year.

Costs: 150FF registration fee; a week of lessons costs 400FF for eight hours or 800FF for 16 hours (ie 50FF an hour).

Facilities: student cafeteria; garden; library; two and a half month beginners sessions starting four times a year.

Accommodation: available in host families (bed and breakfast 2,250FF per month; half-board 3,200FF per month or 3,700FF including weekends) or student residences (1850FF per month for men and 2,700FF for women). Dijon is one and a half hours from Paris on the TGV.

Alliance Française de Lyon

11, rue Pierre Bourdan, 69003 Lyon
Tel: +33 4 78 95 24 72
Fax: +33 4 78 60 77 28
Established: 1985
Level of French: None
Nearest Station: Lyon Part-Dieu
Nearest Airport: Lyon Satolas
Contact: Emmanuelle Benair

1200 students per year; groups of 15 per class, all levels available; preparation for Alliance exams, *Diplôme Supérieur d'Études Françaises* (National Education diploma). Enrol all year round.

Costs: Registration fee 150FF; Beginners' courses from 1,600FF per month for 60 hours of lessons; Intermediate courses from 1,070FF per month for 40 hours; Advanced from 1,120FF per month for 40 hours. Summer courses 1,750FF per month for 60 hours plus 150FF registration fee.

Accommodation: can be arranged with host families. Summer accommodation available in university residences for 1,050FF per month.

Alliance Française de Rouen

79 quai du Havre, 76000 Rouen
Tel: +33 2 35 98 55 99
Fax: +33 2 35 89 98 58
Email: Alliance.Francaise.Rouen@wanadoo.fr
Established: 1983
Level of French: None
Nearest Station: (SNCF) Rouen
Contact: Madame Fatima Labadi

600 students per year; all levels of French; about 12 students per class.

Costs: Registration Fee 200FF. General French classes 480FF per week (15 hours); Easter and Summer courses 525FF per week (15 hours) or 875FF per week (25 hours); au pair courses 210FF per week (six hours; Alliance exam fee 350FF; Business French (280FF per month for eight hours); group deals on demand.

Accommodation: accommodation service available (250FF fee); half-board in host family from 100FF per day; room or studio rental from 1,500FF per month.

Alliance Française Toulouse Midi-Pyrénées

9, place du Capitole,
31000 Toulouse
Tel: +33 5 61 23 41 24
Fax: +33 5 61 23 05 51
Established: 1986
Level of French: None
Nearest Station: (SNCF)
Matabiau - Toulouse
Nearest Airport:
Toulouse-Blagnac
Contact: Madame Viviane
Jambert

Over 900 students per year; 12 in a group; school in the centre of Toulouse; small and friendly.

Cost: Registration fee 200FF; Intensive (three and a half hours every day; 1,900FF for four weeks) and Semi-intensive (five hours per week; 800FF for four weeks). Programmes available at all levels all year; specialist options in literature, civilisation, Business French available (650FF for 16 hours). Alliance exams in December, March and June, fees 300FF; DELF and DALF exam preparation available; each month paid in advance and no refunds.

Facilities: excursions and evening entertainment organised all year round

Accommodation: accommodation available in rooms; bed and breakfast in host families; from 1,400FF for a room and 3000FF for a room with full-board.

Berlitz Champs-Élysées

35 avenue Franklin Roosevelt,
75008 Paris
Tel: +33 1 40 74 00 17
Fax: +33 1 45 61 49 79
Established: 1878
Level of French required: None

Nearest Station: (Métro)
Franklin D. Roosevelt
Contact: Mme Marie-Elisabeth
Crochard

In a modern, streamlined building sandwiched between the Champs Élysées and the Seine sits Berlitz Paris, the company's French flagship. Many have heard of Berlitz but few know its system. The focus is on total oral immersion and helping the learner to communicate. In small groups students are immersed in the language from day one and grammar is only studied once the student can speak. Other than active oral participation, teachers use a variety of other methods, including CD-ROMS and videos. Every new student has an interview to determine their learning objectives and needs, in order to decide which type of class would be suitable. Groups are organised in terms of abilities and, where necessary, nationalities. Europeans, especially Italian and Spanish students, tend to be grouped together, as are Asian students. This is, explains Madame Crochard, to avoid the frustrations that occur when an Italian student, already versed in a Romance language, leaps ahead of a Japanese student. Staff are friendly, helpful and faithful to the system – many have worked at Berlitz for over 15 years. Previous students include Annie Lennox, Gerard Départdieu, Sophie Marceau and Princess Anne.

Such a star-studded list is a reminder that Berlitz has a princely price tag to match. A 'Tonic' course (three hours per day, Monday to Friday, in groups of four or five) costs 7,236FF for four weeks and 13,895FF for eight. A 'Total Impact' course, available from June to

September, costs 5,065FF for two weeks and 9286FF for four (9.30am to 12.30pm and 1.15pm to 3.30pm every day). Business French (taught in two and a quarter hour blocks in groups of two to three people) costs 8,683FF for 20 sessions and the classes can be full or part-time. For the very brave, very devoted and very rich there is also a total immersion option: nine hours a day. One week costs 23,517FF (the price changes according to the number of classes booked). It includes lunch... ou'll need it! At the end of each stage students receive a progress report. None of the prices include materials.

Enrolment takes place all year round. Accommodation, in families, can be arranged at very reasonable rates (149FF per night with breakfast and 198FF with half-board).

To reach Berlitz, take métro line 1 to Franklin D Roosevelt. The avenue Franklin D Roosevelt descends from the Champs-Elysées towards the Seine. Berlitz is on the right. Go upstairs, past the books and T-shirts for sale and you will reach the café-reception area.

Centre Sorbonne Cours de Civilisation Francaise
45, rue des Écoles, 75005 Paris
Tel: +33 1 40 46 22 11
Established 1899
Level of French required: None
Nearest Station: (Métro) Cluny la Sorbonne
Contact: Jean-Louis de Boissieu

This Centre is often confused with the Sorbonne but it is in fact a private institution that has been working within its walls for over 150 years. Nearly every major city in France has a similar school. Such centres offer the best of both worlds to international students: comprehensive language teaching focussed on their needs, along with a university environment, often in gorgeous buildings in the most beautiful parts of the city. Students at this Centre, for example, might not actually be enrolled at the *vrai* Sorbonne, but they can still wander its echoing corridors, drink its disgusting coffee and marvel at its beautiful 19th-century amphitheatres. However, the classes do not actually take place in the old university but in modern buildings sprinkled around the 5th. One distinguishing feature of the Centre is that literary study forms a central part of the curriculum. It offers a solid, traditional course, focusing on the written word, covering not only grammar, translation and phonetics but also literature, history and civilisation. In four months even complete beginners will, according to Jean-Louis Boissieu, be able to communicate. Exams prepared include, obviously, the Sorbonne's own plus the Chamber of Commerce's business exams. Classes are large (maximum 25) and students choose one of two formulae: 10 hours plus two hours of phonetics (5500FF for 12 weeks) or 25 hours (11 500FF). Evening classes (six hours per week) cost 3450FF for 12 weeks. Enrolment is for a minimum of one semester, September-December or February-May. Summer courses are very much *à la carte*, classes can last as little as two weeks or as long as two months. There is an accommodation service and a minimal social programme (ie a choir, but nothing else).

Take métro line 10 to Cluny. Walk up boulevard St Michel, with the Seine behind you. Turn left onto rue des Écoles then right onto rue de la Sorbonne. The entrance is on the left about halfway up the street. Ask the porter how to reach the Centre's main offices which are in the Galerie Richelieu, Salle 9.

CFILC

28, rue des Petites Ecuries (Esc B, 4th Floor), 75010 Paris
Tel: +33 1 48 24 04 10
Fax: +33 1 48 24 04 19
Established: 1996
Level of French required: None
Nearest Station: (Métro)
Chateau d'Eau
Contact: Cecile Vialle

With just two classrooms and an office, this is probably the smallest French language school in Paris. As prices are around 25FF per hour, it is also one of the cheapest. Situated up a dingy stairway, on the fourth floor of a classic Parisian building, CFILC isn't easy to find, nor does it have any of the gloss and glamour of many larger schools. No language labs, no social programme, no café. However, it offers a product, not packaging. Students love it. Established by Cecile Vialle, once FLE teacher, now owner-manager, CFILC runs small classes (with a maximum of ten students per group) in five different levels (Beginners to Advanced). Classes are based on oral and aural comprehension more than grammar, although all aspects of French language and culture, from phonetics to civilisation, are covered. Full-time classes (ten hours in five two-hour blocks) cost 800FF for four weeks, part-time classes (six hours per week) cost 600FF for four weeks and evening classes (one and a half hours twice a week) cost 300FF for four weeks. Teachers use the Panorama books (the cost of which is included in the 130FF enrolment fee) as well as audio-visual

methods. Students' progress is closely followed with a review every three weeks and it is easy to change one's level or timetable if necessary. Since payment is by a block of classes not by period of time, students do not lose classes through absence. Enrolment and evaluation tests take place all year round, although new classes begin every six to eight weeks. The school is open every day and Saturday mornings. CFILC does not organise accommodation.

To reach CFILC, take métro line 4 to Château d'Eau. You will find yourself on boulevard de Strasbourg at its junction with rue du Château d'Eau. Rue des Petites Écuries is the continuation of rue du Château d'Eau.

L'ÉCOLE EIFFEL

3 rue Croce-Spinelli,
75014 Paris
Tel: +33 1 43 20 37 41
Fax: +33 1 43 20 49 13
E-mail: elffelfr@club-internet.fr
Website: www.ccip.fr/club/75/
ecole-eiffel.html
Level of French required: None
Nearest Station: (Métro)
Pernety
Contact: Madame Jouet

The Eiffel in the name of this school is not just an obvious reference to the most famous landmark in Paris. It stands for 'École Internationale de Français et de Formation En Langues'. Such attention to detail defines the school and its objectives. Having worked as a FLE teacher at the Alliance Française and Paris-Langues, Madame Jouet wanted to set up her own. She spent months researching the site and the style, trying to find an area both central yet calm, and the most effective and enjoyable style of teaching, for staff and students. The school is thus close to Montparnasse but in a calm, residential neighbourhood, near a métro station and a small park. It is modern and streamlined, with light classrooms and up-to-date equipment.

The courses are available in several different levels and a student's level will be determined by a placement test. Prices per month are as follows: full-time classes cost 1,700FF per month (ten and a half hours per week divided into three sessions), 2,400FF (20 hours per week divided into five sessions). Part-time classes cost 1,000FF (five and a half hours in three sessions), 1,100FF (seven and a half hours in four sessions), 1,250FF (10 hours in five sessions).

The enrolment fee is 150FF. Beginners can enrol at the start of each month. The school is open from 8.45am to 7pm all year round. Accommodation is available with host families. For a room in Paris, bed and breakfast costs 140FF per day, half-board 188FF and prices increase by 30FF per day with private bathroom.

To reach the school, take métro line 13 to Pernety. Turn left into rue Pernety, right onto rue de l'Ouest, then left again onto rue Croce-Spinelli. Look for the smoked glass windows of the school on the corner on the right.

École de Langue Française pour Étrangers

8 Villa Ballu, 75009 Paris
Tel: +33 1 48 78 73 00
Fax: +33 1 40 82 91 92
Email: contactelfe-paris.com
Website:www.elfe-paris.com
Established: 1984
Level of French: None
Nearest Station: (Métro) Place

de Clichy
Contact: Elizabeth Hannoset

ELFE offers the sort of personalised teaching and small groups found in smaller institutions, but also the external guarantees of teaching quality usually only found in larger schools. Situated in a classic French house, over-looking a tree-filled cobbled courtyard, it is also one of the most attractive schools in the city. One of the founding members of SOUFFLE, it is very close knit and friendly with mini-groups (maximum six students) and two teachers per group. The emphasis is on face-to-face teaching and as a result there is no language laboratory. There is a small coffee bar, a terrace and multimedia and TV equipment at the students' disposal.

Classes start every Monday, except for beginners who can start on the first Monday of every month. New arrivals take a written and oral test and are then assigned a class. Students can choose from 15 hours to 25 hours of classes per week (2,200FF to 5,800FF) in groups, or 10 to 30 hours of individual tuition (from 3,600FF to 10 600FF). Minimum enrolment is two weeks in groups, and one week as an individual. ELFE also offers Business French courses, French teachers' courses and Grandes Écoles preparation. A weekend immersion course (three days, 21 hours of classes and lunches with the teacher) costs 11,000FF. The 400FF enrolment fee covers books, paperwork and excursions (where available). On arrival, students are given a helpful booklet which includes maps of Paris and useful information. At the end of a course students receive an ELFE certificate. ELFE is recommended by the Petite Guide.

LANGUAGE SCHOOLS

Accommodation can be organised with families (1,000FF per week for B and B, 1,750FF for half-board), in hotels (from 2,400FF to 6,800FF weekly) or in student residences (prices on demand). There is a 250FF booking fee for hotels. Fees and enrolment must be paid in full at least four weeks before the start of classes.

Take métro line 13 to Place de Clichy. Walk along rue de Clichy against the traffic. Rue Ballu is the second on the left. Villa Ballu is halfway down on the right.

L'Étoile

38, boulevard Raspail, 75007 Paris
Tel: +33 1 45 48 00 05
Fax: +33 1 45 48 62 05
Established: 1971
Level of French required: None
Nearest Station: (Métro) Sèvres-Babylone
Contact: Madame Rosine Gillard-Sire

It's Friday morning and I walk into a long courtyard overlooked by a huge artist's loft (rented out by John Malkovich not so long ago). I'm looking for a language school but can't see anything. Screams and laughter lead me to a small door on the left and from the relative quiet of the courtyard I arrive in the noisy Étoile family. One of the teachers is leaving today and the class is toasting her with wine, orange juice and cheeses. Rosine shepherds me into her office, though I'm loath to leave the party. Such scenes are part of the daily life of this lively, friendly and homely language school. Offering a lot more than nine levels of French classes, exam preparation and professional teaching, the school is a veritable home from home for its students. There is a

social programme (the cheese and wine were hangovers from the previous evening's "Cinema Night"), accommodation of all types organised by the school and an atmosphere that will ensure that even the most reluctant of learners feels relaxed. Whether to a monk from Tibet or to a Mum from Torquay, the school will feel welcoming.

At 5700FF per trimester (for ten hours a week plus homework) it is also incredible value. Enrolment takes place all year round. Summer courses (four weeks for 3,500FF) take place in July and August. The advanced summer courses combine language learning with the discovery of French culture through specific themes: history; literature; French geography and France through its Monuments. Accommodation can be organised in host families for approximately 4,700FF per month half-board.

To reach the school, take métro line 10 to Sèvres-Babylone. Take the boulevard Raspail exit and keeping Bon Marche behind you and the elegant Hotel Lutetia in front and to the right, turn left and cross rue de Babylone. Keep on the left-hand side, cross rue de Chomel and number 38 is on the left just before a Japanese florist. Go into the courtyard. The school is on the left.

Eurocentre Paris

13 Passage Dauphine, 75006 Paris
Tel: +33 1 40 46 72 00
Fax: +33 1 40 46 72 06
E-mail: 00632.133@compuserve.com
Website: www.clark.net/pub/eurocent/home.htm
Established: 1973
Level of French required: None

**Nearest Station: (Métro)
Mabillon
Contact: Mme Pascale Palaquer**

One of the greatest reasons to choose Eurocentre, other than its reputed teaching and extensive facilities, is that it is an organisation with 31 schools all over the world. Students can pay for a block of 35 weeks of classes and use that time to learn three languages and visit three different countries (this isn't of course, very cheap). Within France, classes can be followed at three sites: Paris, Amboise and La Rochelle. The Paris Eurocentre is situated in a beautiful passageway in the centre of St Germain des Près and the Latin Quarter, with museums, the Sartre/de Beauvoir haunts and the Seine only steps away. The school is in a 19th-century building but its facilities and classes are very 21st century. The standard teaching week is 25 hours (9am to 1pm daily) and students are encouraged to spend their afternoons making use of the language-learning tools at their disposal: computers, videos, laboratories, a *médiathèque* and library. Classes are based around a communicative method elaborated by the centre and its teachers. Commercial systems, whether books or tapes, age too quickly, argues Madame Albrecht, whereas using newspaper articles and a constant series of updated photocopies and texts enables a vivid and up-to-date method of language learning. Students are provided with a folder with all the material. On Thursdays the centre organises activities. Those within Paris are free but for those beyond the city students pay a small fee.

Students can prepare for the DELF, the DALF or the Chamber of Commerce exams in French for Business or French for Tourism. The Eurocentre frequently works with professional groups, such as Finnish journalists or British flight attendants. Enrolment takes place all year round and summer courses are available. All students take a placement test. Accommodation in families is organised and the hosts and students are regularly quizzed to ensure that problems are avoided. Full-time (25 hours per week) classes range from 3,750FF for two weeks (25 hours per week) to 20 5,25FF for 13 weeks. With half-board accommodation these two courses cost 6,198FF and 35,293FF respectively. DELF and DALF preparation is available for a supplement.

Take métro line 10 to Mabillon. Cross boulevard St Germain away from rue du Four and walk up rue de Buci. At Carrefour de Buci take the first left, rue Mazarine. Passage Dauphine is on the right, about halfway up the street, and the Eurocentre is on the right.

Formation Postuniversitaire

**11 rue Tiquetonne, 75002 Paris
Tel: +33 1 40 28 04 03
Fax: +33 1 40 28 49 22
Level of French required: None
Nearest Station: (Métro)
Etienne Marcel
Contact: FPI**

FPI is located in sparse, white rooms, just off the lively rue Tiquetonne. It is somewhat underwhelming both in terms of environment and welcome, but it does not aspire to anything other than teaching French, without any social frills. It was one of the first schools to use audio-visual methods, and now offers four different levels of language classes, a business and written French course and special courses for

FLE teachers. 12.5 hours of classes, over four weeks, costs 1,800FF, four and a half classes over four weeks costs 650FF and a six-hour evening class (three times a week, Monday, Tuesday and Wednesday) costs 1,150FF over four weeks. Groups are a maximum of 16 students. The enrolment fee is 100FF.

Accommodation in host families can be organised.

Take métro line 4 to Etienne Marcel. Walk against the traffic along rue de Turbigo (the diagonal street that goes across rue Etienne Marcel). Turn left into rue Saint-Denis then immediately left again into rue Tiquetonne. FPI is on the left.

France Langue

2, rue de Sfax, 75116 Paris
Tel: +33 1 45 00 40 15
Fax: +33 1 45 00 53 41
E-mail: frlang_p@club-internet.fr
Website: www.france-langue.fr
Level of French required: None
Nearest Station: (Métro)
Victor Hugo

Situated in a classic Parisian building in the chic and expensive 16th, with high-ceilings, long windows and double doors, France Langue seems a long way from the palms of Nice. However, one of the factors which differentiates this school from the competition is that students can choose to transfer their classes from one branch to the other. Spend the winter (which tends to be miserable and grey in Paris) on the coast, and the spring in the capital. This isn't France Langue's only selling point. As one of the larger independent schools it offers a comprehensive selection of courses, and a busy lecture and excursion programme, yet remains very much in touch with its students. And, despite being in one of the least studenty and most expensive *arrondissements* in Paris, the 16th, France Langue is not one of the most expensive. Any student booking for more than 12 weeks and up to a year will pay around 700FF per week.

Beginners classes start every week and there are full-time courses (15 to 30 hours per week) or part-time courses (six to 10 hours per week). 12 weeks, with 15 hours instruction per week, costs 8,400FF, increasing to 126,00FF for 22.5 hours and 16 800FF for 30 hours. The weekly rates for stays over 12 weeks are 700FF (15 hours), 1,050FF (22.5 hours) and 1,400FF (30 hours). Minimum enrolment is two weeks. Groups average 12 students in the intensive classes and 15 to 18 in the extensive. There is an au pair course. Summer courses are also available, including a special intensive session on business French. There are five different levels of ability. Classes are taught through a variety of methods and books used include Cadence, Panorama and Bienvenue en France. Students in the intensive classes are expected to do homework and to spend 45 minutes a day in the *médiathèque*, working on the computer, in a lab or on a film. Payment is by the week and since classes are not fixed to an academic year, missed weeks can be taken at a later date. There is a test at the end of each trimester and students receive a certificate detailing their progress at the end of their course. Facilities include a small café and *médiathèque*.

The school organises accommodation in families, student residences and hotels. A room with half-board in Paris costs 188FF per day (160FF per day for stays longer than three weeks; 140FF for bed and breakfast). A week's bed and breakfast costs 840FF and a week's half-board costs 1,128FF. One week in a university residence (summer only) will cost approximately 700FF to 800FF, in an international foyer with breakfast 1,280FF and in a two-star hotel with breakfast 2,120FF.

To reach the school, take métro line 2 to Victor Hugo. Off the large Place walk along avenue Raymond Poincare (between rue de Sontay and rue Leonardo de Vinci). Rue de Sfax is the first on the left and the school is immediately on the right.

Institut Britannique de Paris

11, rue de Constantine, 75340 Cedex
07 Paris
Tel: +33 1 44 11 73 76
Fax: +33 1 45 50 31 55
Website:
www.bip.lon.ac.uk
Established: 1927
Level of French required: Varies
Nearest Station: (Métro) Invalides
Contact: Varies according to course

The British Institute, snuggled into the same building as the British Council offices in Paris, is possibly better known for its promotion of English language and culture. However, it offers several different courses, open to English and French students, which would be of interest to year abroad students, students considering entering the French education system and linguists seeking a higher degree in translation. The advantage for a British student of following courses in French at the British Institute is that the classes will be easily accredited on returning to the UK. There is no complicated establishing of transfers or trying to explain what the weird letters on the CV mean to the monolingual job interviewer. It is, however, very much a French-style operation. Don't expect the same follow-up and pastoral care that is found in British and American universities. The qualifications are British but the welcome is definitely Parisian; somewhat cold, distant and indifferent.

Courses available include a Masters (in

John James

conjunction with the University of London), Diploma and Certificate in French and English Translation, a Year-Abroad programme (specifically for British University students), a Masters in Contemporary French Studies or in Contemporary French Theatre, practice translation classes for students preparing exams with such a component, and classes specifically for those working as assistants. For the Masters courses you need at least an upper second-class honours degree in a relevant subject or a proven ability or interest in the subject of study. It is also possible to register for a University of London research degree in Humanities, provided the planned subject is one of its special areas of interest. Prices range from £600 for the Assistants Class (26 weeks) to 7,000FF per trimester for the one-year Masters and 3,500FF per trimester for the Masters in translation (over two years). The Year Abroad programme costs from £775 per trimester to £1,150 per year. There is a maximum of 19 students per class.

To enrol, contact the Institut from two to five months before the start date. A written test (to determine a student's level of French) and an application form will be sent out, which must be returned as quickly as possible, with an enrolment fee of 400FF. Full-time enrolment entitles students to a student card. Lists of accommodation will be provided on request.

Take métro lines 8 or 13 to Invalides. The exit is on rue de Constantine. Walk towards the Hotel des Invalides (the big gold dome) and the British Institute is on the left.

Institut de Langue et de Culture Francaises (Institut Catholique de Paris)

12, rue Cassette, 75006 Paris
Tel: +33 1 44 39 52 00
Fax: +33 1 44 39 52 09
E-mail: ilcf@icp.fr
Established: 1841
Level of French required: None
Minimum age: 18 (post-baccalauréat)
Nearest Station: (Métro) Rennes
Contact: Pierre Lefort

The Institut Catholique is probably not as well-known to most foreigners as the Sorbonne or the Alliance Française. However, with these two institutions it forms the historical triumvirate of French language teaching in Paris. They are the *grandes dames* of the FLE family. None of them has the most exciting curriculum or the trendiest teaching methods, but all provide a solid linguistic education, recognised worldwide.

In the heart of the Latin quarter, near St Germain des Prés and Montparnasse, the Institut is, like the CCF at the Sorbonne, a private concern operating within the walls of a public university or, in this case, a 'free' university. It teaches three types of French classes: semesters during the academic year; summer classes in July; and a pre-university course in September for those students about to launch themselves into the unknown waters of the French higher education system. As well as the traditional grammar and civilisation sections, other options include art, theatre, business and fashion. Along with the other Institut Catholiques (in Lille, Lyon and Toulouse) the Parisian branch offers an "Intercatho" diploma which is equivalent to one year of a

DEUG, the first University qualification in France. The ILCF also offers up to 4 hours per week of free conversation classes. A FLE course is also available for those hoping to teach French.

The student population is international (from Japan, America, Germany, Sweden), classes are large (18 to 25 per group depending on the subject) but the Institut aims to keep in close contact with all the students, both academically and personally. Every year, for example, teachers invite their whole class for Christmas dinner at their homes (18 guests!). This is somewhat rare for such a large institution.

The Institut has a huge administrative advantage in that it has a *carte de séjour* service, a bureaucratic nightmare that any student will be glad to avoid. There is a newspaper, Bric-a-Brac, written and edited by the students and many trips connected with the various options. Other facilities include language labs, access to the Institut's library and a café.

Price per semester (15 weeks) is 3,525Ff for six hours instruction, 4,925FF for nine hours, 8,125Ff for 12 hours, 9455FF for 16 hours and 9,760FF for 18 hours. The pre-university course costs 4,685FF for September. The enrolment fee is 350FF to enrol for a semester; write and request the application forms approximately four months in advance (October to November for February). You need to arrive a few weeks before the start of the semester in order to take the placement tests. Accommodation is the students' responsibility, though the Institut can advise.

To reach the Institut, take métro line 12 to Rennes or line 4 to St Placide. Both will lead you to rue de Rennes. Walk away from Montparnasse (the only brown skyscraper in the city so you can't miss it...) and turn right on rue d'Assas. Turn left on rue de Vaugirard and left again onto rue de Cassette. The somewhat unprepossessing entrance to the ICF is on the left.

Institut de Langue Française

3, avenue Bertie Albrecht, 75008 Paris
Tel: +33 1 45 63 24 00
Fax: +33 1 45 63 07 09
Level of French: None
Contact: Valerie Arata
Established: 1986
Nearest Station: (Métro/ RER) Charles de Gaulle Etoile

If you're stuck for a language school, then consider the ILF, but if you have a choice then try somewhere else first. Located in the haughty 8th *arrondissement*, a short distance from the Champs-Élysées, it offers a plethora of courses and a minimal welcome. In the space of 30 minutes, at the end of which my interviewee didn't turn up, I watched both staff and students being treated with the same lack of interest and respect that I received at the hands of the administrative staff. Somehow they manage to enrol around 2500 students per year, in summer courses and more extended programmes.

Hours of study are from four to ten hours per week in the Student/Au Pair Programme (from 1,500FF to 3,500FF per term, with prices decreasing for those enrolling for two or three terms). Intensive programmes (20 hours per week) cost 1600FF for two weeks, 7,500FF for one term, and 20,000FF for three terms. Part-time programmes cost 1,200FF for six hours a week for four weeks, increasing to 3,000FF per term.

INSTITUT PARISIEN

LANGUE & CIVILISATION FRANÇAISES

Picture courtesy of Institut Parisien

the left. Look for the brochures in the ground floor windows.

Institut Parisien
87, boulevard de Grenelle, 75015 Paris
Tel: +33 1 40 56 09 53
Fax: +33 1 40 43 06 46 30
Website:
institut.parisien@dial. oleane.com
Established: 1988
Level of French required: None
Nearest Station: (Métro) La Motte-Picquet Grenelle
Contact: Madame Marie-Christine Simon

There are several options, including Civilisation, Phonetics and Literature which cost an additional fee of 400FF per week over four weeks. The enrolment fee is 200FF. The ILF also runs a DELF preparation course.

Accommodation can be organised in host families, hotels and university residences (summer only). Half-board in a family costs 200FF per day (in Paris) and 140FF per day (breakfast only). The university residences cost 110FF to 140FF per day without breakfast. The hotel rates quoted are rather expensive (400FF) per day.

To reach the school, take métro lines 1, 2 or 6 or RER A to Charles de Gaulle Etoile. Take avenue Hoche from the Étoile and take the second right into Avenue Bertie Albrecht. The ILF is on

Learning a language involves speaking it, a talent which is more effectively developed through the contact between a teacher and a student, not a student and a screen. Such reasoning is behind the lack of computers, language labs and *médiathèques* at the Institut Parisien. "I value the teacher-student relationship above all other learning environments." says the director Marie-Christine Simon. The Institut is not, however, some fusty, dusty old school. It is situated in ultra-modern buildings, with a busy café in the hallway and large, light classrooms leading off a calm, green corridor. I spy on a few classes through the interior glass walls. In both the big au pair class, where there are at least 18 teenage girls, and the small advanced level group, where there are two adults, the atmosphere is one of professional and focussed instruction. The Institut also wins my prize for the most attractive, legible accessible documentation and prices guide.

Full-time courses cost 670FF (10 hours of instruction), 990FF (15 hours) and 1,660FF (25 hours) per week. These prices drop to 590F, 870FF, or 1,460FF when booking five weeks or more. Part-time au pair options (four and a half or nine hours per week) cost 1,950FF/4,190FF per trimester (12 weeks) or 2,850FF/6,120FF per semester (17 weeks) (approximately 270FF/570FF per week). The enrolment fee is 250FF. Classes on French fashion cost 220FF per week. Courses start every Monday (except beginners). Groups are limited to 12 students and each class lasts 55 minutes.

Accommodation is organised in families near the school or hotels. Prices range from 1,220FF for bed and breakfast in a family (1,580FF half-board) to 190FF in a foyer, 385FF per night in a two-star hotel with breakfast or 582FF for a two-person studio.

To reach the Institut, take lines 8, 10 or 6 to La Motte-Picquet Grenelle. At the exit follow the overground métro line along boulevard Grenelle (avenue de la Motte-Picquet on your right and rue du Commerce on your left). The Institut Parisien is about five minutes' walk away on the right.

Langue Onze

15, rue Gambey, 75011 Paris
Tel: +33 1 43 38 22 87
Fax: +33 1 43 38 36 01
Website: www.Langue-onze.com
Established: 1981
Level of French required: None
Nearest Station: (métro) Parmentier
Contact: Thierry Pecot or Karine Kirn

A tiny language school, tucked away up a back staircase in the trendy 11th *arrondissement*, Langue Onze would be a good choice for adults wanting a quick fix of French with no frills. Classes are small (maximum five per

Picture courtesy of Paris École des Roches Langues

Picture courtesy of Paris Langues

group), the focus is on oral communication (literary tenses such as the past historic are not taught on principle) and the teachers and students are determined and focused. A minimal infrastructure (small attic rooms for teaching, no social programme or accommodation service) allows for minimal pricing and maximum concentration on learning French. John Rinehart, a habitual student of Langue Onze, is a US expatriate who could easily take his pick amongst the more dressy and PR-driven language schools. 'I chose this one' he says, 'because I wanted to speak the language and that's what the small groups and teaching encourage. It is a school with a heart, a great secret.' This is very much an adult school, average student age around 28, and there are only 20 students per month. Langue Onze is a member of the Tandem network which works across Europe to put language learners in touch with native speakers.

New students can enrol on the first and third Monday of every month, minimum enrolment is two weeks and prices decrease for longer sessions. A full-time course (four hours per day) costs 1,700FF for two weeks and 3,000FF for a month (the second month costs 2,800FF and the third costs 2,600FF). The school can find you a room in a flat (2,200FF to 2500FF per month) or book hotels (approximately 170FF per day). There is no fee for this service.

There is another Langue Onze school in South-West France, operating with the same objectives. Contact the Paris school or write directly to:

Langue Onze Sud-Ouest, B.P. 31 F. 81500 Lavaur
Tel: +33 5 63 58 40 98
Fax:+33 5 63 58 41 30

To reach the school, take métro line 3 to Parmentier. With rue Oberkampf behind you, walk along Avenue de la Republique. Rue Gambey is second on the left and number 15 is on the right. Go through the heavy blue door. There is a staircase on the right. Press the Langue Onze doorbell and prepare for the walk – four flights of stairs.

Paris École des Roches Langues

6-8 rue Spinoza, 75011 Paris
Tel: +33 1 47 00 99 98
Fax: +33 1 43 57 14 46
Established: 1899/1993
Level of French required: None
Contact: Cecile Jouault

The École des Roches was the first school I visited in France. There is no greater testament to the quality of its welcome than to say that, several months and hundreds of schools later, I remember it vividly. Cecile Jouault, administrator and helpful soul par excellence, embodies the school's personality: friendly, open, thorough. Established four years ago, the school is part of the École des Roches, which is a much respected primary and secondary school in Verneuil sur Avre in Normandy, open to pupils of all nationalities and known to dignitaries and diplomats worldwide. The Paris branch, devoted solely to FLE (French as a Foreign Language), is in an old school building looking out onto a small courtyard with a tree. New arrivals would be forgiven for feeling that they have gone back in time, to a world of satchels and short trousers. The teaching and approach will soon dispel any apprehension, though. Offering courses to suit all students, from au pairs to expatriates, PERL combines the character of a small school with the competence/choice of a large university.

Five levels of classes are available, from beginners to advanced, focusing on communication skills. From level three students can prepare for the DELF, from levels four/five for the DALF, the Sorbonne or the Chambre de Commerce exams. Classes take a maximum of 15 students and students can choose to study in the morning, afternoon or evening. Every month there are two free cultural seminars and a Paris Aventures day-trip (cost varying from 50FF-180FF). The trip is prepared in class and students are then taken on a guided tour of a particular site, gallery or monument in Paris. The school prides itself on its flexibility and friendliness, making sure students are happy, both in academic and personal terms.

Costs range from 2550FF per month for 15 hours of classes, 3000FF per trimester for Business French (six hours per week) and 3000FF per trimester for Sorbonne Exam Preparation (seven hours per week). Full-time classes cost from 1,275FF (two weeks; 15 hours per week) to 24,900FF(24 weeks; 26 hours per week). Part-time classes cost from 740FF (two weeks; six hours per week) to 13,990FF (24 weeks; 12 hours per week).

Beginners classes start at the beginning of each month; more advanced classes begin every week. An evaluation test determines students' levels. There is a free lesson available for all those who want to be absolutely sure this is the place for them.

Accommodation is organised in families or residences, as requested. One week bed and breakfast in a family costs 1,230FF or 1,490FF half-board. A room in a student residence costs 165FF or 180FF with breakfast in an

International Foyer.

To reach the school, take métro line 3 or 2 to Pere Lachaise. At the crossroads follow Avenue de la Republique. Rue Spinoza is first on the right. PERL is on the right.

Paris Langues

FIAP Jean Monnet, 30 rue Cabanis, 75014 Paris
Tel: +33 1 45 65 05 28
Fax: +33 1 45 81 26 28
E-mail: Parislangues@com-puserve.com
Level of French required: None
Nearest Station: (métro) Glacière
Contact: Brigitte Verpraet

For those who hate getting up in the morning and are not too fond of commuting, Paris Langues is ideally situated. The school is in the basement of an international foyer, the FIAP, thus for those students who so desire, accommodation is available in the same building as the classes. There is also a restaurant and café. Even with a longer commute Paris Langues offers much to the budding French speaker. It is cheap, cheerful and communal. There is nothing high-tech about it and this is reflected in the price. Classes are small (maximum 12) and the focus is on communicating and learning oral and written language skills, using up-to date texts, role-play and audio-visual techniques.

Full-time and part-time courses are available, including an au-pair programme. 15 hours per week for two weeks costs 1,650FF, increasing to 2960FF for four weeks and 7,440FF for three months. 21 hours per week plus one cultural activity costs 2,320FF for two weeks, increasing to 3,920FF for four weeks and 9,770FF for three

months. There is also an intensive programme (25 hours plus one activity is 2,920FF for two weeks and 5,620FF for four weeks) and an afternoon programme (ten hours plus one activity costs 1650FF for two weeks and 2960FF for four weeks). The ten-week Au-Pair programme (six hours per week) costs 2600FF. The enrolment fee of 200FF includes study materials. Due to its location Paris-Langues is an ideal place for groups (minimum age 16), and special rates for school-children and adults are available on request. Weekly activities include trips to art museums, learning how to make Tarte Tatin in a French home and visiting the Assemblee Nationale.

Accommodation in the FIAP is available for those who want it. Bed and breakfast costs 180FF per night in a shared room or 270FF single (only on request). Half-board costs 226FF or 330FF respectively. Staying with a French family is also an option: bed and breakfast 163FF and half-board 215FF.

To reach Paris-Langues, take métro line 6 to Glacière. You are on boulevard A. Blanqui. Keeping the métro exit behind you, find rue de la Sante and turn left. Rue Cabanis is the first right and the FIAP is on the right. Paris-Langues is in the basement.

Université de Paris III: Sorbonne Nouvelle

46, rue Saint-Jacques, 75005 Paris
Tel: +33 1 40 46 29 29
Fax: +33 1 40 46 29 30
Level of French: All levels, except Beginners, specialising in Advanced
Nearest Station: (Métro) Cluny la Sorbonne
Contact: Mlle Wagner

A cross between the CCF at the Sorbonne, in terms of school and class structure, and every public university in France, in terms of architecture: ie. you are paying to spend time in a multi-storey car-park disguised as a university. If you are planning to enrol for a semester this is one of the places to consider, since it is cheaper than the Old Sorbonne and the ICF and there are fewer students overall (around 140). Don't imagine that you will find frills for your money, however. Language laboratories are the only high-tech equipment. Otherwise prepare for 15 hours per week of grammar, translation, literature and oral expression. Groups are large (18-20), students are international and teaching is serious. The social programme is as good as you make it: nothing is organised by the University. This is the closest you will get to a public French university without actually enrolling in one. Contact the University at least three months before the start of the semester (October or January) to enrol. Acceptance for a second semester depends on completion of the first Accommodation can be organised through the CROUS once enrolment has been completed.

NORTH-EAST
Centre International d'Étude de Langues
'Le Concorde', 4 quai Kléber, 67000 Strasbourg
Tel: +33 3 88 22 02 13
Fax: +33 3 88 75 73 70
E-mail: cielfrancais@ strasbourg.cci.fr
Website: www.strasbourg.cci.fr
Level of French: All levels
Nearest Station:
(SNCF) Strasbourg
Contact: Christine Bartier

CIEL is affiliated to the Chambre de Commerce de Strasbourg, the Alliance Française and is a Souffle-registered school. It is located in modern buildings in the centre of the city and is a good alternative to the IIEF for those who want a shorter, non-academic course.

The Centre offers courses all year round. New classes start every two weeks. All levels are available. Two-week courses start from 1,950FF for 15 hours of tuition (10 students per group) during the academic year and 2,400FF for 20 hours of tuition (15 students per group) in the summer. An intensive two-week course, with 55 hours of tuition, costs 3,950FF. Options include Commercial French (3,000FF for two weeks), Teaching French as a Foreign Language and French for the Hotel and Tourism industry (2,900FF for two weeks). Prices decrease for longer stays.

You must be at least 18 years old. A deposit of 1,500FF must accompany the registration form and be sent at least two weeks before the course start date. The deposit will be refunded if enrolment is cancelled at least ten days before the start date. Payment can be made by cash, cheque, bank transfer or credit card.

Accommodation is available in families (from 140FF per day half-board to 2,000FF for a month's bed and breakfast), hotels (from 150FF per night), studios or, in the summer, in University residences (from 80FF per night to 1,100FF per month).

CIEL is located in the centre of Strasbourg, easily accessible from the train station.

Centre de Linguistique Appliquée de Besançon

6, rue Gabriel Plançon, 25030
Besançon, Cedex France
Tel: +33 3 81 66 52 00
Fax: +33 3 81 66 52 25
Website: www.univ-fcomte.fr/
cla/cla.html
Established: 1958
Level of French: All levels
Nearest Station: (SNCF)
Besançon
Nearest Airport: Bâle-Mulhouse
Contact: Dependent on course
chosen

CLA, as it is known in its lovely brochures, is in one of those French cities that few tourists and foreigners know about, but which is a classic example of what this country has to offer, in terms of architecture, history and local countryside. Besançon, known as the greenest city in France, is practically an island (circled by the river Doubs) and is the capital of Franche-Comté. The region shares its borders with Switzerland, Alsace and Rhône-Alpes, and the Vosges, Alps, Black Forest and Jura are all within reach, as is the city of Dijon and the Burgundy vineyards. The city is towered over by the Citadel, designed by Louis XIV's architect, Vauban. Famous locals include Louis Pasteur and Victor Hugo.

The CLA (which is part of the University of Besançon) is located in modern buildings beside the river, and near the centre of town. It offers a multitude of courses, which are all neatly laid out, with prices, dates and number of hours, in simple-to-follow brochures, unlike the scrappy documents provided by many language schools. The information provided is extremely comprehensive.

As an applied research centre, with an academically active and involved teaching staff, the CLA is always up-to-date with new pedagogical methods and approaches. Such research forms the basis of much of the teaching methodology and materials used at the Centre. However, teaching remains pragmatic not theoretical, focused on the needs of the students. A month-long intensive course, with 100 hours of tuition (and a maximum of 18 students per group) costs approximately 4,000FF, depending on the time of year. Two-week intensive courses (for non-beginners only) cost approximately 3,000FF, for 60 hours of tuition with around 15 students per group. There are approximately 3500 students in total per year. Other options include a four-week, pre-university French course (80 hours of tuition; 18 students per group; 4,100FF), a year-long two-semester course (October-February; February-June; 5,300FF per semester), DELF and DALF courses (120FF per exam unit) and French Teachers courses' (several options are available throughout the year, from one month to two semesters, from 4,600FF to 12,000FF). Facilities available to students include individual work stations (audio, video and computer equipment), language and computer laboratories and a *médiathèque*. Students have free access to the internet and email (if they have their own account). The CLA is a member of Souffle and ADCUEFE.

Enrolment must be completed at least four weeks before the course start date. Students must be 16 years old. A 50 per cent deposit is payable at the time of enrolment which, in the event of cancellation, may be kept as a credit towards another course or returned (minus a 350FF handling fee). Fees should be paid by international money order or by cheque (in francs).

Accommodation is available with host families (half-board from 105FF to 120FF per day), in university residences (summer only: private rooms approximately 1,000FF per month), in studio apartments (approximately 2,563FF per month) or in shared student flats (summer only: about 900FF per person per month). Hotel and hostel accommodation is also an option: the brochure lists several possibilities in detail.

The Centre recommends that new arrivals take a taxi to the Centre (students staying with families will often be met at the station/airport).

Institut International d'Études Françaises

Université des Sciences Humaines de Strasbourg, 9 place de l'université, Palais, Universitaire, 67084 Strasbourg
Tel: +33 3 88 25 97 56
Fax: +33 3 88 25 08 63
E-mail: ief@ushs.u-strasbg.fr
Website: 130.79.140.19/ default.html
Established: 1919
Level of French: None
Nearest Station: (SNCF) Strasbourg
Contact: Madame Catherine Schwentzel

The cities of Strasbourg and Alsace, whether under snow or sun, eating *Flammenkuchen* or *choucroute*, are both incredible, with a character so distinct from France yet so much part of it. Like the Sorbonne, the IIEF is a private institute attached to a public university. It offers an academic schedule in two semesters as well as summer courses for teachers and students. One semester costs 4,300FF and an academic year costs 7,350FF. There is an additional fee of 889FF for university registration and 1,020FF social security. A student summer course costs 3100FF for four weeks and 1,800FF for two weeks, or 3300FF or 1,900FF for teachers of French. Courses are focused on written French, grammar, phonetics and textual study (through literature and history) and classes are large (from 20 in a grammar class to 70 in a lecture). Applications must be received by mid-September for the October semester and by early December for the January semester. Summer course enrolment must be completed by mid-June. Students for the academic programme must have the equivalent of a *baccalauréat*. The IIEF organises very reasonably priced accommodation for summer students in a private student residence (1300FF for the month) and reservations should be made by the beginning of June (the form is with the IIEF brochure). Those enrolling for an academic semester are left to the mercy of CROUS. The IIEF is an ADCUEFE member and recommended by the Petit Guide.

The IIEF is in the Palais Universitaire, a grand Germanic stone building in the centre of the city, just south of the European Parliament and east of the cathedral.

Université Charles-de-Gaulle Lille III–Département des Étudiants Étrangers

BP 149 – F 59653 Villeneuve

d'Ascq Cedex
Tel: +33 3 20 41 62 96
Fax: +33 3 20 47 23 62
E-mail: dee@univ-lille3.fr
Level of French: None
Nearest Station: (SNCF) Lille
(served by both TGV and
Eurostar)

An hour away from Paris, linked to London by Eurostar and close to Brussels, Cologne and Luxembourg, Lille is one of the most European of cities. Like Strasbourg, its border position gives it an extra edge over many other French towns. A mix of Belgium and France, it has an 18th-century Flemish centre that offers the best in French, Flemish and Belgian traditions, whether cafés or brasseries. Anyone studying here would be in a great position to get a flavour of both France and the rest of the continent, without even leaving Lille.

The Université de Lille III, like many other state universities, offers French language courses in its Département des Étudiants Étrangers (DEE). It runs a two-semester programme plus a summer school. Classes are available in five different levels and levels 3-5 are diploma courses. Students with a *baccalauréat* equivalent can sit the level five diploma after attending two consecutive semesters. The diploma offers options in French Literature, Dutch and Arab, and can, eventually, be considered as the equivalent to the first year of a DEUG. Teaching is based on texts such as 'Nouveau Sans Frontières' (level five), photocopied articles and multimedia tools. In level five students follow options in art and literature in addition to language classes. The department has a classroom devoted to EAO. (*Enseignement Assisté par Ordina-*

teur: Computer-Aided Teaching), aimed at students in the first three levels, a specialist library and a language laboratory. One semester costs 3,300FF and two 6,00FF. It pays to know in advance that you wish to enrol for both since the price drops to 5,500FF. Fees must be paid in full at the time of enrolment and are non-refundable. Enrolment takes place in September for the Autumn semester and in early January for the Spring semester. The department is a member of ADCUEFE and listed by the Petit Guide. The university does not organise accommodation.

The department is on a modern campus in the centre of Lille. The nearest métro stop is Pont de Bois which is on line 1, direction 4 Cantons.

Université de Nancy 1: Cours d'été pour étudiants étrangers

Université de Nancy 2, 23
boulevard Albert 1ér, BP 33-97,
54015 Nancy Cedex
Tel: +33 3 83 96 43 92
Fax: +33 3 83 96 70 19
E-mail: taveneau@clsh.u-
nancy.fr
Established: 1938
Level of French: None
Nearest Station: (SNCF) Nancy
Nearest Airport: Nancy/Metz
Contact: François Taveneaux

Nancy gave birth to art nouveau, and though not as well-known as its Alsatian neighbour Strasbourg, it is a very classic French city. Situated in Champagne, to the east of Paris, the west of Alsace and just north of Burgundy, it is also close to some of the most spectacular regions of France. During the summer the University runs an extremely successful language course and, for those exasperated by the endless permutations available in most schools and colleges, its simple packages will come as a welcome relief. Choosing a language course seems much easier when there are only seven options available. Prices and packages are the same, whether for a beginner or a French teacher: only the level changes. Teaching covers grammar, written French, oral comprehension and options include literature, business French and the media. The four-week programmes also offer students (maximum 18; conversational-intermediate French required) the chance to practice their thespian skills in the theatre workshop. Every year a small group prepares a project to be performed at the Conservatoire de Nancy. The University is an ADCUEFE member.

Package A, including approximately 23 hours of classes per week for four weeks, accommodation, breakfast, two meals a day in the University restaurant from Monday to Saturday, excursions, Sunday visits to Alsace and the Vosges, evening entertainment including a cinema club, picnics and a three-day trip to Paris, costs 7,500FF. Packages B and C, which are shorter versions of the same, cost 6,500FF and 4,900FF for three and two weeks respectively. D, E and F offer the same packages (four weeks 6,900FF, three weeks 6,000FF and two weeks 4,600FF) without the university restaurant meals. Only A and D (the four week programmes) include the Paris trip. It is also possible to pay for just tuition at 950FF per week.

Summer enrolment is limited to 120 students which ensures a friendly atmosphere but means those interested should apply early. Applications (the form is at the back of the University brochure) should be accompanied by a 1,000FF deposit with the balance payable either in advance or at the beginning of the course. In the event of a cancellation deposits will be refunded minus banking charges.

Students will be met from the station the day before the start of classes.

Université de Nancy 2: Service Universitaire des Étudiants Etrangers (SUEE)
Université Nancy 2, 23 boulevard Albert 1er, B.P. 3397, 54015 Nancy Cedex
Tel: +33 3 83 96 70 05
Fax: +33 3 83 96 70 19
Level of French: None
Nearest Station: (SNCF) Nancy
Contact: SUEE

Over 300 students from 50 different countries attend classes at the SUEE in Nancy. It is situated on the Arts campus in the centre of the city, close to the University gym, swimming pool, cafeterias and library. The SUEE offers an academic programme, with two 14-week-long semesters, starting in October or February. It is possible to attend for one semester (3,387FF) or the whole academic year (5,657FF). Classes are taught by academics who are specialists in their fields and up-to-date with recent methodology. Teachers use different materials, rather than a fixed method, depending on students' needs and motivations but the large groups (20 maximum) suggest that the classes are more teacher-led rather than interactive.

Seven different levels are available from beginners to the Diplome Superieur de Langue Francaise (one year course). Students have 15 hours of classes per week plus five extra hours in the

Language Centre and homework. From level five onwards students choose the General French option or the Literature and Culture option. The DELF and DALF enrolment is free for those following the General French option. Successful completion of the DSEF course may be recognised as equivalent to parts of the DEUG in Humanities (contact the SUEE for details of dates and procedures). Each level has an exam at the end of each semester, which must be passed in order to follow a second semester. Facilities include a *médiathèque* with a video, audio and computer equipment, and an advice service. Budding thespians can get involved with the SUEE's theatre workshop. The SUEE is a member of ADCUEFE.

To enrol, students must be at least 17 years old, have finished their secondary education and have proof of their eligibility/acceptance for university. Originals and translations of the following are required: birth certificate; secondary education diplomas; proof of eligibility for university entrance; university grades where applicable. Students should arrive in the middle of September (for the October semester) or the middle of January (for the February semester).

There is no accommodation service but limited places are available in University residences (650FF per month; apply before 1st April for the following year). The SUEE brochure includes a list of addresses and information to help with finding somewhere to live.

The SUEE is about five minutes away from the centre of Nancy and the train station.

Université de Picardie Jules Verne: Service Universitaire des Étudiants Étrangers (SUEE)

Chemin du Thil – campus – 80025 – Amiens Cedex 1
Tel: +33 3 22 82 72 51
Fax: +33 3 22 82 78 59
E-mail: None
Website: www.u-picardie.fr/
Established: 1989
Level of French: None
Nearest Station: (SNCF) Amiens
Nearest Airport: Charles de Gaulle
Contact: Nicole Gauthier

Amiens is about one hour from Paris, close to Lille, Champagne and the Channel coastline. The S.U.E.E. at the University of Picardie is one of the smallest and cheapest of the university semester courses. However, it is not for the beginner since all courses are in French. Two levels are available, the *Certificat Pratique d'Études Françaises* (CPEF which is slightly more advanced than the DELF) or the *Diplôme d'Études Françaises* (DELF which is equivalent to the DALF). Both courses cover grammar, phonetics, oral and written comprehension, literature and civilisation. There are approximately 130 students enrolled in a two-semester programme, and about 20 per class. Each semester lasts 12 weeks, with 15 hours of lessons per week, and costs 1,600FF. An additional 999FF enrolment fee is payable to the university. Minimum qualification is a *baccalauréat* equivalent and there are no beginners courses. Facilities include a language laboratory. The University is an ADCUEFE member.

The SUEE. is on a campus outside Amiens. There a university bus service into the city. No accommodation service is available and students are advised to contact CROUS, 25 rue Saint Leu 80038 Amiens, tel: +33 3 22 71 24 00.

Interested applicants should write and ask for information at least one month before the course start date, although Madame Gauthier recommends that non-EU candidates start the application process three months in advance. Payment is due on arrival.

Université de Reims (Centre International d'Études Françaises)

17, rue du Jard, 51100 Reims
Tel: +33 3 26 47 04 11
Fax: +33 3 26 47 04 50
E-mail: None
Website: None
Established: 1971
Level of French: None
Nearest Station: (SNCF) Reims
Contact: Monsieur Bernard Mathieu/Mlle S. Suanthong-Dargaud

The Centre International d'Études Françaises has two glasses of Champagne on the back of its brochure, reminding prospective students of the region's most famous attributes. It runs a two-semester programme, summer courses and an intensive class in September. During the academic year there are five different levels of classes, each with approximately 15 hours of lessons per week plus an advanced DSEF (*Diplôme supérieur d'études françaises*) option over two semesters, with approximately 20 hours of lessons per week. The DSEF is equivalent to the first year of a DEUG and successful candidates may be admitted directly into the second year. The 14-week semesters are run very much on the Sorbonne model, with emphasis on grammar, written French, phonetics,

civilisation and literature. Each one costs 3,700FF plus 500FF enrolment fee. A programme of events and excursions costs an additional 800FF. Students who are eligible to sit the advanced diploma pay 2,300FF for the second semester.

Summer courses, which last one month, with 15 hours of classes per week every morning from nine to twelve, cost 2,900FF including excursions and social events. In the afternoons students are encouraged to take part in different activities, both academic (translation classes) and amusing (cookery classes and theatre workshops). The intensive September course, which lasts one month with 26 hours of classes per week, costs 2,400FF plus an additional 600FF for those taking part in the programme of excursions and events. Students need a *baccalauréat* equivalent for the DSEF but otherwise there are no required qualifications. Minimum age is 18. The Centre is a member of ADCUEFE.

Accommodation is available in the summer (July to September) in university residences (875FF per month) and the university will organise reservations. Students can eat at the campus restaurants (13,70FF per meal). During the academic year students will be put in contact with residences but must make the reservation themselves.

Students should enrol at least a month in advance (more for non-EU candidates) enclosing a completed application form and a 500FF non-refundable deposit.

NORTH-WEST

Centre d'Études de Langues de St Malo

Centre Christian Morvan, BP 6,
35430 Saint Jouan des Guerets
Tel: +33 2 99 19 15 46
Fax: +33 2 99 81 48 78
Nearest Station: (SNCF) St
Malo/Port of St Malo
Level of French: None
Contact: Sophie Chaillon

49008 Angers Cedex 01
Tel: +33 2 41 88 30 15
Fax: +33 2 41 87 71 67
Established: 1947
Level of French: From
beginners to advanced
Nearest Station: (SNCF) Angers
Contact: Mme Renée Cochin

St Malo is one of the prettiest small towns on the Brittany coast, and probably one of the most pleasant for a short language break. It has all the character and charm of the sea-side but none of the crowds. At the CEL you will have plenty of time to appreciate the miles of local beaches whilst learning how to speak the language.

Students study for four hours every morning and have afternoons free. Intensive (25 hours per week) and semi-intensive (20 hours) sessions are available and all levels are welcome. Most of the students are young European professionals (average age 30 to 35). The Centre looks after everything including accommodation and transport to and from class (the centre is 7km outside of the town). The emphasis is on making students feel welcome. Sophie Chaillon points out that the maximum intake of 250 over the summer is deliberately limited to ensure that no one feels anonymous. Prices range from 3120FF for two weeks (semi-intensive) or 5,500FF including accommodation in a family. Accommodation in hotels, youth hostels and apartments can also be organised on request. There is a reduction in the class rate for those booking several weeks.

Centre International d'Études Françaises: Université Catholique de l'Ouest
3 place André Leroy, BP 808,

Angers and the Val de Loire (in the West of France) are reputed for the purity of the French spoken. You'll still have to learn the difference between *tu* and *vous* but at least there will be no Provencal twang or Alsatian tongue to decipher on top of the usual Gallic gurgles.

The Centre International d'Études Françaises, in the centre of Angers, has been teaching this supposedly neutral French to thousands of international students for over 50 years. Located on a city campus that combines lovely Angevin classic architecture and modern facilities, it offers courses throughout the summer and the academic year. The Centre prides itself on its communicative approach. Teaching covers the basics as well as more esoteric options, from language, grammar and literature to art, musicology and philosophy. Month-long courses cost 3,600FF with 80 hours of tuition (July/August) and 4,200FF for 90 hours (September). A semester course from October to December, with 20 to 22 hours of tuition per week, costs 7200FF, or 7,800FF for the slightly longer option (October to January; February to June). Beginners are accepted onto the summer courses and at the beginning of each semester whereas other students can start a class (whether two weeks long or two months) at any stage. Transfer credits may be available for foreign university students. Teachers' courses, including cultural workshops and language improvement classes, are available in July for three or four weeks, costing from 3,100FF. An intensive pre-university course, with two weeks of tuition, costs 2,000FF. Students receive a certificate at the end of their course and the CIDEF is also an accredited CCIP, Alliance Française, DELF and DALF exam centre. There are 20 students per group. Summer students must be aged 16 or over and semester students need to have completed secondary (post-*baccalauréat*) education. Facilities include a computer room, language laboratories and a library. The Centre organises excursions across the region as well as sporting events, theatre evenings and seminars. It is recommended by the Petit Guide.

An accommodation service promises to provide students with an address before they leave their home countries. Options include bed and breakfast/half-board/full-board in families (from 2,800FF in July and 2,850FF in September) or rooms in university residences with meals taken on campus. During the academic year student rooms cost approximately 1,450FF per month.

Enrolment takes place all year round. Students must send a 1,400FF non-refundable deposit (banker's draft or international money order in French francs) with the application form at least four weeks before the course starts. Semester students must also send proof of their completed secondary education.

Angers is in the heart of château country, about two hours from the sea and 90 minutes from Paris on the TGV.

LANGUAGE SCHOOLS

The CIDEF is in the centre of the city on a campus that is both modern and classic.

Centre International d'Étude des Langues-Brest

BP 35, rue du Gué Fleuri, 29480 Le Relecq-Kerhuon
Tel: +33 2 98 30 57 57
Fax: +33 2 98 28 26 95
E-mail: chateau@ciel.fr
Website: www.ciel.fr
Established: 1987
Level of French: All levels
Nearest Station: (SNCF) Brest
Contact: Dominique Chateau

You couldn't ask for a more beautiful site for a language school. Located in a 19th-century manor in a park looking out over the sea, CIEL Brest is at the North-Western tip of France. The renovated buildings are beautiful and so is the view. Distractions after class include sailing and other water sports. Facilities include a *médiathèque*, video library, multimedia workstations, a cafeteria, and self-service language laboratory.

All levels are catered for. Weekly (20 or 25 hours tuition per week) and trimestriel (20 hours per week for ten weeks) courses are available. Other programmes include Refresher courses for teachers (two three-week sessions in July and August) and CCIP courses (two three-week summer courses with 30 hours of tuition and exams). There are 12 students maximum per group. Beginners classes begin on very specific dates.

CIEL organises individual and group sessions on demand. A programme of excursions is organised by the Centre. CIEL is a member of Souffle and a Vis-à-Vis partner school.

Students must be aged 16 or over. Semi-intensive courses (20 hours per week) cost from 2,700FF tuition only or 4,660FF with accommodation included. Intensive courses (25 hours per week) cost from 3,100FF course only or 5,060FF with accommodation included. There is an additional 220FF fee for materials. A trimester costs 8,650FF tuition only plus 980FF per week for accommodation. CCIP, teachers and pre-university summer sessions all cost 4,900FF for three-four weeks of tuition or 7,840FF including accommodation. A 1,000FF deposit must be sent with the enrolment form and full payment must be received at least a month before the course begins. A full refund will be given up to ten days before the start date. Payment can be made by eurocheque or bank cheque (in francs), credit card or banker's draft.

CIEL organises accommodation in families and students will be welcomed at the railway station/airport by the host family. Other options include youth hostels, university residences and hotels.

Students arriving independently should be aware that the centre of Brest is about 15 minutes away from Le Relecq-Kerhuon.

CIREFE: Centre International Rennais d'Études du Français pour Étrangers

Université Rennes 2-Haute Bretagne,
6 Avenue Gaston Berger, 35043 Rennes Cedex
Tel: +33 2 99 14 13 01
Fax: +33 2 99 14 13 10
E-mail: christine.davette@uhb.fr
Website: www.uhb.fr/cirefe
Established: 1963

**Level of French: All levels
except Beginners
Nearest Station: (SNCF) Rennes
Contact: Marcelle Lieury**

Rennes is a small town with a huge student population (over 70 000). It is probably one of the best places to spend a university year: lively and young as well as beautiful and well-positioned. The historic capital of Brittany, it is two hours from Paris, one hour from St Malo and the Brittany coast, and one hour from La Baule, which is apparently the longest beach in Europe. If all this wasn't enough, CIREFE runs a university course for international students, not a language school, and its programme is one of the most reasonably priced available.

The CIREFE is unusual in that it offers a year long course rather than semesters. Four different levels are available, with 16-18 hours of weekly tuition (including language classes and options). Classes lead to national university diplomas – the *Certificat Pratique de Langue Française*; the *Diplôme d'Etudes Françaises* or the *Diplôme Supérieur de Langue Française*. The total cost is 4,800FF. In September there is also an intensive programme. There are 25 students per group but less than 15 in oral classes. CIREFE is listed in the Petit Guide.

Applicants must have the equivalent of the *baccalauréat* and be over 18 years old. There are no courses for absolute beginners. Enrol as soon as possible. No deposit is payable. Students must pay the full amount of fees after the placement tests.

There is no accommodation service. Students should contact: CROUS, 7 rue

Hoche, BP 115, 35002 Rennes Cedex before 31 August. University rooms through CROUS cost 1200FF monthly. Rooms in the city cost from 1,200FF to 1,500FF per month. The CIREFE is located on the Villejean campus, just outside the city centre.

Centre Linguistique pour Étrangers, Tours

**7-9 place de Châteauneuf,
37000 Tours
Tel: +33 2 47 64 06 19
Fax: +33 2 47 05 84 61
E-mail: cle@lenet.fr
Website: www.cle.fr
Established: 1985
Level of French: All levels
Nearest Station: (SNCF) Tours
Contact: Isabelle and Hervé Aubert**

A classic Loire city, with ashlar buildings and slate roofs, Tours is a perfect place to study French. Like Angers it is renowned for its relatively pure French accent and it is close to Paris and the Loire valley, within easy reach of Châteaux such as Chambord and Chenonceaux. CLÉ (French for key) is a small, friendly language school in an 18th-century building in the centre of the city. It is listed in the Petit Guide.

Classes are run on an intensive basis, with 20 hours of tuition per week and small groups (maximum seven). Sessions are from one to 11 weeks long and you can enrol for any number of sessions. One week costs 2,050FF, 11 costs 17,300FF. DELF exam courses are available. There are specific start dates for beginners. Minimum age 18. Facilities include a library, video library, language laboratory and multi-media computers.

Accommodation is available in families,

costing from 950FF per week for a private room with breakfast. Fully-equipped studios cost from 4,740FF per month and flats from 6,210FF per month (these prices are not cheap... in fact they are more expensive than Paris, so if you're capable of finding this sort of accommodation yourself do so, especially if you're on a budget, or stay with a family).

CLE is located in the centre of Tours, easily accessible from the train station.

Centre Via Langues
13 rue de Vincennes, 35700 Rennes
Tel: +33 2 99 87 53 51
Fax: +33 2 99 36 06 45
Level of French: None
Nearest Station: (SNCF) Rennes
Contact: Monsieur Etechami

The Centre Via Langues is a cheap and flexible school, situated in the University campus at the centre of Rennes. Rather than offer fixed courses, the school sells French classes in 30-hour blocks. All levels, from beginners to more advanced, pay the same price (1860FF or 62FF per hour) and are taught in small groups (from three to eight people). If a student enrols during a period when there is no class already established at his/her level, the Centre will start a class for that student (personal tuition for 62FF per hour!). The student can also decide whether to organise the classes intensively or extensively.

Packages (comprising classes, accommodation, activities and excursions) range from 5,000FF to 6,000FF per person for three weeks (these prices depend on group size, time of year and the excursions). Students take an evaluation test, receive a Certificate of Attendance and can prepare for the DELF and DALF. When enrolling students should specify when they would like to attend and whether they wish to follow one 30-hour block or several in sequence. There are no hidden extras, such as books, since teaching is based on teachers' individual methods (photocopies are provided) with audiovisual support. Help with accommodation is available.

École de Langues Inlingua
31, rue Marechal Joffre, 35000 Rennes
Tel: +33 2 99 67 50 50
Fax: +33 2 99 67 54 90
Level of French: None
Nearest Station: Rennes
Contact: Monsieur Sarrazin

Rennes is one of the most lively and friendly cities in France and it is, according to Monsieur Sarrazin from the Inlingua language school, one of the best places to learn French. Small enough to enable a sense of community (and by extension, a chance to practice one's French) but large enough to offer students a social life, it is also close to Paris (two hours on the TGV) and the Brittany coast.

The school, situated in the city centre near to both the historic and modern quarters, strives to create an atmosphere that reflects its locality's character. Like many such organisations, Inlingua, a Swiss organisation with 300 language schools worldwide, runs courses throughout the summer. However, unlike many, they have a deliberate strategy of teaching students in very small groups (five to six maximum) in order to keep classes as personal as possible. Each two-week block (minimum enrolment two weeks, maximum eight) is divided into one week of grammatical study and one week of oral practice. Each week includes three hours of daily classes (except Wednesday when students have eight hours), an excursion and an evening's entertainment. The weeks are structured in such a way that students can arrive at any moment without fear of missing classes.

One week's tuition (26 x 45 minute units) costs 1,925FF. Accommodation is organised (1,330FF per week half-board) and Monsieur Sarrazin stresses that they only place students with 'gastronomic families': the sort of hosts that will introduce students to the region and its specialities. The school can prepare students for the Inlingua International Certificate, which is especially useful in Europe. Facilities include a language laboratory but no multimedia equipment. Teachers use the Inlingua books which students can buy.

Institut de Touraine
1, rue de la Grandière, 37000 Tours
Tel: +33 2 47 05 76 83
Fax: +33 2 47 20 48 98
E-mail: institut.touraine@wanadoo.fr
Established: 1912
Level of French: All levels
Nearest Station: (SNCF) Tours
Contact: Béatrice Capon

Established in 1912, and registered by Souffle, the Institut Touraine has a pedigree worthy of its grand location. Here, in a 19th-century mansion, redolent of TV costume dramas, students can learn what is reputed to be the purest French in the country. Tours itself is a historic, medieval city on the River Loire, easily accessible from Paris and close to the châteaux.

Courses are available throughout the year for seven different levels. Teaching

Picture courtesty of Institut de Touraine

balances written and oral French, using traditional and modern methods. There are four-week sessions throughout the year as well as trimesters and speciality courses. Two-week summer courses (with 50 hours of tuition) cost from 3,400FF tuition only, to 5,300FF tuition including half-board accommodation with a family (not available for beginners). Month-long courses, with 88 hours of tuition cost 4,400FF during the academic year and 4,600FF in July/August/September. Trimester sessions, with 19-24 hours of tuition per week, run from October to December, January to March and April-June, cost 10 200FF (payable in three instalments). Four–week CCIP courses in French for Business, Tourism and Secretaries, as well as the Institut's own course for French teachers all cost 5,200FF for 88 hours of tuition. The Institut welcomes over 2,500 students per year. Most groups have about 15 students except oral/phonetic classes which tend to have around seven to eight. Excursions and weekly sporting activities are organised. Every student receives a certificate of attendance, and there are also several exam options available including the DELF, DALF and the Institut's own Certificat d'Études Françaises. Credit transfers are possible and the Institut has links with the University of Bristol in UK and University of Georgetown in the US. The school has 35 classrooms, three video rooms, a multimedia studio, a library and *médiathèque*.

Minimum age for two-week courses is 18. No qualifications needed. Enrolment throughout the year. A 2,000FF deposit should be sent with the registration form and the balance is payable a week before the course start date. Payment by bank transfer, cheque in French francs or postal order.

Accommodation is available in families (from 950FF per week room only or 1100FF per week room and half-board), university residences and foyers, (prices and availability vary depending on the time of year: monthly rates from 1,030FF in the summer to 2,950FF with breakfast during the academic year).

The Institut is in the centre of the city, within easy reach of the railway station.

La Maison des Langues
1, place Marechal Juin,
35000 Rennes
Tel: +33 2 99 30 25 15
Fax: +33 2 99 30 34 54
Web: www.oda.fr.aa.maison-deslangues
Level of French required: None
Contact: Monsieur Lefaix
Nearest Station: (SNCF) Rennes

One of the great advantages of learning French in a small town like Rennes is that, unlike big cities and tourist sites (especially the South coast), you are much more likely to use your new-found skills rather than talk to other foreigners. Close to the Loire valley, the coast and Mont St Michel (one hour away) and only two hours from Paris, Rennes offers a busy social life (it is full of students) as well as beautiful scenery. At La Maison des Langues French courses are offered in two formulas: semi-individual groups (maximum five) or medium-sized groups (from 10 to 15 students). Students can choose 15, 20 or 30 lessons a week (in blocks of 45 minutes). Minimum enrolment is two weeks and prices decrease for longer stays. Accommodation can be arranged in families for approximately 700FF (half-board) or 900FF (full board) per week. Teachers choose their own pedagogical support (including computers, videos and television) and at the end of the course each student is issued with a Certificate of Attendance. Facilities include a language laboratory and computers.

SOUTH-EAST

Bordeaux Language Services

1 cours Georges Clemenceau, 33000 Bordeaux, France
Tel: +33 5 56 51 00 76
Fax: +33 5 56 51 76 15
E-mail: bls@imaginet.fr
Website: www.worldwide.edu/ France/bls/index/html
Established: 1992
Level of French: Beginners to Advanced
Nearest Station: (SNCF) Bordeaux-St Jean/Bordeaux
Nearest Airport: Merignac
Contact: Corinne Woodward

Bordeaux Language Services makes the most of its location. Situated in a 19th-century building in the centre of Bordeaux, it offers more than just French language classes. Over six days students can follow an intensive wine-tasting course, in a region that is home to some of the most famous wine houses in the world (such as Château Margaux and Mouton Rothschild). 15 hours of lectures and wine-tastings at the school are complemented by another 20-25 hours taught by professionals in the châteaux. Lunches, excursions to several châteaux, wine-tasting lessons are all included in the 7000FF fee (special prices available for groups). Students pass a test at the end of the session and receive a certificate. Classes are taught in French and translated into English and numbers are limited to 12 participants.

For those who want a more traditional (and somewhat cheaper) experience of the French language BLS runs several general courses. The school is an Établissement libre d'enseignement Supérieur (thus recognised by the Bordeaux education authorities). Teaching provides a balance between conversation, reading, listening and writing using a mixture of library, video and audio material.

General French courses (minimum enrolment two weeks) are available in blocks of 15, 20, 25 hours tuition per week, costing from 2,700FF for two weeks. A three-month course with 20 hours per week costs 13,620FF and there is the possibility of preparing the DELF or DALF. Students can also choose a combined course and board package, living and learning in a teacher's home (from 5,500FF for 15 hours per week). An A level revision course, (during half-terms and British summer holidays) costs 1,550FF for 15 hours of tuition and a cultural programme. Students receive a certificate at the end of the course. Beginners start on the first Monday of every month. Enrolment fee is 320FF.

The school has over 650 students per year. Class size is limited to five and the average student age is 30. Accommodation can be organised in families (bed and breakfast 875FF per week; half-board 1,050FF) or hotel residences (ask for prices).

Enrol at least three weeks before the start of the course enclosing 3,000FF deposit.

The school is located in the centre of Bordeaux near Place Gambetta and within walking distance of the River Garonne. An additional fee is payable for transfers from the airport and

LANGUAGE SCHOOLS

train station (220FF and 160FF respectively).

CAREL: Centre Audiovisuel de Royan pour l'Étude des Langues

48, boulevard Franck Lamy, BP 219C, 17205 Royan Cédex
Tel: +33 5 46 39 50 00
Fax: +33 5 46 05 27 68
E-mail: carel@hermes.univ-poitiers.fr
Website: www. univ-poitiers.fr/carel/
Established: 1966
Level of French: From Beginners to Advanced
Nearest Station: (SNCF) Royan
Contact: Pierrette Cotty

Royan is an architectural gem, combining 19th-century period houses and the Le Corbusier style of the 1950s. It is in fact one of the oldest sea-side resorts in France, and was one of the first to offer 'ocean bathing'. More than 160 houses are listed buildings and the oldest lighthouse in France (dating from the 14th-century) is along the Royanese coast. Positioned south of La Rochelle and north of Bordeaux it is also one of the sunniest places in France, more sheltered than the rest of the Atlantic coast. The area is famous for cognac and oysters, which is probably why Picasso, Zola and Sarah Bernhardt spent time here. Like the town, the Centre Audiovisuel de Royan pour L'Étude des Langues is well-established and well-equipped. It has over 30 years of experience and a Souffle recommendation, is accredited by the University of Poitiers and is one of Vis-à-Vis selected schools.

The CAREL offers intensive language courses for adults, all year round (there are also programmes for teenagers).

Minimum enrolment is two weeks. There are 22 classrooms, a TV studio, five language laboratories and a multimedia resource centre. Students have access to email.

A general French course, with five hours a day of tuition costs 2,450FF for two weeks. Personal tuition, with 30 hours of tuition per week, costs 13,000FF for two weeks. Classes take place all year round and each group has a maximum of 15 students. Courses for teachers of French cost from 3585FF for 30 hours of tuition per week for two weeks to 4130FF for 25 hours of tuition per week for four weeks. These take place, depending on the level, in January, July and August. Students must be aged 18 or over. Application forms must be accompanied by a non-refundable deposit of 750FF (for enrolment of less than 12 weeks) or 1,000FF (for more than 12 weeks). Enrolment must be received at least two weeks before the start of courses. DELF and DALF preparation is available (examination fees are extra).

Accommodation can be organised in families (from 125FF per day half board per night), in studios (from 1,000FF for two weeks) and in flatshares (from 700FF for two weeks).

The CAREL is a big modern purpose-built building in the centre of Royan, about ten minutes away from the railway station and 15 minutes from the sea.

Centre d'Enseignement du Français Langue Étrangère/Département d'enseignement Français Langue Etrangère, Université de Toulouse –

Le Mirail

**5 allée Antonio Machado,
31058 Toulouse Cedex 1
Tel: +33 5 61 50 42 38
Fax: +33 5 61 50 41 35
E-mail: cefle@cict.fr
Website: www.univ-
tlse2.fr/cefle
Established: 1978
Level of French: None
Nearest Station: (SNCF)
Toulouse Matabiau
(Métro) Mirail Université
Contact: Mme Sandrine
Dulot/Christian Depierre**

'See in Paris. Have in Lyon. Play in Bordeaux. Learn in Toulouse' If this Renaissance saying is to be believed, Toulouse has always been considered a centre of learning. However, playing and seeing are not exclusive to Paris and Bordeaux. Known as the 'rose city' because of its warm orange bricks and roofs, Toulouse is renowned as one of the most beautiful cities in France. Warm all year round, it combines friendliness with sophistication. It is near the Pyrenees yet the capital is only a few hours away on the TGV. For food lovers, the city is within easy reach of the vineyards of Languedoc-Roussillon and the Perigord, France's most renowned gastronomic region. The university was established in 1229 and Rabelais (and possibly Montaigne) was a student in the 16th-century. It moved to a modern campus in 1968 (driven out by *soixante-huitard* protestors?) and now welcomes over 23,000 students, with over 600 enroling in the Centre for French as a Foreign Language. The University is an ADCUEFE member.

During the academic year, the CEFLE (soon to be DEFLE) offers seven different levels of general French language classes, from Beginners to Advanced, plus two Written French options. Other courses include Teaching French as a Foreign Language, Linguistic Preparation for Higher Education and workshops in writing and conversation. At present (1998-99) students can only enrol for a whole year (two semesters) but as of 1999 enrolment will be possible for either semester. Prices were unavailable (for 1999) at time of going to press. Students must be 18 or over with a *baccalauréat* equivalent qualification.

Summer courses run in July, August and September. Students choose 15 or 21 hours of lessons per week and prices range from 2,700FF per month for tuition only to 5,500FF for a complete package including tuition, accommodation in a student residence and three meals a day from Monday-Friday. The month-long courses for Teachers' and University preparation cost 4,250FF and 4,800FF for tuition only or 6,250FF and 6,800FF including accommodation and meals. There are approximately 15 students per class and students must be over 17 years old. Students receive a CEFLE diploma on completing the course. No qualifications are required. Accommodation is only organised for the summer courses.

A deposit of 1,000FF should be sent with the application form at least one month before the start of classes. Proof of this payment must be provided at registration on arrival. Enrolment takes place throughout the year.

The CEFLE is 10 minutes outside the city centre on the modern Mirail campus. The nearest métro is Université.

Institut d'Études Françaises de La Rochelle

102, rue de Coureilles – Les Minimes, 17024 La Rochelle Cedex 1- France
Tel: +33 5 46 51 77 50
Fax +33 5 46 51 77 57
E-mail: ief@ief-la-rochelle.fr
Established: 1931
Level of French: None
Nearest Station: (SNCF) La Rochelle
Contact: Le secrétariat of the IEF

The IEF combines a long history with a twentieth-century outlook. It is part of the Université de Poitiers, which was established in 1431 and counts Francis Bacon as an alumnus. Situated in La Rochelle, a historic port on the Atlantic coast, it has been running summer language courses for over 60 years. Teaching is based on a combination of written and audio-visual materials and classes take place on a modern campus in premises shared with the ESC business school. After class students will find plenty to amuse themselves... the beach is only 200 metres away.

Most of the Institut's courses run in July and August. General French language classes are available in four-week semi-intensive or two-week intensive programmes (5,360FF and 4,100FF respectively). A four-week DELF/DALF preparation course costs 5,360FF (20 hours of lessons per week). Students receive proof of attendance and an Institut diploma. There are two Chambre de Commerce de Paris options. The 'Certificat Pratique' course lasts four weeks (20 hours per week; 5,415FF plus 400FF examination fee). The *Diplôme Supérieur*, which is for advanced students only, is very intensive with 30 hours of classes per week for a month (6,300FF plus 500FF examination fee). The IEF also offers two-week literature and civilisation options for advanced students (4,100FF or 2,315FF per week for 30 hours of lessons). Two-week and month-long teachers' programmes cost 2,715FF and 5,415FF respectively with 20 hours of lessons per week. Intermediate and advanced students can also enrol for a whole semester, either in January or October, and take optional classes at the Business School (12,600FF). There are approximately 12 students per group in beginners courses and around 15 in others.

Accommodation is available in University residences (1,270FF for two weeks, 2,540FF for a month) or families (from 1,020FF for one week to 4,455FF for a month, depending on the number of meals provided by the host). Students will be met at the station/La Rochelle airport by their hosts where applicable.

Only students over 18 can enrol. For summer courses applications (and a preliminary deposit of 1,500FF: see brochure) must be received by May whereas enrolment for a semester ends in the month preceding the start date.

La Rochelle has its own airport and is situated south of Nantes, to the west of Poitiers and north of Bordeaux.

Université Michel de Montaigne-Bordeaux III

Domaine Universitaire, 33405 Talence CEDEX
Tel: +33 5 56 84 50 44
Fax: +33 5 56 84 51 05
Email: defle@montaigne.u-bordeaux.fr
Level of French: None
Contact: Mlle Durand

Nearest Station: (SNCF)
Bordeaux

Language students at the Universite de Bordeaux III have more opportunities than most to practise their new-found linguistic abilities. On Radio Campus, the student radio station, they have their own live broadcast, Frequence Galaxy, which they produce and present themselves. French learners from all over the world talk to the campus population about their own countries and their experiences in France. Such focus on aural and oral skills continues in the classroom.

Nine levels from beginners to *perfectionnement* are offered and the first six are taught exclusively by audiovisual techniques. In levels seven to nine classes in translation, phonetics, literature, civilisation and written expression are introduced. There are two sessions per year, from October to January, February to June, with approximately 400 students each and students can enroll for one or both. Classes lead to the University's own diplomas and, although DELF and DALF preparation is available, an extra payment is necessary. Fees for one semester are 2,630FF and 4,800FF for both (+85,650FF for a student card). The university is recommended by the Petit Guide and is a member of ADCUEFE.

Accommodation is the student's responsibility except during the intensive summer sessions. The modern campus is situated about 20 minutes away from the centre of the city.

SOUTH-WEST

Actilangue-Nice
2, rue Alexis Mossa, 06000

Nice
Tel: +33 4 93 96 33 84
Fax: +33 4 93 44 37 16
E-mail: actilang@imaginet.fr
Established: 1977
Level of French: All except
Beginners.
Nearest Station: (SNCF) Nice
Nearest Airport: Nice
Contact: Paul Ceccaldi

If you think that Nice is a wonderful place to stay and study, then you have a lot in common with the thousands of others who head to the Cote d'Azur for the same reasons. Nice is probably one of the most cosmopolitan of French cities but, like Paris, it suffers as a result from the FLE syndrome: you are more likely to meet foreigners than the French. However, this is the only drawback which is easily compensated for by the incredible year-round weather, the proximity of the sea and Provence and Nice's lively atmosphere (patronised by the likes of Elton John).

Actilangue is a small language school in the centre of town near the beach. With 100 students a year, taught in small groups of eight, teaching emphasises spoken and conversational French and students are grouped according to age and interests. The materials used are developed in-house and are periodically reviewed. The school looks after accommodation, whether in hotels, university residences (limited number of places), families (single or double rooms, with breakfast, half or full board) or flats; organises trips to Monaco, Grasse, Cannes, St Tropez and sporting activities including biking, hiking and diving.

There are three basic programmes which run throughout the year, except Easter, July and August: general (20 hours of weekly lessons: 2,270FF for two weeks); semi-intensive (25 hours; 3,130FF for two weeks) and intensive (30 hours, 3,750FF for two weeks). A 12-week course, during which suitable candidates can prepare the DELF, costs 8,810FF, 12,180FF and 14,600FF for 20, 25 and 30 hours respectively. Easter and Summer courses cost from 3,150FF (20 hours per week for two weeks) to 10,420FF (30 hours per week for four weeks). A special combination package is available at Easter and during the summer. 28 hours of lessons plus two weeks of activities and excursions costs 6,590FF including transport, insurance, equipment and the guides.

Actilangue is also the official CCIP examination centre in Nice. Preparation for the *Certificat Pratique de Français Commercial et Économique*'lasts eight weeks, with 24 lessons per week, and costs 9830FF plus 500FF registration fee. Exams take place in April, June, September and December. Private one-to-one courses start every Monday. Prices range from 6,180FF per week for 20 lessons (45 minutes each) to 15,450FF per week for 50 lessons. Accommodation is available with host families and in student residences. Bed and breakfast with a family costs 1,820FF for two weeks or 2,210FF for half-board. Each extra week costs 980FF (bed and breakfast) or 1,190FF (half-board). Full-board is also available for an extra 175FF per week. A room in a student residence costs 800FF per week during the academic year and 1,100FF in the summer. Hotel rooms and flats can also be organised. The School will organise all accommodation requirements.

Applications should be sent as early as possible enclosing a 1,000FF deposit.

Full settlement of course fees and lodging must be paid at least two weeks before the course begins. The deposit will not be refunded in the event of cancellation.

The centre of Nice is easily accessible from the train station and there is a shuttle service from the airport. Actilangue can organise a transfer to and from either for 170FF.

Alpha.B Institut Linguistique

7, boulevard Prince de Galles. 06000 Nice
Tel: +33 4 93 53 11 10
Fax: +33 4 93 53 11 20
E-mail: alpha.b@WEBSTORE.fr
Website: www.alpha_b.fr
Established: 1993
Level of French: From Beginners to Advanced
Nearest Station: (SNCF) Nice
Nearest Airport: Nice
Contact: Mlle Anja Denysiuk

Situated in a 19th-century house with a garden, between the Musée Matisse and Musée Chagall and ten minutes from the beach, Alpha.B is well-placed for the discovery of all Nice has to offer, culturally and socially. A medium-size language school, with approximately 550 students per year, it runs French classes at all levels, using a direct and conversational style.

There are four different formulas available. 'Français Continu' is a general French language course and the cheapest option. 20 language lessons per week cost from 2,250FF for two weeks to 3,900FF for four (975FF extra per week from week four onwards). Français Intensif combines language study with learning about French culture. The 20 hours of language classes per week are complemented by 10 hours of practical group discussions and debates on various subjects, including literature, history and French life (from 3,050FF for two weeks to 5,700FF for four weeks; 1,425 FF per additional week). The Français Combiné option is for those who wish to back up learning in a group with more focused, individual classes. 26 hours of lessons (20 in groups in the morning and six private in the afternoon) cost from 4200FF for two weeks to 7900FF for four weeks. A 12-week DELF course costs 17 000FF; sessions begin in March, June and September. Classes are small (maximum ten students per group), students are grouped in five different levels and new courses start every two weeks. Custom-made classes are available on demand. Prices include enrolment fee, course book and photocopies, placement test and certificate. The school organises a series of activities and excursions, including cinema evenings, bowling, discos and guided museum visits (free apart from museum entrance and day trips). Students must be aged 16 or over.

Accommodation is available in flat shares (90FF per night), host families (165FF half-board per night), hotels (two-star from 280FF per night) and in fully-equipped studios (from 1500FF per week).

Apply using the application form in the school's brochure. Full payment is due before the course begins or, at the very latest, at the start of the course.

The school is located in the Cimiez area of Nice, near the Université des Sciences, in the centre of the city.

Campus International
BP 133 83957 La Garde Cedex

Tel: +33 4 94 21 12 82
Fax: +33 4 94 14 30 52
Established: 1977
Level of French: Beginners-Advanced
Nearest Station: (SNCF) Toulon
Nearest Airport: Toulon/Hyeres
Contact: Nathalie Perez

Situated between Toulon and Hyères, in 75 acres of grounds, Campus International is one of four SOUFFLE recognised schools on the Côte-d'Azur. For those who want to enjoy the advantages of the area, be it the weather, the scenery or the food, but who don't want to be located in a town or city, this is the perfect option.

Campus offers comprehensive courses all year round. A typical 15-hour week will include four hours of language classes, two hours of conversation, two hours of literature, three hours of culture and civilisation and four hours of regional studies. In the summer an intensive course (25 hours per week: beginners to advanced) costs 1450FF per week and a semi-intensive course (15 hours per week) costs 1100FF. In the winter a semi-intensive week (15 hours) costs 800FF or 750FF for bookings over nine weeks. Teaching French as a foreign language courses are available for both qualified teachers and those planning a career. Sessions run in July and August, for two to four weeks. One week costs 1450FF for 23 hours of tuition. Beginners classes only run in the summer months. Students can enrol in singing, silk painting, photography and cookery workshops, for a 250FF supplement, and there is a weekly programme of excursions and sporting events.

Alliance Française, CCIP and DELF

exams can all be prepared at Campus (an additional exam fee is payable). Students receive a course certificate at the end of the session. Minimum booking two weeks. Facilities include audiovisual rooms, a language laboratory; computer rooms and a library. There are 12 students per group, approximately 750 per year and students must be at least 16 years old.

In the summer accommodation is available in the campus residence. Single and double studios (equipped with a kitchenette, bathroom, direct line telephone, linen and towels) cost from 2,600FF for a double (half-board for two weeks), and 3,300FF for a single (half-board two weeks). The residence has a bar-restaurant with cybercafé, tv and pool tables, information office and travel agency. During the rest of the year Campus can organise accommodation with families, for 120FF per day (half-board during the week, full board at weekends) or 2,500FF per month.

Accommodation must be fully paid at least 30 days before the start of stay. Course fees must be paid at the time of registration by cheque or bank transfer. There is a 1,100FF cancellation fee.

Students will be met at Toulon station or Toulon/Hyères airport by school representatives (if staying on campus) or the host family.

Cavilam

BP 2678, 14, rue du Marechal Foch, 03206 Vichy-Cedex, France
Tel: +33 4 70 58 82 58/+33 4 70 30 81 30
Fax: +33 4 70 58 82 59/+33 4 70 30 81 31
E-mail: 106112.1000@ compuserve.com
Website: www.isp-riviera.com/ cavilam
Established: 1964
Level of French: Beginners to Advanced
Nearest Station: (SNCF) Vichy/Lyon-Satolas
Nearest Airport: Clermont-Ferrand
Contact: Anne Laudereau/Marie Fradin

Vichy is the Bath of France, a spa town that has been frequented by some of the most notable figures in French history. In the 18th-century, the court reconstituted itself here whereas in more recent years Pétain set up his wartime government in this small and beautiful city. Its historic pedigree and attraction is mirrored at Cavilam, a large language school that is both Souffle registered and affiliated to the University of Clermont-Ferrand. With five well-equipped buildings all over the city, it teaches French to over 2,500 students per year.

Courses are available all year round and start every Monday; except for beginners, who can only start on the first Monday of every month. The basic course unit throughout the year is 22 hours a week of teaching, including six hours in themed language workshops, for 1,200FF. Other courses include CCIP exam preparation (four weeks: 4,350FF), DELF and DALF options, intensive university preparation (which assumes a good level of French), and learning French with radio. Classes take place in the morning and there are four levels: beginners; elementary; intermediate; advanced. Courses for French teachers take place in July and August and sessions last from one to eight weeks. Participants have 28 hours of classes to choose from and can select a programme in terms of their own objectives and priorities. It is also possible to follow a year-long course (the *Diplôme d'université pour enseignants étrangers de français*) in teaching French as a foreign language. Non-exam students receive a certificate of attendance and level of ability. Classes are limited to 15 participants maximum and students must be at least 16 years old.

Each building has a range of audio-visual materials and students have access to four language laboratories, a self-service multi-media resource centre including a reading room and computer room. Cavilam provides new arrivals with a booklet listing information about Vichy, including where to eat, how to get around and where to get discounts with the school's student card.

Accommodation is available in families (from 110FF per night bed and breakfast or 140FF half-board), university residences (80FF per night), studio flats (110FF per day single or 150FF for a couple) and hotels (from 100FF per day).

Applicants must do a language test (enclosed with the brochure) and return this with full payment (in francs) before the course start date.

Students should check which of the five buildings to go to on arrival.

Centre de Cours Internationaux Avignon/Universite d'Avignon

1, avenue de Saint Jean, 84000 Avignon
Tel: +33 4 90 86 61 35
Fax: +33 4 90 85 08 08
Level of French: None
Contact: Caroline Casseville

Nearest Station: (SNCF) Avignon

Although part of a much bigger structure, the University of Avignon, the CCIA is a small, friendly centre, with around 50 students and four teachers sharing a family atmosphere. It offers three different options for learning French: a single semester with 200 hours tuition; two consecutive semesters with 400 hours tuition or short intensive sessions of two or three weeks. There are four levels and the upper two, Intermediate and Advanced, prepare students for the DELF. The classes, especially Beginners and Elementary, emphasise practical communication, stressing oral and phonetic skills more than translation or written work. Students can also follow courses at the University. There is a maximum of 15 students per group. A semester costs 3500FF, the year costs 5,000FF and short two week courses vary from 1,00FF to 2,00FF. The CCIA also runs a week-long course for French teachers in July for 2,000FF. Accommodation in University residences is organised by the Centre.

Centre d'Études Linguistiques d'Avignon

16, rue Saint-Catherine, Avignon, 84000 France
Tel: +33 4 90 86 04 33
Fax: +33 4 90 85 92 01
Web: www.avignon-et-provence.com/cela
Contact: Mme Marie-France Greene
Nearest Station: (SNCF) Avignon

The CELA offers enough to tempt the most reluctant of language-learners. Situated in an extraordinary 19th-

> If there is one city in the world where one can enjoy the gentle way of life in an agreeable and friendly society, it must be Chambery!
>
> JJROUSSEAU, Les Confessions, Livre V

century stone house, surrounded by gardens and next to the Pope's Palace in Avignon, it is an extremely lively, friendly small school, working with classes of around 12 students and a maximum of 110 at any one time.

There are classic French language courses, open to everyone. One week, with 20 hours of tuition in medium-sized groups (12 maximum), costs 1,500FF. (This price increases to 1800FF in July during the Festival d'Avignon and decreases to 1050FF in November and December).

The centre also arranges specialised, closed courses, for groups, individuals or companies, combining French with a particular subject. Almost any combination is possible, for any group. Journalists, medics, bankers, musicians, scientists can all be catered for and the focus of the stage will be on their particular professional interests. There are, of course, tourist options such as Christmas in Provence (discovering everything, for example, about the Provencal tradition of 13 desserts whilst learning the perfect tense), Provencal Cuisine, Horse Riding and Canoeing. Finally, there is a special course for Teachers of French as a Foreign Language. Price for 20 hours of classes per week is 1800FF, reduced to

1260FF in November and December and increased to 2160FF in July. Those booking for more than five weeks receive a discount. The CELA is recommended by the PETIT GUIDE.

Once out of the classroom, there are lots of weekly activities, excursions, and social events, including a Friday lunchtime aperitif when the whole school congregates to say goodbye to departing students. Accommodation is available in families (85FF bed and breakfast; 130FF half-board; 160FF full-board), hotels (from 160FF per night) as well as studios and campsites. There is an accommodation arrangement fee (250FF). Enrolment takes place all year round... the school never closes!

Centre International Antibes Institut Prevert

28, avenue du Château, 06600 Antibes
Tel: +33 4 93 74 47 76
Fax: +33 4 93 74 57 11
E-mail: cia@imcn.com
Established: 1985
Level of French required: None
Nearest Station: (SNCF) Antibes
Contact: Iona Nechiti

Antibes Juan-les-Pins (two different parts of the same town) sit on either side of the Cap d'Antibes, offering the best of the Côte d'Azur's character, both Provence and the Riviera. Juan-les-Pins is a classic Southern resort, full of nightlife and beautiful people whereas Antibes moves at a more relaxed pace, an old port that was once home to Picasso. The Centre International Antibes Institut Prevert language school makes the most of such surroundings. Situated close to Antibes in an old stone house, it offers French classes at all levels, both indoors and outdoors! And it is not just a pretty face: the courses are all Souffle guaranteed.

The Centre offers packages, combining accommodation and language classes, or just lessons. Courses with individual accommodation range from 2,500FF per week to 5800FF (depending on the time of year and lodging chosen), including breakfast, airport/train transfer and 20 hours of lessons. Sharing a room reduces the price range to 2,100FF to 3740FF. Lessons-only cost from 1,340FF for 20 hours per week to 3,055FF for the Managers course (30 hours per week in groups of four). The Centre runs special preparation packages, for the DELF, Alliance Française diplomas and Chambre de Commerce de Paris exams. Twelve-week DELF or Alliance Française programmes, with single room accommodation and 30 lessons per week, are 37,980FF, whereas an eight-week Chambre de Commerce course with accommodation and 30 hours of teaching costs 25,320FF. There are approximately ten students per group. All levels are available throughout the year, although there are more specific start dates for beginners and exam courses.

The school has a pick-up service from Nice airport (which they describe as 'more expensive than the bus but much cheaper than a taxi) and buses run from Nice to Antibes.

Centre International d'Études Françaises– Université Lumière Lyon 2
16, quai Claude Bernard, 69365 Lyon cedex 07
Tel: +33 4 78 69 71 35
Fax: +33 4 78 69 71 36

E-mail: Aliette.Jeannez@ univ-lyon2.fr
Website: signserver.univ-lyon2/cief/cief.html
Established: 1947
Level of French: All levels
Nearest Station: (SNCF) Lyon-Perrache or Part-Dieu
Contact: Aliette Jeannez

Sited by the Romans at the conjunction of the Rhône and Saône, Lyon is France's second largest city with the second largest student population. It is the capital of the Rhone-Alpes region, two hours south of Paris on the TGV, two hours north of the Mediterranean and two hours west of Geneva, thus within reach of sea, ski and sight-seeing.

The University centre, which is a member of ADCUEFE, offers a semester programme during the academic year, a summer course and a pre-university course. Classes combine units on language, literature and civilisation and are valid in the European Credits Transfers System. Two semesters and three levels are available (12 hours tuition for 14 weeks, 16 hours for advanced students, 3,700FF each). Each level leads to a national university diploma – the *Certificat Pratique de Langue Française*; the *Diplôme d'Études Françaises* or the *Diplôme Supérieur de Langue Française* – and for interested students to the DELF and DALF. There are 18 students per group. A summer school runs in July, for Beginners and Intermediate-Advanced, and there is also a pre-university course in September. Both run for 18 hours per week for four weeks, costing 2,700FF for students and 4,050FF for teachers. During the year various evening classes are available including a CCIP Business French course preparation (two semesters, four hours per week, 1,500FF per semester). The university organises a cultural programme and has established a service called 'Alter Ego', which aims to increase contact between French and English students.

Applications are only accepted from students aged over 18 who have proof of completion of secondary education. Students are advised to enrol as early as possible (starting from 1st April for the autumn semester and 1st September for the Spring semester). A 500FF deposit (refundable in the event of cancellation, unless a student cancels due to a visa refusal) should be sent with the registration form and full payment is expected in the week preceding the course start date. Pay by cheque or postal order in French Francs. No eurocheques.

The university only organises accommodation in the summer in university residences. A single room for a month costs 1,200FF including breakfast.

The Centre is 10 minutes away from the mainline train stations.

Centre Méditerranean d'Études Françaises

Chemin des Oliviers, BP 38, 06320 Cap d'Ail
Tel: +33 4 93 78 21 59
Fax: +33 4 93 41 83 96
E-mail: centremed@ monte-carlo.mc
Website: www.monte-carlo.mc/centremed
Established: 1952
Level of French: All levels
Nearest Station: (SNCF) Monaco

The Centre Méditerranean has some of the most stunning views of any language school. Situated on a hillside terrace, in a park full of olive trees and pines facing the Mediterranean, some of its classes take place in an open-air Greek amphitheatre, designed by the artist Jean Cocteau. 2 km from Monaco and 15km from Nice, the Centre combines all the advantages of a Côte d'Azur school with a village atmosphere.

All levels of French are catered for. Courses last from two weeks to three months. Beginners courses, with 28 hours of tuition, start once a month and the objective is to enable students to acquire a basic knowledge of French and to become accustomed to French civilisation. Non-beginners and advanced students have 20 hours of study covering written and oral expression, grammar, and work on documents in all formats, written, visual and audiovisual. Refresher courses for teachers are available in the summer. There are about 15 students per group. At the end of each course participants receive a certificate indicating level and ability. Preparation for the Alliance Française exams, DELF, DALF and *Certificat Pratique de langue Française 1er degré* is available. During the academic year, there is a commercial French option available (595FF for three hours personal tuition). Facilities include a computer room and library. A social programme is organised during each session. In 1998, a new summer junior programme was launched: the Monte Carlo Sports Academy. A two-week course combining 15 hours of French and a sports programme in handball, tennis or football costs 7,400FF. The Centre has been recognised by French Ministry of Education since its opening and is a Vis-à-Vis school partner.

You must be over 18 to enrol (except of

course for the junior programme!). One week's tuition, at any level, costs 1480FF per week plus 40FF annual subscription to the centre. After five weeks there is a 10 per cent discount on tuition and accommodation fees. Application forms (in the brochure) should be returned with 25 per cent deposit of the total fees paid by cheque (no credit cards). The balance is payable on arrival. Deposits (minus 400FF administration fees) will be returned up to two weeks before the course start date. Students should arrive on the Sunday before the Monday class begins.

Accommodation is available at the Centre in twin-bedded rooms. A week's full-board costs 1,645FF per week and half-board costs 1,435FF. The supplement for single occupancy is 210FF per week (not available in July or August). There is a regular bus service from Nice airport towards Nice and Cap d'Ail. Menton is the closest train station.

Collège International de Cannes

**1, avenue du Dr Pascal,
06400 Cannes
Tel: +33 4 93 47 39 29
Fax: +33 4 93 47 51 97
E-mail: cic@imaginet.fr
Website: www.daftari.com/cic
Established: 1931
Level of French: All levels
Nearest Station: (SNCF) Cannes
Nearest Airport: Nice-Côte
d'Azur
Contact: Andréas Schweitzer**

The word 'campus' in France often refers to a concrete building a long way from the centre of a city. This is not the case with College International's campus, which is right in the middle of town and which would only be closer to the beach if it were actually on it. Claiming to be the only self-contained campus (in its category) exclusively devoted to teaching French as a foreign language, the College was founded by Paul Valéry in 1931, and is recognised by the Academy of Nice. It offers everything a prospective language student could hope for: well-organised, comprehensive courses that lead to qualifications without paying more, on-site accommodation, a team of organisers dealing with practical, academic and social information, a language exchange club and a network of shops that not only give student discounts but also actively welcome foreigners practising their French.

The school is open all year. Academic sessions run from September to June and summer schools in July and August. The core course is a 15-hour per week unit in groups of 10 to 12 students and this can be supplemented by several options, from history of art to business French. Students can customise their courses according to their own goals and objectives. Preparation for DELF, DALF and Alliance Française exams can be incorporated into the classes without additional fees. The facilities are impressive and self-contained: language laboratories; auditorium; library; bar with terrace; gym. The social programme is organised in terms of five different sections, the contents of which differ in terms of the time of year: sport; excursions; week-end trips; museum visits; soirees. The Collège is listed by the Petit Guide.

Most sessions are four weeks long, though it is possible to enrol for two weeks. A four-week summer course costs 4,000FF for 15 hours of weekly tuition. Complementary language courses (an extra six hours per week) cost 620FF per session. An academic year course costs 3,500FF per four-week session for 15 hours of tuition. A 1,500FF non-refundable deposit must be returned with the application form. Payment can be made by bank transfer, French franc cheque or eurocheque or traveller's cheque. Students must be aged 16 or over.

Over 85 per cent of students live on campus. Half-board costs from 8,750FF per session and full-board costs from 9,800FF. The prices decrease for those staying over a month.

Rooms in families and studios are also available and are much cheaper. Bed and breakfast with a family costs from 3,550FF and rented studios cost from 5,000FF per session. Rooms are cleaned and linen is provided.

Cannes is easily accessible by train and by shuttle bus from Nice-International airport.

IFALPES: Institut Français de Chambery
371, rue de la République, 73000 Chambery
Tel: +33 4 79 85 83 16
Fax: +33 4 79 85 13 56
Email: ifalp73@instituts-ifalpes.icor.fr
Web: www.ifalp.icor.fr
Level of French: None
Contact: Clare Donnelly

A picturesque and very French town, surrounded by lakes and mountains, Chambery in itself would be motivation enough to study at the IFALPES, but the institute's teaching, facilities and social programme are as tempting as its location. The most apt word to describe what it provides is 'choice'. It offers three-month sessions starting in January, February, April, September and October, an academic two-semester programme and month-long sessions in the summer.

Teaching emphasises that the students must speak for themselves and in addition to the basic units of grammar, writing and oral classes, the students do group-work, hold debates and presentations and use audio-visual equipment. Everyone is entered for the Institut's exam (which is a diploma from the Catholic University of Lyon) although students pay extra if they wish to.

In addition to the four hours of classes per day, the Institut has an incredibly comprehensive and cheap social programme. Trips are planned to nearby ski resorts, including Meribel, to Lyon and Beaujolais, to the Chartreuse distillery, to the Cannes film festival and to the Venice carnival. Free facilities include conversation classes, email and CD-Rom loan. Trimester prices range from 4500FF (two for 8,750FF), university semester prices from 4,950FF (two for 9,400FF) and summer months from 2,500FF. All sorts of accommodation are organised by the school whether in families, apartments, shared studios or university residences (prices from 1600FF per month for self-catering flats, not including bills, to 3,000FF in a family with meals included). IFALPES undertakes to find accommodation for all enrolled students. If all of this wasn't already enough, points out Clare Donnelly, the Institut is relocating to a castle.

ISEFE: Institut Savoisien d'Études Françaises pour Étrangers

Université de Savoie, Domaine universitaire de Jacob Belle-combette, Bat No 10, B.P. 1104, 73011 Chambery Cedex France
Tel: +33 4 79 75 84 14
Fax: +33 4 79 75 84 16
Email: isefe@univ-savoie.fr/isefe/
Web: www.univ-savoie.fr/isefe/
Established: 1974
Level of French: None
Nearest Station:
(SNCF) Chambery
Contact: Mme Monique Clapier
(+33 4 79 75 84 14)

Many University language institutes are associated to ADCUEFE. Many smaller schools are members of Souffle. L'isefe belongs to both which suggests that it has extremely high standards of language teaching. It is also situated in one of the most beautiful regions of France, ten minutes from the centre of Chambery, surrounded by the Alps and close to the Lac d'Annecy. It is in fact a skier's paradise, close to the biggest skiable area in the world. With slopes only 30 minutes drive away, students can practise their slalom and their subjunctive.

The Institut offers three types of language courses. In the summer there are intensive sessions in July and August. Each one lasts three weeks with 20 hours of classes per week from 9am to 1pm Monday to Friday. Many of the units cover aspects of the DELF and DALF. There are several optional afternoon workshops on different themes, including phonetics, conversation, debates and videos. Classes are medium-sized (average 15 per group) which facilitates teaching that focuses on oral practice whilst integrating written French and grammar. In August there is an additional session for French language teachers, aimed at both those already working in a school and those interested in the profession. During the academic year the Institut runs two 15-week semesters. Students can take 15 or 20 hours of classes per week and preparation for the DELF or DALF is included. It is also possible to spend the semesters preparing the Parisian Chamber of Commerce (CCIP) exams. The school will also organise group programmes, combining language lessons and skiing.

The summer sessions cost 3,300FF for one, or 6,300FF for both, and the August teacher's course costs 3,500FF. The 15-hour per week semester costs 7,200FF and the 20-hour costs 9500FF and it is also possible to enrol for both (13,900FF or 18,500FF respectively). Preparation of the CCIP exams (five hours per week over 15 weeks) costs 2,800FF. Sessions are open to anyone over 18. Application forms must be accompanied by a deposit made out in French francs.

Accommodation can be organised in families, university residences, student flats and rented studios. Prices range from 1,000FF for three weeks in a university residence over the summer, 1,600FF per month for a room with a family during the academic year, to 2,500FF per month for a one-person studio. There are excursions organised on Wednesday and Saturday afternoons.

The Institut is situated on the Université de Savoie campus, and this apparently facilitates exchange between French and international students. That's the theory but you are probably more likely to see them disappearing off for the weekend than taking you with them.

Chambery is three hours from Paris by TGV, and Geneva and Lyon Satolas airports are approximately 80km away. The small Voglans-Bourget du Lac airport is 8km away but may not be accessible from international routes.

Novalangue
43, rue de l'Université 34000 Montpellier
Tel: +33 4 67 60 92 09
Fax: +33 4 67 60 92 09
E-mail:
novalangue@hotmail.com
Established: 1997
Level of French: Beginners to Advanced
Nearest Station: (SNCF) Montpellier
Nearest Airport: Fregorjue
Contact: Florence Gaudry

If you want to combine French lessons with cooking classes, close to two of the most interesting foodie regions of France, Gascony and Provence, then Novalangue's Gastronomic French course would be a perfect choice. Situated in a traditional old building, five minutes from the centre of Montpellier, Novalangue is a young language school (started in June 1997) which offers both general French classes and special options. Groups and intake are kept small in order to retain a family atmosphere and teaching focuses on communicative learning within a relaxed and friendly environment. The city of Montpellier itself is one of the loveliest places to visit in the South of France. It is close to the Mediterranean (15 minutes by bus) yet small enough to be friendlier than most of the big coastal cities.

General French courses are available from beginners to advanced level. Beginners classes, with 15 hours of tuition per week, cost from 900FF (one week) to 3,000FF (four weeks). Intermediate and Advanced classes, with 20 hours of tuition per week, cost from 1,200FF (one week) to 4,000FF (four weeks). It is also possible to book classes for a semester, starting in March or September (13 weeks; 15 hours of tuition per week; 6,800FF). Students receive a certificate at the end of the course. Classes are available all year round, except at Christmas.

The specialised French courses are aimed at students who have already followed French language classes and wish to improve their skills for professional reasons. The Business French course covers both linguistic and topical subjects, giving students a grounding in the language and culture of the French economy. A 25-hour week of classes costs 1,700FF increasing to 5,800FF for four weeks. The Gastronomic French course includes 15 or 20 hours of language teaching plus two cookery afternoons. A one-week course costs 1,400FF (15 hours) or 1,700FF (20 hours), increasing to 5,000FF or 6,000FF (four weeks). There are also courses in French for Secretaries or for Tourism (one week, 25 hours tuition, 1,700FF), Translation (one week, 20 hours, 1,400FF) and French for French Teachers (one week, 20 hours, 1,400FF). All of these courses follow a fixed schedule. A DELF and DALF programme is also available.

Accommodation can be organised in families (from 140FF per night half-board), independent studios (prices on demand), student residences (2,600FF per month: only in the summer; very limited availability so apply well in advance) and hotel residences (from 1,500FF per week).

To enrol, return the school's application form with a 50 per cent deposit. The school is open all year round except Christmas. It is 15 minutes from the railway station on foot.

Université Jean Monnet Saint Étienne: Centre International de Langue et Civilisation (CILEC)

30, rue Ferdinand Gambon, 42100 Saint-Étienne
Tel: +33 4 77 46 32 00
Fax: +33 4 77 46 32 09
E-mail: chalabi@univ-st-etienne.fr
Established: 1976
Level of French: None
Nearest Station: (SNCF) Saint Étienne Châteaucreux
Contact: H. Chalabi

A member of both Souffle and ADCUEFE, the Centre International de Langue et Civilisation has an impeccable guarantee and it is located in one of the most beautiful parts of France. Students in St Étienne have the best of every world, the advantages of living in a small city plus easy access to the Auvergne, the Alps, and Lyon, the second biggest city in the country.

The Centre runs French language classes all year round. Teaching focuses on grammar, written and spoken French, using audio-visual and laboratory methods. A three-month semester, with 18 hours of lessons for 12 weeks, costs from 3,700FF to 4,540FF (420FF a week). A full academic year with five

hours of lessons for 34 weeks costs 5,960FF (190FF per week). The Au Pair programme, which also lasts a year with five hours of lessons for 34 weeks, costs 3,240FF (110FF per week). A two-week summer course, available in July, August and September, costs 1,700FF (1,100FF per week) for 24 hours of lessons per week whereas a four-week course, with 18 hours of lessons, costs 2,100FF (650FF per week). An additional 500FF deposit must be sent with the application form. DELF and DALF enrolment costs 850FF. Class size is limited to 15 students. There are no beginners classes during the summer.

Accommodation can be organised by the university. A furnished room in a hall of residence costs 850FF per month for under 26-year-olds or 1,100FF per month for over 26-year-olds or 610FF/820FF for two weeks. A room and half-board in a family costs 3,000FF per month and those choosing this option need to contact the Centre as early as possible.

Apply at least three weeks before the course start date enclosing a 500FF non-refundable deposit (payable by International reply coupons not eurocheques or travellers cheques) and two passport photos.

The CILEC is on a modern campus 10 minutes outside the city centre.

Université de Perpignan–Centre d'Études Françaises

52, avenue de Villeneuve, 66860 Perpignan Cedex
Tel: +33 4 68 66 20 10
Fax: +33 4 68 66 20 19
E-mail: cef@gala.univ-perp.fr
Established: 1988

Level of French: None
Nearest Station: Perpignan
Contact: Madame Hélène
Guisset

If you don't mind learning an accent with a twang, Perpignan is a wonderful place to study French. With the Mediterranean on one side and the Pyrénées on the other, it is one of the most southern cities in France, so far south it's practically in Spain. The university was established in the 14th-century but is now sited on a modern 20th-century campus. It runs a two-semester programme and a summer school. Teaching focuses on written and oral French, civilisation and literature, grammar and vocabulary. There is a language laboratory and audiovisual support. Six different levels are available. Levels one to three are non-diploma courses aimed at beginners. Level four leads to the *Certificat Pratique de Langue Francaise*, Level five to the *Diplôme d'Études Francaises* and Level six, which can only be taken at the end of two semesters, leads to the 'Diplôme Supérieur d'Études Françaises'. One semester costs 3650FF and one academic year costs 6259FF (ie. those who know they are staying for a whole year will save 1000FF). The summer course is very intensive: classes run from Monday to Saturday, with 24 hours of lessons. Two weeks cost 2,700FF, three 3,900FF and four 4,900FF. The intensive September course (75 hours of classes over three weeks) costs 3,500FF.

There are 15 to 20 students in a group. Minimum age is 17. Complete beginners are not accepted for the second semester. The Centre is a member of ADCUEFE and Petit Guide recommended. Applications should be accompanied by a 700FF non-refundable deposit (1,500FF for the intensive September course and 1,000FF for the summer courses). Accommodation can be organised for summer students (from 1,200FF for two weeks in a university residence) but those enroling during the academic year will be given a list of available rooms and flats. The campus is just outside the city centre.

Vis-à-Vis
24 Stoneleigh Park Road,
Stoneleigh, Epsom, Surrey,
KT19 0QR
Tel: (0181) 786 8021
Fax: (0181) 786 8210
E-mail: dquk@dircon.co.uk
Website: www.teclata.es/ visavis
Established: 1996
Level of French: None to
Advanced
Contact: Vis-à-Vis

If you can't quite face contacting a language school yourself in order to organise a study trip, try Vis-à-Vis, a company that acts as an agent for schools in France, Belgium and Canada. The staff can give advice on courses available and help students to find a class that suits their objectives and priorities. Schools have been vetted by Vis-à-Vis. At present there are seven schools in France, one in Brussels and one in Montreal including Actilangue Nice, Institut Parisien and Carel. The company organises everything for the student, booking both courses and accommodation at the various centres. Students gain the advantage of being able to pay in sterling, rather than having to transfer money, send a banker's draft or worry about exchange rate fluctuations, but must pay £40 to Vis-à-Vis in addition to school and accommodation costs. This is a great way of having your hand held whilst organising a trip but it also might prove more expensive, depending on the course and exchange rate. For example, Actilangue's two-week standard intensive course costs 2,270FF or £252 (using exchange rate of 9FF to the pound current at the time of going to press) whereas Vis-à-Vis charges £305 plus £40 booking fee. The school's eight-week business course which costs 9,830FF plus 500FF enrolment fee, or £1,147 (9FF to the pound) costs £1,326 plus £40 booked through Vis-à-Vis.

There are, of course, many other language schools to consider. This is a list of some of them, sorted alphabetically.

OTHER SCHOOLS

ADCUEFE/UNIVERSITY CENTRES
Service Commun d'Enseignement du Étudiants Étrangers Université de Provence
29, avenue Robert Schuman
13621
Aix Cedex 1
Tel: +33 4 42 59 22 71/
+33 4 42 95 32 16
Fax: +33 4 42 20 64 87

Azurlingua
25, bvd Raimbaldi
06000 Nice
Tel: +33 4 93 62 01 11
Fax: +33 4 93 62 22 56

CAFOL
Centre d'Acceuil et de Formation Linguistique
32/34, rue de Saurupt
BP 3106
54013 Nancy Cedex
Tel: +33 3 83 58 45 35
Fax: +33 3 83 56 11 54

Centre d'Études des Langues

Chambre de Commerce et d'Industrie de Bayonne Pays Basque
50-51, Allées Marines
BP 215
64102 Bayonne Cedex
Tel: +33 5 59 46 58 10
Fax: +33 5 59 46 59 70

Centre d'Études Françaises pour l'Étranger – Université de Caen
14032 Caen Cedex
(also a member of SOUFFLE)
Tel: +33 2 31 45 55 38
Fax: +33 2 31 93 69 19

Centre International des Langues
166, avenue du Majoral Arnaud
04100 Manosque
Tel: +33 4 92 72 46 19
Fax: +33 4 92 87 82 81

Centre International d'Études Françaises – Université de Bourgogne
36, rue Chabot-Charny
21000 Dijon
Tel: +33 3 80 30 50 20
Fax: +33 3 80 30 13 08

Centre International d'Études Pédagogiques (CIEP)
1, ave Leon Journault
92318 Sèvres Cedex
Tel: +33 1 45 07 60 00
Fax: +33 1 45 07 60 01

Centre International Linguistique et Sportif (CILS)
1, route de Paris
51700 Troissy
Tel: +33 3 26 52 73 08
Fax: +33 3 26 52 72 07

Centre Universitaire d'Études Françaises – Université Stendhal-Grenoble III

BP 25 38040 Grenoble Cedex 9
(also a member of SOUFFLE)
Tel: +33 4 76 82 43 27
Fax: +33 4 76 82 41 15

Centre Universitaire de Formation Continue – Université d'Angers

5, bvd Lavoisier
49045 Angers
Cedex 01
Tel: +33 2 41 35 21 90
Fax: +33 2 41 35 21 80

Ecolangues

18, rue de Bretagne
49100 Angers
Tel: +33 2 41 60 43 21
Fax: +33 2 41 60 57 44

École Méditerranéenne

31, rue de l'Argenterie
34000 Montpelier
Tel: +33 4 67 66 14 51
Fax: +33 4 67 66 12 01

Ecole Suisse Internationale de Français Appliqué

10, rue des Messageries
75010 Paris
Tel: +33 1 47 70 20 66
Fax: +33 1 42 46 34 57

ELFCA Institut d'Enseignement de la Langue Française sur la Côte d'Azur

66, ave de Toulon
83400 HyèresTel: +33 4 94 65
03 31
Fax: +33 4 94 65 81 22

Études Françaises pour Étrangers

UFR des Lettres, Atrs et
Sciences Humaines
Université de Nice
98, bvd Edouard Herriot
Nice Cedex
Tel: +33 4 93 37 54 57
Fax: +33 4 93 37 54 98

Eurocentre Amboise

9 Mail St Thomas
BP 214
37402 Amboise Cedex
Tel: +33 2 47 23 10 60
Fax: +33 2 47 30 54 99

Eurocentres La Rochelle

Avenue Marillac
17024 La Rochelle
Cedex 01
Tel: +33 5 46 50 57 33
Fax: +33 5 46 44 24 77

Eurofaec International

Association européenne
d'éducation et de culture
47A Les Rivages de Maguelone
34250 Palavas
Tel: +33 4 67 68 20 15
Fax: +33 4 67 50 60 90

European Language Services

35, rue Emile Brault
BP 831
53008 Laval Cedex
Tel: +33 2 43 69 52 52
Fax: +33 2 43 69 55 00

Idhee Clarife

Campus St Raphael
87, bvd
59800 Lille
+33 3 20 57 92 19
+33 3 20 15 29 30

INSA Lyon
Service de Français
Bât 601
20, ave A Einstein
69621 Villeurbanne Cedex
Tel: +33 4 72 43 83 66
Fax: +33 4 72 43 88 95

Institut Catholique de Toulouse (IULCF)
31, rue de la Fonderie
BP 7012
31068 Toulouse
Cedex 7
Tel: +33 5 61 36 81 00
Fax: +33 5 61 25 82 75

Institut de Langue et de Culture Françaises (ILCF)
Université Catholique de Lyon
31, place Bellecour
69288 Lyon Cedex 02
Tel: +33 4 72 32 50 53
Fax: +33 4 72 32 51 82

Institut d'Enseignement de Français Langue Etrangère de Nice
11, rue Rostan
06600 Antibes
Tel: +33 6 09 55 88 49
Fax: +33 6 09 55 75 7

Institut des Étudiants Étrangers – Université Paul Valéry
BP 5043
34032 Montpellier
Cedex
Tel: +33 4 67 14 21 01
Fax: +33 4 67 14 23 94

Institut Franco-Scandinave
9, cours des Arts et Métiers
13100 Aix-en-Provence
Tel: +33 4 42 26 46 08
Fax: +33 4 42 26 31 80

Institut Français d'Annecy
Centre de Résidence
Les Marquisats
52, rue des Marquisats
74000 Annecy
Tel: +33 4 50 45 38 37
Fax: +33 4 50 45 86 72

Institut International de Rambouillet
48, rue G. Lenotre
78120 Rambouillet
Tel: +33 1 30 46 53 20
Fax: +33 1 30 46 53 13

Institut Linguistique du Peyrou
3, rue Auguste Comte
34000 Montpellier
Tel: +33 4 67 92 05 55
Fax: +33 4 67 92 30 10

Institut Meditérranean d'Études Françaises
Espace Universitaire Albert Camus, 21, ave du Professeur Grasset 34093 Montpellier Cedex 5
Tel: +33 4 67 91 70 00
Fax: +33 4 67 91 70 01

International House
62, rue Gioffredo
06000 Nice
Tel: +33 4 93 62 60 62
Fax: +33 4 93 50 53 09

La Cardère Bourgogne
Institut Culturel de Langue Française
71580 Frontenaud
Tel: +33 3 85 74 83 11
Fax: +33 3 85 74 82 25

Langue et Communication
16, rue de Penhöet
35065 Rennes Cedex

Tel: +33 2 99 78 15 62
Fax: +33 2 99 79 33 91

La Sabranenque
Rue de la Tour de l'Oume
30290 Saint-Victor-la Coste
Tel: +33 4 66 50 05 05
Fax: +33 4 66 50 12 48

Sud-Langue-Méditerranée
8, place de l'opéra-Comédie
34000 Montpellier
Tel: +33 4 67 66 30 11
Fax: +33 4 67 66 30 11

SUEE - Faculté des Lettres
Ave Poplawski
64000 Pau
(also a member of SOUFFLE)
Tel: +33 5 59 92 32 22
Fax: +33 4 93 37 54 98

SUEE – Université de Blaise Pascal
34 ave Carnot
63000 Clermont-Ferrand
Tel: +33 4 73 40 64 97
Fax: +33 4 73 40 62 83

SUEE – Université de Nantes – Ensemble Administratif 'L'
Chemin de la Sensive
du Tertre
BP 1025
44036 Nantes Cedex 01
Tel: +33 2 40 14 10 30
Fax: +33 2 40 14 10 05

Université de Droit, d'Economie et des Sciences d'Aix-Marseille,
Institut d'Études Françaises
pour Etudiants Etrangers,
23, rue Gaston de Saporta
13625 Aix-en-Provence Cedex 1
Tel: +33 4 42 21 70 90
Fax: +33 4 42 23 02 64

Université de Poitiers – Centre de Français Langue Étrangere (CFLE)
95, ave du recteur Pineau
86022 Poitiers Cedex
Tel: +33 5 49 45 32 94
Fax: +33 5 49 45 32 95

Université d'Été de Boulogne-Sur-Mer
BP149
59653 Villeneuve d'Ascq Cedex
Tel: +33 3 20 91 97 66
Fax: +33 3 20 41 66 25

Université d'Été de Menton Office du Tourisme
BP 329
06506 Menton Cedex
Tel: +33 4 92 41 76 72
Fax: +33 4 92 41 76 82

Student Story

"They say that the best way to learn a language is to go and live in the country concerned. As long as you socialise with the people rather than only talking to fellow foreigners in English, then in my experience, this is very true. Six months at Perpignan University and I could talk the hind leg off the proverbial donkey – in French.

Perpignan is situated in the south-west of France very near the Spanish border, the Pyrénées and the beach. As I drove through Spain and into France a feeling of tranquillity settled over me. It was October, 28 degrees; I had the window wide open inhaling deeply the smells of the balmy south. The autoroute was practically deserted and unpolluted, unlike motorways in the UK.

The only problem was the tolls. Driving a right hand drive car on the right means that you are on the wrong side for putting your money in the machine. To the amusement of other drivers I either had to climb over all my clutter on the passenger seat or get out the car and walk around. The adventure of living in another country had well and truly started.

My home for the next 6 months was a rather spartan room in a rather spartan hall of residence. However, it was cheap, clean and warm. I had a huge window which provided a stunning view of Le Canigou – although not the highest peak in the Pyrénées, its distinctive shape is easily recognisable. As the sun streamed in and the room reverberated to the hum of the cicadas I felt like I was in a set for a Marcel Pagnol film.

The first week, I had to decide what subjects to do. Translation – never my strong point – was, unfor-tunately, compulsory. As was grammar. For my options I chose World 20th Century History and 20th-century European Culture and Civilisation – the latter because I'd heard that it involved watching lots of videos and looking at slides.

The first couple of weeks passed in a blur of getting to the right classroom at the right time, finding the local supermarket, piling as many people into my car to go to the beach and checking out the local bars. We felt it our duty to sample some of the local wines; the Languedoc Roussillon area produces some very fine examples. My social life became an important part of improving my language skills. After a few glasses you lose any inhibitions and prattle away at a vast rate of knots.

I soon realised that my A Level French had left me poorly equipped to deal with being lectured in French, not to mention the thick, guttural local accent. Thankfully, after a couple of weeks my ear became attuned to the melodious musings of lecturers and shop-keepers.

The biggest test of my language skills was learning Russian through the medium of French. Having started to learn the Cyrillic tongue before coming to France, I did not want to forget what I'd learnt. As the university did not offer Russian, my tutor arranged for me to go to the local high school. The shock of learning a foreign language in a foreign language was not as great as going back to school!

I have to say that my French really did improve. My grammar was still punctuated with a poor choice of preposi-tions and pronouns, but, by the end of the 6 months I was fairly fluent. My British accent became less pronounced although I never managed to acquire the local accent. Probably not a bad thing as I'm not sure how well it would have gone down in my final oral exams. "

Yolande Taylor

Professional and Vocational Courses

Learning the classics of French culture (whether art, food or wine) is one way to experience the country or even to grasp the language. However, it is also possible, whether or not you speak much French, to gain professional and vocational experience and/or qualifications. Rather than spending a year on a university course, why not follow a passion, learn a new skill or develop an existing career? Theatre, make-up, fashion design and business can all be studied for short periods of a month to a year. For the determined they may lead to a different profession.

Range of Schools

Theatre, role, scene, mime, vaudeville, spectacle, ballet – French is the very language of performance. In the country that produced The Phantom of the Opera, Quasimodo and Cyrano de Bergerac, the theatrical arts have a long history and a lively present scene. Whilst other countries cut budgets and projects, France continues to support cinematic, stage and musical productions. For those interested in a performing arts career, Paris is still one of the most creative cities in the world. Who better to teach the art of dramatic mime than Jacques Lecoq, the man who developed his skills alongside Nobel prizewinner Dario Fo and taught Jeffrey Rush how to Shine? And why not learn acting at the École Florent, the school that trained Daniel Auteuil and Isabelle Adjani? Year-long programmes are available and the École Florent runs summer schools.

Make-up and Beauty

In the country of Marcel Marceau, 'off'-stage skills are as prized as 'on'. Make-up schools, teaching everything from the basics of colour and shape to the arts of body painting and prosthetics, offer short and long courses. In three to six months a complete novice could learn to be a beautician or a make-up artist for stage, screen or studio. Who better to teach stage make-up than the make-up artist from the Opera de Paris? Prices are competitive and facilities are impressive.

Fashion

The fashion houses in France have been taken over by British designers but it is still a country renowned for its style and couture. Budding John Gallianos and Stella McCartneys will increase their skills and their credibility by spending a summer or a semester learning dress-making and designing in a Parisian *atelier*. Many studios offer month-long sessions.

Business

The MBA is a very American qualification, but some of the best business schools are European. France is home to several, including Insead and Essec, and all of them offer international programmes in English. Many of them are one-year courses which makes them more economical (albeit still very expensive) than the two-year transatlantic equivalents. Insead also has two intakes per year, one in September and one in January.

Typical Prices

Professional courses demand an investment in time, cost and commitment. All the schools listed are private, which makes them a lot more expensive than the French public sector. However, in general the prices are lower than those in the North American/British private colleges and, as education is historically free in France, paying students are treated with respect and courtesy.

Level of French

In the theatre schools an intermediate level of French is a prerequisite. It is unlikely that a non-French speaker will manage the auditions let alone the classes. Make-up and beauty schools run classes in French but the visual nature of demonstrations make them very accessible and popular with international students.

The same applies to fashion studios and schools. All the business schools listed run their programmes in English.

Level of Expertise

All of these schools will operate a selection procedure to determine a student's capabilities and motivation. Beauty schools are the least stringent, business schools the most. Admission to theatre and fashion design courses will depend on evidence of a passionate interest in the subject and some previous experience.

Certificates and Awards

The complete diversity of professional and vocational programmes open to international students leads to a plethora of different qualifications, none of which, excepting those offered by theatre schools, is specific to France. However, studying abroad adds an immeasurable extra dimension to the learning experience. MBA candidates will already know the value of the degree but those considering an international/European career may need to determine the value-added gains of living in a foreign culture and improving language skills and European connections. Theatrical training offered by Florent and Lecoq is internationally renowned and very much determined by the character of the teachers and founders. The certificate and exams provide evidence but it is the personality of the particular school that will form technique. This is also the case for fashion design, with the added proviso that, as with all art, France and especially Paris, has a history and style which are unsurpassed. Make-up schools benefit from links with the Opera de Paris and France's fashion and film industries.

Paris or the Provinces?

Many of the schools in this chapter are one-offs, and thus the question of whether to study in the capital or the provinces doesn't arise. In terms of concentration of schools and connections, Paris is the obvious choice. The decision to head to a provincial city or the countryside is a very personal and practical one. Beyond the capital living expenses fall dramatically whereas the opportunity to integrate into French life increases. Lyon, for example can offer both a big city lifestyle and contacts, but also a provincial tempo, including access to the mountains and coast.

BUSINESS

ESSEC

**Avenue Bernard Hirsch, BP
105, 95021 Cergy-Pontoise
Tel: +33 1 34 43 32 26
Fax: +33 1 34 43 32 20
Email: mba@edu.essec.fr
Website: www.essec.fr**

Contact: Isabelle Miramon
Nearest Station: (RER)
Cergy-Pontoise
Level of French: Intermediate
(teaching is in English)

Cergy-Pontoise is a modern metropolis on the outskirts of Paris, filled with brick buildings, geometric gardens and landscaped lakes. The ESSEC group isn't the easiest to find but strolling around the grounds whilst looking for it is far from stressful unless, that is, you hate modern architecture. Essec offers three bilingual study programmes: IMHI, an MBA in Luxury Brand Management and an MBA in Food Management. It is the only school in the world which offers an MBA specifically directed at working with names such as Armani, Dior and Möet et Chandon. Applicants must take the Gmat test, have three years professional experience and a university degree or equivalent qualification, attend a series of interviews and present written work. The school's teaching aims to 'blend the rigor of North American quantitative methods with the history, scope and creativity of European Social Sciences.' The core programme covers Marketing, Management, Critical Thinking and Group Dynamics and students also lead field projects for the luxury goods companies who work with the school. Alumni tend to find jobs with international companies such as Yves Saint Laurent, L'Oreal and Prada.

There is a maximum of 40 students per class and 80 per cent are international. The one-year MBA programmes cost 120,000FF, start at the end of August and last 11 months. Cheap student accommodation is available.

INSEAD: The European Institute of Business Administration

Boulevard de Constance, 77
305 Fontainebleau
Cedex, France
Tel: +33 1 60 72 40 00
Fax: +33 1 60 74 55 00/01
E-mail: mba@insead.fr or admissions@insead.fr
Website: www.insead.fr
Established: 1959
Level of French required: ntermediate
Nearest Station: (SNCF) Fontainebleau
Contact: Samia Safir

Insead has one of the most beautiful campuses and one of the best MBA courses in the world. Situated about 60km south of Paris, the school is in a largely self-contained campus surrounded on three sides by the forest of Fontainebleau. It teaches an integrative management approach to prepare executives for working in an international environment. There are approximately 520 students, from all over the world, and over two-thirds of the participants speak more than one language. Such a broad mix of candidates establishes a worldwide focus that serves to emphasise the teaching strategies. The programme runs a core course in business fundamentals, including Managerial Behaviour, Financial Accounting, Economic Analysis and Corporate Strategy, and students choose a minimum of seven electives from a wide range of possibilities such as Strategies for Pacific Asia, Managing Global Competition and Advanced Business Languages (French, Spanish and German). The campus is somewhat unique for a European business school: it is not only beautiful but also well-equipped. There is an extensive information centre where students have access to books, publications and periodicals in more than ten languages, a bar, a fitness centre and self-service restaurant. Information about accommodation is available through an agency and students' families are welcome to take advantage of campus facilities.

Students can start in January or September and the programme, unlike many American MBAs, lasts 10 months. Applications begin to be considered up to one year in advance so early submission is encouraged. Students need to have passed the Gmat and Toefl (where necessary), have an undergraduate degree, a working knowledge of French and fluent English and professional experience (most applicants have approximately four and a half years). Total cost is 155,000FF. There is a career management service which aims to give students access to a large network of recruitment opportunities. Insead an also provide information about study loans.

Informal information sessions are arranged on Fridays, from 4pm to 7pm. The easiest way to reach the school is by car or taxi, although this isn't the cheapest option (approximately 600FF from Orly). From central Paris trains leave for Fontainebleau/Avon (direction Sens) from the Gare de Lyon. From the train station take a taxi or bus to the campus.

MIB-Ecole Nationale des Ponts et Chaussées

**28, rue des Saints-Pères, 75343 Paris Cedex 07
Tel: +33 1 44 58 28 52
Fax: +33 1 40 15 93 47
E-mail: mib.admit@paris.enpc.fr
Website: www.enpc.fr/mib/**

**pres.htm
Established: Ecole des Ponts 1747; MIB 1988.
Level of French required: None: all the classes are in English
Nearest Station: (Métro) Saint-Germain des Prés
Contact: Mayalene Crossley**

The École Nationale des Ponts et Chaussées is the oldest French Grande École, and its situation in an 18th century building in one of the most renowned historic quarters of Paris, St Germain des Prés, reflects this. However, since 1988 its flagship program has been the MIB, a general European MBA that aims to provide professionals with an overall understanding of the major issues of contemporary business management. The MIB courses are divided into four main streams: finance, strategy and marketing, technology management and general management. There are also three regional options: Eastern and Western Europe, the Pacific Basin and North America which aim to give participants an understanding of local issues within a context of global international business. The course lasts 14-16 months, including nine months in Paris and abroad and a personal professional project that allows students to apply their skills on a consulting project. This must take place in a country other than the participant's home. Exchange opportunities exist within Canada, Europe, Asia and the Americas.

The course is full-time, costs 110 000FF and begins in October. The intake is small (around 45 per year) which enables a close student community to develop. Applicants need to pass the Gmat, provide three letters of recommendation and provide evidence of

PROFESSIONAL & VOCATIONAL STUDIES

their ability in English. Personal interviews take place in Paris or with an MIB representative abroad. There are four to eight assistantships each year which offer reduced tuition fees in exchange for administrative support in MIB offices. A limited number of scholarships are also available (including a fellowship scheme offered by the Royal Academy of Engineering to British engineers and life scientists). There are three application deadlines, in March, May and August. Early applications are encouraged.

Student accommodation is available through Crous.

To reach the ENPC, take métro line 4 to St Germain des Prés. Walk along boulevard St Germain against the direction of the traffic. Rue Saints-Pères is the third on the right and the ENPC is on the left.

FASHION AND BEAUTY

Centre de Formation de Modelistes
23, rue Vasco-de-Gama, 75015 Paris
Tel: +33 1 45 58 04 54
Fax: +33 1 44 26 32 64
Established: 1981
Level of French required: Intermediate
Nearest Station: (Métro) Lourmel
Contact: Mlle Laure Luxey

A *modeliste* is a dressmaker, and this private school in a Parisian side-street excels in training dressmakers for France's fashion industry. When couture houses need dressmakers for their salons, they come to the Centre to look for them. The school is tiny, with a total of 50 students over two years, three teachers and an assistant, and is renowned for its excellent training. To be accepted, you must attend an interview, answer questions – and sew (they will watch how you handle a needle and they're looking for neatness and precision). The course lasts for two years, during which you learn pattern-cutting, styling and Moulage (fitting on a mannequin). Students research and make 12 dresses which are copies of famous designs from portraits, films or weddings. These are judged by professionals from the fashion world and displayed at the School's end

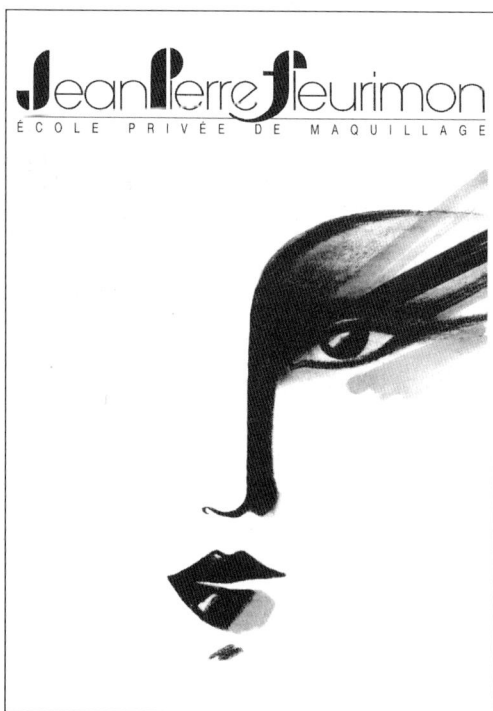

Jean Pierre Fleurimon
ÉCOLE PRIVÉE DE MAQUILLAGE

of year show which is supported by everyone from Agnès B to Yves Saint Laurent. Those who make 12 successful copies, pass the exams with a grade of at least 12/20 and complete one month's probation working for a company will be awarded the BTS. It is far from easy – usually 50 per cent of students fail. To succeed, says the senior tutor, you need to be logical, innovative and aim for perfection. Most of the school's students are French but there are a few from overseas.

The two-year BTS course costs 23,700FF in the first year and 29,500FF in the second. The enrolment fee is 2,500FF. The Centre also offers professional three-month or one-year options for those interested in furthering their skills but not gaining a qualification. In order to be considered, applicants need the equivalent of the *baccalauréat*.

Take métro line 8 (direction Balard) to Lourmel. With rue de Lourmel on the right and Avenue Felix Faure on the left, walk along Felix Faure. Rue Vasco-de-Gama is the first on the left. The Centre is on the left.

École Professionnelle Privée de Maquillage Jean-Pierre Fleurimon

274-276, rue St Honoré, 75001 Paris
Tel/Fax: +33 1 42 61 29 15
Established: 1962
Level of French: Conversational
Contact: Jean-Pierre Fleurimon
Nearest Station: (Métro) Palais Royal, Musee du Louvre

Established in 1962, this is one of the most well-known make-up schools in Paris and one of the few that is autho

Student story

"A couple of years ago, Yolanta came to our make-up school. She had abandoned her native Poland – at that time under a communist regime. Being quite sensitive, she seemed so lost in the vast metropolis that is Paris.

She was always on time for class and was also the last to leave. She was so dedicated to her studies that I ended up discussing with her how she managed to survive in Paris. She told me that to pay for her classes and living costs she worked as a receptionist at "Aux Caves de la Tour d'Argent" – an annex of a famous Parisien restaurant where tourists can buy souvenirs after eating on one of the most beautiful roofs of Paris.

Once she'd finished her studies with us, Yolanta moved on but came back regularly to tell us what she was doing. I thus learnt that she had been the make-up artist for the model on the poster of the famous "Nuit des publivores". She also did the make-up for the famous French singer, Julien Clerc, for all of his concerts.

I didn't see or hear of her for a while until last Saturday when I happened to buy the magazine Madame Figaro and her name appeared. She had done the make-up for the cover and a lot of the models in the photos throughout. I have to admit that I was very proud; in seeing the cover I recognised my technique that Yolanta had adapted to her own style and personality.

Jean Pierre Fleurimon

rised by the Minister of Education. It is situated in a 17th-century listed building, just across from the Jardin des Tuileries and next to the Palais Royal. Beyond the cobbled courtyard is the studio, which, installed in 1997, is far from historic. Large and light, it has a modern theatre for demonstrations and lots of individual workstations. Classes take place morning and afternoon and are taught by artists working in all areas of the profession, including television, theatre and film. Students follow classes in Make-Up for Photos, Television, Cinema and Theatre, as well as Face and Body Painting and Working with Latex.

Short and long courses are available. Two-thirds of the students study for nine months whereas the rest follow three to six month courses. A complete course lasts three months. Students come from all over the world, including Japan, Russia and Canada. Make-Up Stylist courses are available in four formats: one-week (2000FF), three months (12,000FF); six months (20,000FF) and nine months (25,000FF). Sessions begin in September, January and April. Students enrolling for a minimum of three months will receive a complete rofessional make-up box, which remains their property, and a portfolio of their work.

The very visual nature of the demonstration means that students can manage with minimal French and Jan Bos, the Artistic Director, can also provide translation. Accommodation is the student's responsibility. Applicants should enrol as early as possible

John James

because courses fill very quickly. No previous expertise is necessary but students need to be very motivated.

Take métro line 1 to Palais-Royal Musée du Louvre. Walk away from the Louvre into the Place du Palais Royal and turn immediately left. Once beyond Place André Malraux stay on the right-hand side of the rue St-Honore. 274 is on the right. Look out for a door and doorbell. The school is not obvious from the street.

Funcreation Parfumeurs

**Les Baux, 06750 Seranon
Tel: +33 4 93 42 73 11
Fax: +33 4 93 42 40 52
Level of French: Conversational
(translator available for an
extra fee).
Contact: Mme Michelle Funel
Nearest Station: (SNCF) Grasse
+ 40 km (but Mme Funel is
mobile).**

The South of France is renowned for its wine, but there is another liquid produced in this region which needs an equally expert nose: perfume. Perfume has been made in Grasse since the Middle Ages, when tanners, dismayed at the scent of the skins they used, developed it to make their products smell sweeter. It is now the world capital of this expensive elixir, combining a perfect sunny climate with a proliferation of plant life. Mme Michelle Funel is one of only 40 *parfumeurs* in the world and when she's not mixing secret potions (she refused to tell me whether she knew the Chanel recipes) she offers short courses in perfumery. In her laboratory in an 18th-century farmhouse in Seranon, 40 km north of Grasse, students spend two and a half hours learning about the history of perfume and the basic theory before mixing up their own recipe, which they take away with them at the end of the session. For more determined aromaphiles a block of three half-days is also available and Mme Funel will also run classes anywhere in the region, for those who cannot reach Seranon. Each session costs 200FF (not including tax) and they are available every day except Monday, all year round.

Institut Français de la Mode

**33, rue Jean Goujon,
75008 Paris
Tel: +33 1 56 59 22 22
Fax: +33 1 56 59 22 00
Email: com@ifm-paris.org
Web: www.textiles.fr
Established: 1986
Level of French required:
Intermediate to Advanced
Contact: Laurence Sudre;
Maria Neves
Nearest Station: (Métro)
Alma-Marceau**

If you are interested in fashion management, not design, if you want to work in business but in a creative industry, there is only one place to go. The Institut Français de la Mode, situated close to the Seine, the Grand Palais and the Champs-Élysées, is one of only two schools in France which offers a one-year course in Textile and Fashion Management. (The other is in Lyon and is much more sociological). The programme is cross-disciplinary, covering design classes (which are followed in order to understand the process involved) and classes in the Culture of Fashion. The teaching staff includes both permanent staff and associated professors, who work in fashion management and design.

Students need the equivalent of a *baccalauréat* plus four further years of study and a determined, motivated personality. Applicants tend to be both creative and business-minded. The course costs 55,000FF (which is cheap when compared to other more general management programmes) and since the Institut has many partnerships with companies there are also grants available, which were established to ensure that the recruitment process remains as fair as possible. There are 40-50 students per year, from various backgrounds, including engineering, education and business, and each year is divided into smaller groups for the optional courses. Application is based on a dossier and an interview, both in French. 10% of the yearly intake is from abroad. Job prospects are good because the school helps students network with past students and with the Institut's commercial partners. Help in finding accommodation is available.

Take line 9 to Alma-Marceau. Walk away from the river along avenue Montaigne. Rue Jean Goujon is first on the right. Number 33 is on the left-hand side.

Studio Bercot

29, rue des Petites Écuries, 75010 Paris
Tel: +33 1 42 46 15 55
Fax: +33 1 48 01 07 02
Email: studio-bercot@calva.net
Website: www.enterprises.fr/bercot
Established: 1955
Level of French: Intermediate
Contact: Madame Joelle Cotonnec
Nearest Station: (Métro) Château d'Eau

The Bercot system involves learning to make the most of very little, and it obviously works in the Parisian fashion world. Once they have finished their first two years of studies, apprentices from this fashion design studio may find themselves training with Chanel, Lacroix, Rykiel and Kenzo. What differentiates Bercot from others is that it is purely a studio. There are no marketing or management courses and students spend all of their time focusing on designing. The studio is 300m^2 and situated in the heart of the Parisian rag trade, surrounded by couture studios and haberdasheries. It is also within reach of the city's flea markets. Students work around large tables and in groups. The teachers are all professionals, who work in design, styling or photography, and they emphasise letting the students put their ideas into practice, in order to learn through hands-on experience. Bercot prides itself on its family atmosphere, and in order to preserve this it only enrols a small number of students.

The course takes two years and leads to the Studio's own diploma, and students are expected to spend about 24 hours per week in the studio. In the third year the school finds apprenticeships (unpaid) for all its students, often offered by previous generations of students who have established themselves in the fashion business. No expertise is necessary but students must be passionate about fashion and design. Mimimum age for enrolment is 18. 60 per cent of the students are foreigners and there are approximately 60 in each of the two years of study. Each year costs 39,000FF (payable in three instalments) and this does not include materials. Students are advised on the best shops in which to buy supplies. Enrolments begin in January via a questionnaire and mandatory interview although written applications will be considered from international students. There is no accommodation service though the school can offer help and information.

Take métro line 4 to Château d'Eau. You will be at the junction of rue Château d'Eau and boulevard de Strasbourg. Walk against the traffic along rue Château d'Eau which turns into rue des Petites Écuries. 29 will be on the left-hand side.

Sup'Maquillage F.I.L.M.

3 bis rue des Marroniers,
69002 Lyon
Tel: +33 4 78 42 09 89
Fax: +33 4 78 37 24 37
Nearest Station: (SNCF)
Lyon-Perrache et Lyon-de-la-Part-Dieu
Contact: Monsieur Rodolphe Voiron/Madame Bidet
Level of French: Conversational

The Sup'Maquillage school, part of the Université Professionnelle Peyrefitte in Lyon, demonstrates that big institutions can be welcoming. Many similar schools, especially in Paris, couldn't be bothered to talk about their work, whereas the staff at F.I.L.M. (Formation Internationale Lyonnaise de Maquillage) were more than helpful, despite the fact that they were in the midst of a large end-of-term party. It is the only professional make-up school in the Rhône-Alpes region. Offering a short three-month Beautician course and a nine-month Make-Up Artist course, the school aims to develop professionals who are equipped to work in theatre, cinema, fashion,

advertising and television. Classes are taught in studios in a converted coaching inn steps away from the paved streets of the centre of France's second largest city. The nine-month programme costs 19,500FF, and enrolment begins in January.

PERFORMING ARTS

École Florent/Formation de l'Acteur
40 rue Mathis, 75019 Paris
Tel: +33 1 40 36 37 57
Fax: +33 1 40 38 27 30
Established: 1967
Level of French required: Advanced
Nearest Station: (Métro) Crimee
Contact: Brigitte Descormiers

Situated in the north-east of Paris, far from the artistic *arrondissement* of Montparnasse but close to Montmartre, passers-by would be unaware of this school's existence, though they might wonder why there was a cluster of young people so early in the morning in this non-studenty neighbourhood. Years ago that cluster would have included Daniel Auteuil and Christophe Lambert. Or Sophie Marceau and Isabelle Adjani. The school's list of alumni is so impressive that it is difficult to decide who to cite as an emblem of its success. Such a grand roll-call would imply that this acting school is exclusive and expensive. It is neither. For a start it runs a yearly competition for a free year of study, the Classe Libre which can, for those good enough, lead to a second year. To be considered students must enrol by November of the previous year (for a 300FF fee) and then perform at three different auditions (in November, December and January). International students attend the same auditions (in French) and also present a scene in their own language. This generous scheme bears witness to the spirit of the school's founder, François Florent, who considers theatre to be as fundamental to our society as thought and therefore a practice that should be open to everyone.

For those not lucky enough to be accepted into the Classe Libre, there are several other options. A probationary Beginners class, lasting three weeks, is open to anyone who has no theatrical experience. Two summer courses, 'The Actor and the Camera and The Actor and the Theatre, each lasting eight days (4-6 hours of classes daily), take place in July and August and cost 2135FF (+ 750FF enrolment fee) and 2045FF (+ 650FF enrolment fee) respectively. The successful completion of each one enables direct entry into the 'Formation' programme which lasts from one to three years and costs 1,690FF per month in the first year (+610FF yearly enrolment fee). Students, whether enrolled in summer or academic year classes, are entitled to be in the school's Casting books which are regularly consulted by agents and directors from TV, cinema and the theatre.

Enrolment takes place all year round.

Take métro line 7 to Crimee, which is at the junction of rue Mathis and rue de Crimee. The École Florent is right at the end of the street, on the right-hand side.

École Lecoq

57, rue du Faubourg St Denis, 75010 Paris
Tel: +33 1 47 70 44 78
Fax: +33 1 45 23 40 14
Established: 1956
Level of French required: Inter-mediate
Nearest Station: (Métro) Strasbourg St Denis
Contact: Fay Lees Lecoq

Geoffrey Rush is on the walls here, in a clown's costume. The now famous star of Shine, once a student at the Ecole Lecoq, is in illustrious company. Nobel Prize laureat Dario Fo and playwright and actor Stephen Berkoff also studied here, and their combined and diverse talents alone inform the novice that this school is extraordinary. It is situated in the only remaining Victorian gymnasium in Paris, where young boxers used to train. The ring is no longer there but students can still tread the same boards, and watch from the same gallery, like 19th-century audiences before them.

The large, airy space is perfect for the sort of theatre taught by Jacques Lecoq. Focusing on the creative as well as the physical aspects of movement, students are encouraged to express and develop their talents across the theatrical spectrum, as writers, directors and actors. His technique draws on his varied career. Trained as a physical education teacher and physiotherapist, he became interested in the theatre of mime and mask in the 1940s. After spending eight years in Italy, helping to found the Piccolo Teatro School in Milan, he returned to Paris and started his own school. His 'mimo-dynamic' methods apply the laws of movement to creation and acting, encouraging the student through the use of masks, mime and acrobatics how to use the body as a dramatic object.

Students come from the world over to study the Lecoq technique and the only entrance requirement is motivation.

Many are already working in theatre and have decided to take a sabbatical at the school. Once accepted students cannot rest on their laurels: at the end of the first trimester 2/3rds of the class are selected to continue until June. Students have 20 hours of classes per week and are expected to spend an additional ten hours rehearsing in small groups to prepare a weekly performance project which will be presented to the class on Friday. At the end of the first year students perform a show and those considered good enough can enrol for a second year. Many students have either continued or returned for a third year of pedagogical training and then opened their own schools or worked in universities.

The one-year programme costs 10,600FF per trimester for a daily four-hour class plus 970FF for enrolment. The regime is strict: attendance registers are kept and lateness is not tolerated. To enrol, contact the school as early as possible before the start of the academic year. Approximately 80 students are enrolled per year and in November 1997 the October 1998 class was already a quarter full.

Send a CV with precise details of previous theatrical experience and workshops followed, a photo and a letter of recommendation.

Take métro lines 4/8/9 to Strasbourg St Denis and take the rue St Denis/Faubourg St Denis exit. Walk past the large stone arch (Porte St Denis) and along rue Faubourg St Denis. Number 57 is on the left and the school can be reached by walking through the courtyard.

École Supérieure du Spectacle

31, avenue Parmentier, 75011 Paris
Tel: +33 1 48 06 68 01
Fax: +33 1 47 00 74 41
Web: www.oda.fr/aa/forum-du mouvement.
Established: 1975
Level of French: Conversational
Contact: Chris Pages
Nearest Station: (Métro) Alexandre Dumas (Dance); Voltaire (Singing/Theatre).

Established 21 years ago in the trendy East of Paris, the École Supérieure is one of the few places which offers training in theatre, song and dance. Students spend 35 to 40 hours per week following a variety of classes including Modern and Contemporary Dance, Voice, Improvisation and Music Study. It is possible to spend equal amounts studying each discipline or to focus on one in particular. The school is small enough to be familial but large enough (between 60-80 students per year) to provide a troupe for the end of year shows. Students work in groups in a big 180m^2 dance studio. A basic knowledge of French is helpful and the school is full of international students who spend a year brushing up both their linguistic and lyrical skills. Motivation is more important than stage experience. Students need to enrol before 1st October for the whole academic year (33,000FF) though it is possible to enrol for two terms beginning in January (14,000FF per term). The school can help with finding accommodation.

Take métro line 9 to Voltaire. At the exit, cross Place Leon Blum and head up Avenue Parmentier. Number 31 is on the left.

PROFESSIONAL & VOCATIONAL STUDIES

Universities

DEGREES AND CYCLES

A university education is divided into three different cycles and several different diplomas. The *premier cycle* (first cycle) is a basic orientation and training period, preparing students for the *deuxième cycle* and, in some cases, serving as a launchpad for access into competitive entry schools. At the end of two years students sit the DEUG (Diplôme d'Etudes Universitaires Générales). Equipped with a DEUG students remaining in the university sector continue onto the *deuxième cycle*, a period of professional specialisation lasting one year (licence, roughly equivalent to a BA) or two (*licence* and *maîtrise*, roughly equivalent to a Master's). Most students in this sector will stop at a *maîtrise*. The *troisième cycle* comprises the DEA and the DESS. The DEA (*Diplôme d'Etudes Approfondies*) is a one-year research degree which leads to careers in research and/or the preparation of a doctorate. The DESS (*Diplôme d'Études Supérieures Specialisées*) is a one-year professional course leading to a career in a specific sector. Education trajectories, and the jobs they lead to, are measured in terms of how long a student has remained in post-secondary education e.g. a 'bac+4' student has spent four years in higher education post-*baccalauréat*.

Fondation Nationale des Sciences Politiques: Institut d'Études Politiques

27 rue Saint-Guillaume, 75007 Paris
Tel: +33 1 45 49 50 50
Fax: +33 1 45 44 12 52
Email: programmes@international.sciences-po.fr
Web: www.sciences-po.fr
Established: 1872
Level of French required: Advanced
Nearest Station: (Métro) St-Germain-des Pres
Contact: Secretariat des Étudiants Étrangers (Tel: +33 1 45 49 50 47; Fax: +33 1 45 44 12 52)

The Institut d'Études Politiques, more commonly known as 'Sciences Po', is one of the only Grandes Écoles, France's most prestigious educational institutions, to openly invite international applications. Over 800 of its 4000 students come from abroad. Located in St Germain des Prés, in several 17th- and 18th-century mansions, the school offers pluridisciplinary broad-based social sciences programmes which are reputed for training professionals for several different sectors, including public

Premier cycle	Deuxième cycle	Troisième cycle
DEUG – Two years	Licence/maitrise – one or two years	DEA or DESS – one year

administration, business, media and research. It is renowned for the quality and style of its comparative, synthetic analytic education. Unlike most of the French higher education system, Sciences Po teaches its courses through small tutorials, or *'conferences de methode'*, combined with lectures.

There are several different one-year, two-year, semester and summer programmes available for international students. The International Program in Political and Social Sciences is a two-semester course aimed at undergraduates who have already completed two years of university study. The semesters are consecutive but independent, and students choose whether they wish to obtain the International Program Diploma (which involves following an extra one-year lecture course plus language training or options) or the Certificate, which is awarded on completion of one or two semesters. Students are evaluated on the basis of written exams and participation. There is also a one-year Undergraduate Program, aimed at first years who subsequently plan to follow the Sciences-Po Diploma. The International Graduate Program can be followed for one or two years depending on the students' objectives. The first year is open to any student who has completed a degree in another institution and who wishes to further their knowledge across the social science spectrum. Successful completion of year one is required in order to follow the second year which leads to a Master's degree. For students continuing their education beyond Master's level, the Institut offers doctoral programmes, including a DEA and a Research Seminar Program in the Social Sciences. The 12-16 month DESS is aimed at those seeking professional not research training. There is also a bilingual nine-month MBA course which is the only one in France that is part of a major university. The International Program,

Kirsten Chapman

International Graduate Program, Master's Program (Cycle du Diplome) and Undergraduate Program all cost 5850FF and the semester program costs 2925FF.

Sciences Po is an extremely selective Institut. The Undergraduate Program has an entrance exam and the DESS course only accepts 130 students from over 1000 applications. Enrolment is minimised to ensure maximum opportunity for its graduates. Prospective applicants should contact the Institut as early as possible to find out the respective requirements and documents needed for the specific programme. Every candidate must pass a three-hour French language proficiency test, either in the French consulate in their home country in February of the year of application, or at Sciences Po in May. A limited number of scholarships are available from the French Foreign Ministry. Contact the French Embassy in the home country.

Take métro line 4 to St-Germain des Près. Keeping the church on your right-hand side walk along the boulevard. Rue

"I came to France from the Czech Republic. I felt that at home the study of politics has not really had time to acquire the breadth and scope of courses in Western institutions. I decided to come to France because I had studied French before, and also because France has a reputation for political freedom. I did need to improve my French very quickly when I first arrived."

Andrea

Saint Guillaume is the third on the left. Turn left and Sciences Po is on the left.

For more information on applying to French Universities, please see the 'Applying to Study' Chapter. On the following pages there is a comprehensive listing of the universities in France, by region, complete with contact details.

PARIS

Université Panthéon-Sorbonne: Paris 1
12, place du Panthéon,
75231 Paris cedex 05
Tel: 01 46 34 97 00
Fax: 01 46 34 20 56

Université Panthéon-Assas: Paris 11
(droit-economie-sciences sociales), 12 place du Panthéon,
75231 Paris cedex 05
Tel: 01 44 41 57 00
Fax: 01 44 41 55 13

Université de la Sorbonne Nouvelle: Paris 111
17, rue de la Sorbonne,
75230 Paris cedex 05
Tel: 01 40 46 28 97/99
Fax: 01 43 25 74 71

Université Paris-Sorbonne: Paris 1V
1, rue Victor Cousin,
75230 Paris cedex 05
Tel: 01 40 46 22 11
Fax: 01 40 46 25 88

Université René Descartes: Paris V
12, rue de l'Ecole de Medecine,
75270 Paris cedex 06
Tel: 01 40 46 16 16
Fax: 01 40 46 16 15

Université Pierre et Marie Curie: Paris V1

4, place Jussieu,
75252 Paris cedex 05
Tel: 01 44 27 44 27
Fax: 01 44 27 38 29

Université Denis Diderot: Paris V11

2, place Jussieu,
75251 Paris cedex 05
Tel: 01 44 27 44 27
Fax: 01 44 27 69 64

Universite Paris Dauphine: Paris 1X

Place du Marechal
de-Lattre-de Tassigny,
75775 Paris cedex 16
Tel: 01 44 05 44 05
Fax: 01 44 05 41 41

Universite de Marne-La Vallée

5, boulevard Descartes,
Champs-sur-Marne,
77454 Marne-La-Vallee cedex 2
Tel: 01 60 95 75 00
Fax: 01 60 95 75 75

Universite Paris Vincennes: Paris V111

2, rue de la Liberte,
93526 Saint-Denis cedex 02
Tel: 01 49 40 67 89
Fax: 01 48 21 04 46

Université Paris-Val-de-Marne: Paris X11

61, avenue du General-de
Gaulle, 94010 Creteil cedex
Tel: 01 45 17 10 00
Fax: 01 42 07 70 12

Université Paris-Nord: Paris X111

Avenue Jean-Baptiste Clement,
93430 Villetaneuse

Tel: 01 49 40 30 00
Fax: 01 49 40 38 93

Université de Cergy-Pontoise

33, boulevard du Port,
95011 Cergy-Pontoise cedex
Tel: 01 34 25 60 00
Fax: 01 34 25 61 01

Université d'Evry-Val d'Essonne

Boulevard Francois Mitterrand,
91025 Evry cedex
Tel: 01 69 47 70 00
Fax: 01 64 97 27 34

Université Nanterre: Paris X

200, avenue de la Republique,
92001 Nanterre cedex
Tel: 01 40 97 72 00
Fax: 01 40 97 75 71

Université Paris Sud: Paris X1

15, rue Georges Clemenceau,
91405 Orsay cedex
Tel: 01 69 15 67 50
Fax: 01 69 15 61 35

Université de Versailles Saint-Quentin-en-Yvelines

23, rue du Refuge,
78035 Versailles cedex
Tel: 01 39 25 40 00
Fax: 01 39 25 78 01

NORTH-EAST

Amiens

Université Picardie –Jules-Verne: Amiens

Chemin du Til, 80025 Amiens
cedex 1
Tel: 03 22 82 72 72
Fax: 03 22 82 75 00

Université de Technologie de Compiegne

(école extérieure aux universités)
Centre Benjamin-Franklin,
rue Roger-Cottolenc-BP 649,
60206 Compiegne cedex
Tel: 03 44 23 44 23
Fax: 03 44 23 43 00

Besançon

Université de Franche-Comté: Besançon

1, rue Goudimel,
25030 Besançon cedex
Tel: 03 81 66 66 66
Fax: 03 81 66 50 25

Dijon

Université de Bourgogne: Dijon

Campus universtitaire de
Montmuzard- BP 138, 21004
Dijon cedex
Tel: 03 80 39 50 00
Fax: 03 80 39 50 69

Lille

Université d'Artois

(Arras, Bethune, Douai,
Lens) 9, rue du Temple –
BP 665,
62030 Arras cedex
Tel: 03 21 60 37 00
Fax: 03 21 60 37 37

Université des Sciences et Technologie de Lille: Lille 1

Cite scientifique, 59655 Vil-
leneuve-d'Ascq cedex
Tel: 03 20 43 43 43
Fax: 03 20 43 49 95

Université du Droit et de la Sante: Lille 11

42 rue Paul Duez, 59800 Lille
Tel: 03 20 96 43 43
Fax: 03 20 88 24 32/20

Université Charles-de-Gaulle: Lille 111

(sciences humaines, lettres et
arts) Domaine universitaire
litteraire de Villeneuve d'Ascq,
Pont-de-Bois – BP 149,
59653 Villeneuve-d'Ascq cedex
Tel: 03 20 41 60 00
Fax: 03 20 91 91 71

Université du Littoral

9, quai de la Citadelle – BP
1022, 59375 Dunkerque cedex 1
Tel: 03 28 23 73 73
Fax: 03 28 23 73 13

Université de Valenciennes et du Hainaut-Cambresis

Le Mont-Houy – BP 311,
59304 Valenciennes cedex
Tel: 03 27 14 12 34
Fax: 03 27 14 11 00

Nancy-Metz

Université de Metz
Île du Saulcy – BP 794,
57012 Metz cedex 1
Tel: 03 87 31 50 50
Fax: 03 87 31 50 55

Pole Universitaire Europeen de Nancy-Metz

34, cours Leopold 54052
Nancy cedex
Tel: 03 83 17 67 67
Fax: 03 83 17 67 65

Maison du Pole

2, rue Winston Churchill,
57000 Metz
Tel: 03 87 65 81 40
Fax: 03 87 65 81 41

Université Henri Poincare: Nancy 1
2-30, rue Lionnois – BP 3069,
54013 Nancy-cedex
Tel: 03 83 85 48 00
Fax: 03 83 85 48 48

Université Nancy 11
Rue Baron Louis – BP 454,
54001 Nancy cedex
Tel: 03 83 34 46 00
Fax: 03 83 30 05 65

Institut National Polytechnique de Lorraine
2, avenue de la Foret-de-Haye
–BP 3, 54501 Vandoeuvre-les-
Nancy cedex
Tel: 03 83 59 59 59
Fax: 03 83 59 59 55

Reims

Université de Reims Champagne-Ardenne
Villa Douce, 9 boulevard de la
Paix, 51097 Reims cedex
Tel: 03 26 05 30 00
Fax: 03 26 05 30 98

Université de Technologie de Troyes
12, rue Marie Curie – BP 206,
10010 Troyes
Tel: 03 25 71 76 00
Fax: 03 25 71 76 77

Strasbourg

Université de Haute-Alsace: Mulhouse
2, rue des Freres Lumiere,
68093 Mulhouse cedex
Tel: 03 89 33 63 00
Fax: 03 89 33 63 19

Université Louis Pasteur: Strasbourg 1
4, rue Blaise Pascal,
67070 Strasbourg cedex
Tel: 03 88 41 60 00
Fax: 03 88 60 75 50

Université des Sciences Humaines: Strasbourg 11
22, rue Rene Descartes,
67084 Strasbourg cedex
Tel: 03 88 41 73 00
Fax: 03 88 41 73 54

Université Robert Schumann: Strasbourg 111
1 place d'Athènes – BP 66,
67045 Strasbourg cedex
Tel: 03 88 41 42 00
Fax: 03 88 61 30 37

NORTH-WEST

Caen

Université de Caen
Esplanade de la Paix,
14032 Caen cedex
Tel: 02 31 56 55 00
Fax: 02 31 56 56 00

Nantes

Université d'Angers
30 rue des Arenes – BP 3532,
49035 Angers cedex 01
Tel: 02 41 23 23 23
Fax: 02 43 83 30 77

Université de Nantes
1 quai de Tourville – BP 1026,
44035 Nantes cedex 01
Tel: 02 40 99 83 83
Fax: 02 40 99 83 00

Orleans-Tours

Université d'Orleans
Château de la Source – BP
6749, 45067 Orleans cedex 2

Tel: 02 38 41 71 71
Fax: 02 38 41 70 69

Université François Rabelais: Tours
3, rue des Tanneurs,
37041 Tours cedex
Tel: 02 47 36 66 00
Fax: 02 47 36 64 10

Poitiers

Université de Poitiers
15, rue de l'Hotel Dieu,
86034 Poitiers cedex
Tel: 05 49 45 30 00
Fax: 05 49 45 30 50

Université de la Rochelle
23, avenue Albert Einstein,
17071 La Rochelle cedex 9
Tel: 05 46 45 91 14
Fax: 05 46 44 93 76

Rennes

Université de Bretagne Occidentale: Brest
Rue des Archives – BP 808,
29285 Brest cedex
Tel: 02 98 01 60 00
Fax: 02 98 01 60 01

Université de Bretagne Sud (Lorient-Vannes)
12, avenue Saint-Symphorien,
56000 Vannes
Tel: 02 97 68 16 20
Fax: 02 97 68 16 39

Université Rennes 1
2, rue du Thabor, 35065 Rennes
cedex
Tel: 02 99 25 36 36
Fax: 02 99 25 36 00

Université de Haute Bretagne: Rennes 11
6, avenue Gaston Berger,
35043 Rennes cedex
Tel: 02 99 14 10 00
Fax: 02 99 14 10 15

Rouen

Université du Havre
25, rue Philippe Lebon – BP
1123, 76063 Le Havre cedex
Tel: 02 35 19 55 00
Fax: 02 35 21 49 59

Université de Rouen
1, rue Thomas Becket, 76821
Mont-Saint-Aignan cedex
Tel: 02 35 14 60 00
Fax: 02 35 14 63 48

SOUTH-EAST

Aix-Marseille

Université de Provence: Aix-Marseille 1
3, place Victor Hugo,
13331 Marseille cedex 3
Tel: 04 91 10 60 00
Fax: 04 91 10 60 06

Université de la Mediteranee: Aix-Marseille 11
Jardin du Pharo, 58 boulevard
Charles-Livon, 13264 Marseille
cedex 07
Tel: 04 42 17 27 18
Fax: 04 42 64 03 96

Université de Droit, d'Economie et des Sciences: Aix-Marseille 111
3, avenue Robert Schumann,
13628 Aix-en-Provence cedex 01
Tel: 04 42 17 27 18
Fax: 04 43 64 03 96

Université d'Avignon et des Pays du Vaucluse

Site Universitaire Sainte-Marthe, 74 rue Louis Pasteur, F-84029 Avignon cedex 01
Tel: 04 90 16 25 00
Fax: 04 90 16 25 10

Clermont-Ferrand

Université d'Auvergne: Clermont-Ferrand 1

49, boulevard Gergovia – BP 32, 63001 Clermont-Ferrand cedex 1
Tel: 04 73 34 77 77
Fax: 04 73 35 55 18

Université Blaise Pascal: Clermont-Ferrand 11

34, avenue Carnot – BP 185, 63006 Clermont-Ferrand cedex 1
Tel: 04 73 40 63 63
Fax: 04 73 40 64 31

Grenoble

Université de Savoie: Chambery

27, rue Marcoz – BP 1104, 73011 Chambery cedex
Tel: 04 69 75 95 85
Fax: 04 79 75 85 55

Université Joseph-Fourier: Grenoble 1

621, avenue Centrale, Domaine universitaire de Saint-Martin-d'Heres/Gieres, BP 53 X, 38041 Grenoble cedex 9
Tel: 04 76 51 46 00
Fax: 04 76 51 48 48

Université Pierre Mendes-France: Grenoble 11

(sciences sociales) 151, rue des universités, Domaine universitaire de Saint-Martin-d'Hères, BP 47, 38040 Grenoble cedex 9
Tel: 04 76 82 54 00
Fax: 04 76 82 56 54

Université Stendhal: Grenoble 111

Domaine universitaire de Saint Martin d'Hères, BP 25, 38040 Grenoble cedex 9
Tel: 04 76 82 43 00
Fax: 04 76 82 43 84

Institute National Poly-technique de Grenoble

46, avenue Felix Viallet, 38031 Grenoble cedex 1
Tel: 04 57 45 00
Fax: 04 76 57 45 01

Lyon

Université Claude Bernard: Lyon 1

43, boulevard du 11 novembre 1918, 69622 Villeurbanne cedex
'La Doua'
Tel: 04 72 44 80 00
Fax: 04 72 43 10 20
'Rockefeller'
Tel: 04 78 77 70 00
Fax: 04 78 77 71 58

Université Lumiere: Lyon 11

86, rue Pasteur, 69365 Lyon cedex 07
Tel: 04 78 69 70 00
Fax: 04 78 69 56 01

Université Jean Moulin: Lyon 111

1, rue de l'Universite – BP 0638, 69239 Lyon cedex 02
Tel: 04 72 72 20 20
Fax: 04 72 72 20 50

Université Jean Monet: Saint-Etienne

34, rue Francis Baulier,
42023 Saint-Etienne cedex 02
Tel: 04 77 42 17 00
Fax: 04 77 42 17 99

Montpellier

Université Montpellier 1

5, boulevard Henri 1V – BP
1017, 34006 Montpellier
cedex 1
Tel: 04 67 41 20 90
Fax: 04 67 41 74 56

Université Montpellier 11

(sciences et techniques du
Languedoc)
Place Eugène Bataillon,
34095 Montpellier cedex 5
Tel: 04 67 14 30 30
Fax: 04 67 14 30 31

Université Paul Valéry: Montpellier 111

Route de Mende, 34199 Mont-
pellier cedex 5
Tel: 04 67 14 20 00
Fax: 04 67 14 20 52

Université de Perpignan

52, avenue de Villeneuve,
66860 Perpignan cedex
Tel: 04 68 66 20 00
Fax: 04 68 66 20 19

Nice

Université de Nice; Sophia Antipolis

Parc Valrose, 28 avenue de
Valrose, 06108 Nice cedex 2
Tel: 04 92 07 60 60
Fax: 04 92 07 66 00

Université de Toulon et du Var

Avenue de l'Universite – BP
132, 83957 La Garde cedex
Tel: 04 94 14 20 00
Fax: 04 94 14 21 57

Bordeaux

Université Bordeaux 1

(Sciences et technologies)
351 cours de la Liberation,
33405 Talence cedex
Tel: 05 56 84 60 00
Fax: 05 56 80 08 37

Université 'Victor Segalen' – Bordeaux 11

146, rue Leo Saignat,
33076 Bordeaux cedex
Tel: 05 57 57 10 10
Fax: 05 56 99 03 80

Université Michel de Montaigne: Bordeaux 111

Domaine universitaire,
Esplanade Michel de Montaigne,
33405 Talence cedex
Tel: 05 56 84 50 50
Fax: 05 56 84 50 90

Université Montesquieu: Bordeaux 1V

(droit, sciences sociales et politiques, sciences economiques
et de gestion)
Avenue Leon Duguit,
33608 Pessac cedex
Tel: 05 56 84 85 86
Fax: 05 56 84 83 20/56

Université de Pau et des Pays de l'Adour

Domaine universitaire, Avenue
de l'universite – BP 576,
64012 Pau cedex
Tel: 05 59 92 30 00
Fax: 05 59 80 83 80

Limoges

Université de Limoges
Hotel Burgy, 13 rue de Genève,
87065 Limoges cedex
Tel: 05 55 45 76 01
Fax: 05 55 45 76 34

Toulouse

Université des Sciences Sociales: Toulouse 1
Place Anatole France,
31042 Toulouse cedex
Tel: 05 61 63 35 00
Fax: 05 61 63 37 98

Université Toulouse-Le Mirail: Toulouse 11
5 allees Antonio Machado,
31058 Toulouse cedex
Tel: 05 61 50 42 50
Fax: 05 61 50 42 09

Université Paul Sabatier: Toulouse 111
118 route de Narbonne,
31062 Toulouse cedex
Tel: 05 61 55 66 11
Fax: 05 61 55 64 70

Institut National Polytechnique de Toulouse
Place des Hauts-Murats – BP
354, 31006 Toulouse cedex
Tel: 05 62 25 54 00
Fax: 05 61 53 67 21

UNIVERSITIES NOT IN MAINLAND FRANCE

Corsica

Université Pascal Paoli: Corse
7, avenue Jean Nicoli – BP 52,
20250 Corte
Tel: 04 95 45 00 00

Fax: 04 95 46 03 21

French Guiana

Université des Antilles-Guyane
Boulevard Legitimus – BP 250,
97157 Pointe-a-pitre cedex
Tel: 05 90 91 99 46
Fax: 05 9- 91 06 57

Réunion

Université de La Reunion
Campus universitaire du
Moufia, 15 avenue René
Cassin, 97715 Saint-Denis
Messag, cedex 9
Tel: 02 62 93 80 80
Fax: 02 62 93 80 06

French Polynesia

Université du Pacifique
BP 4635, 98713 Papeete, Tahiti
Tel: 06 89 42 12 43
Fax: 06 89 41 01 31

Appendix

If you are planning a stay in any country, it is always advisable to make some attempt at learning the basics of the language before you go. It would be a shame if you spent the first month of a 3-month course not following a word because you have no idea at all of the language. Remember, however, that it will take a little while for you to adjust. After several weeks you will probably be amazed that you can understand every word in the 19th Century Art lecture. Below are some words and phrases for use both in study and leisure time . . .

Things you might want to ask or say . .

How many students are there in the class?
Il y a combien d'étudiants dans la classe?

What level is the class?
La classe est à quel niveau?

I want to improve my spoken French
Je voudrais améliorer ma compétence orale en français

I want to work on my grammar
Je voudrais travailler la grammaire

Are there any books that you recommend?
Est-ce qu'il y a des livres que vous recommendez?

I'm sorry but I don't understand
Je m'excuse, mais je ne comprends pas.

Could you explain that in English, please?

> Qui ne connaît pas de langues étrangères
> ne connaît pas la sienne.
> *(Goethe – Maximen und Reflexionen)*

Pouvez-vous me donner une explication en anglais, s'il vous plaît?

I'm sorry but I don't understand what I'm supposed to be doing.
Je m'excuse mais je ne comprends pas ce qu'il faut faire.

Do we have any homework?
Est-ce-qu'il y a des devoirs?

What page are we on?
Nous sommes à quel page?

How do you spell it?
Comment ça s'écrit?

Which room is it in?
C'est dans quelle salle?

Could you speak more slowly, please?
Pouvez-vous parler plus lentement, s'il vous plaît?

I'm sorry, I haven't done my homework
Je suis vraiment desolé mais je n'ai pas fait mes devoirs.

Things the teacher might say to the group. . .

Listen to the tape
Écoutez la cassette

Fill in the blanks
Remplissez les blancs
Put your hand up
Levez la main

Answer the questions
Répondez aux questions

Match the phrases
Reliez les phrases

Come up and write it on the board
Allez l'écrire au tableau

Listen up everybody
Écoutez bien s'il vous plaît

Turn to page 50
Tournez à la page 50

Work in pairs/groups of four
Travaillez en paire/à quatre

Next week we're having a test
Il y aura un petit examen la semaine prochaine

Times

1 o'clock	*une heure*
13.00	*treize heures*
2 o'clock	*deux heures*
14.00	*quatorze heures*
3 o'clock	*trois heures*
15.00	*quinze heures*
4.15	*quatre heures et quart*
16.15	*seize heures quinze*
5.30	*cinq heures et demi*
17.30	*dix-sept heures trente*
6.45	*sept heures moins le quart*
18.45	*dix-huit heures quarante cinq*
morning	*le matin*
afternoon	*l'après midi*
evening	*le soir*
night	*la nuit*
midday	*midi*
midnight	*minuit*

What time does the class start/finish?
À quelle heure commence/finit la classe?
How long is the class?
La classe dure combien de temps?
Is there an earlier/later class?
Est-ce qu'il ya une classe plus tôt/ plus tard?
Do you do evening courses?
Est-ce qu'il y a des cours le soir?

Numbers

1	un/une	**11**	onze	**21**	vingt-et-un/une
2	deux	**12**	douze	**22**	vingt deux
3	trois	**13**	treize	**30**	trente
4	quatre	**14**	quatorze	**40**	quarante
5	cinq	**15**	quinze	**50**	cinquante
6	six	**16**	seize	**60**	soixante
7	sept	**17**	dix-sept	**70**	soixante-dix
8	huit	**18**	dix-huit	**80**	quatre-vingts
9	neuf	**19**	dix-neuf	**90**	quatre-vingt dix
10	dix	**20**	vingt	**100**	cent

200	deux cents	**100000**	cent mille
300	trois cents	**1000000**	million
1000	mille	**10000000**	dix millions
10000	dix mille	**100000000**	milliard

Days of the Week

Monday	*lundi*
today	*aujourd'hui*
Tuesday	*mardi*
tomorrow	*demain*
Wednesday	*mercredi*
day after tomorrow	*le lendemain*
Thursday	*jeudi*
yesterday	*hier*
Friday	*vendredi*
day before yesterday	*l'avat-hier*
Saturday	*samedi*
weekend	*le weekend*
Sunday	*dimanche*

What days are the wine tasting courses on?
Les cours de dégustation sont aux quels jours?

When shall we meet?
Quand est-ce qu'on va rencontrer?

Months and Dates

January	*janvier*
January 1st	*le premier janvier*
February	*fevrier*
February 2nd	*le deuxième fevrier*
March	*mars*
March 3rd	*le troiusième mars*
April	*avril*
April 4th	*le quatrième avril*
May	*mai*
May 5th	*le cinquième mai*
June	*juin*
July	*juillet*
August	*août*
September	*septembre*
November	*novembre*
December	*décembre*

What's the date today?
Quel est la date aujourd'hui?

When's your birthday?
C'est quand votre anniversaire?

When were you born?
Quel est votre date de naissance?

When does the language course start?
Le cour de langue commence à quelle heure?

Health

doctor	*le médecin*
pharmacy/chemist	*la pharmacie*
prescription	*l'ordonnance (la)*
medecine	*les médicaments*

I've got	*J'ai...*
stomache ache	*mal au ventre*
a headache	*mal à la tête*
earache	*mal aux oreilles*
backache	*mal au dos*
toothache	*mal à la dente*
a sore throat	*mal à la gorge*

It hurts	*Ça fait mal*
I'm sick	*Je suis malade*
I've got asthma	*Je suis asthmatique*
I've got a temperature	*J'ai une fièvre*
I'm diabetic	*Je suis diabétique*

My glands are swollen
J'ai une inflammation des ganglions
I've got tonsilitis *J'ai une angine*
Do you have any aspirin?
Est ce que vous avez de l'aspirin?
Do you have a plaster?
Est ce que vous avez du sparadrap?

I'm sorry I missed class yesterday. I was ill
Je suis desolé(e) d'être absent(e) hier. J'etais malade

Can I leave early – I've got a headache?
Est ce que je peux partir tôt – j'ai mal à la tête?

Socialising

Hello	*Bonjour*
Goodbye	*Au revoir*
Please	*S'il vous plaît*
Thankyou	*Merci*
Yes	*Oui*
No	*Non*

What's your name?
Comment vous appellez-vous?
My name's Vivienne
Je m'appelle Vivienne

Where are you from?
D'où venez-vous?

I'm from Great Britain
Je suis Britannique
the USA   *Je suis américain(e)*
Australia   *Je suis australien(ne)*
New Zealand   *Je suis néo-zélandais(e)*

What do you do?
Que faites vous dans la vie?

What do you think of the course?
Que pensez-vous des cours?

Would you like to go for a drink later?
Tu veux aller boire quelque chose plus tard?
Are you doing anything this weekend?
Est-ce que tu vas faire quelque chose ce weekend?
Do you fancy going to see a film?
Tu veux aller au cinéma?
Shall we go for a coffee after class?
Tu veux prendre un café après le cours?

Food

Finding your way around the menu in a foreign country is half the fun of being abroad. Having survived the waiter's haughty disdain at your halting French and mispronunciation of some famous dish, you're not always sure what you've ordered. This section provides only a taster of some of the dishes on offer. You probably don't want the voyage of discovery spoilt in any way. Some of the translations below, however, may help you to avoid some gastronomic disasters . . .

knife	*le couteau*
salt	*le sel*
plate	*l'assiette (la)*
fork	*la fourchette*
pepper	*le poivre*
bowl	*le bol*
spoon	*la cuillère*
sugar	*la sucre*
glass	*le verre*

I've dropped my knife – please could you bring me another?
J'ai laissé tomber mon couteau – pouvez-vous m'en apporter un autre?

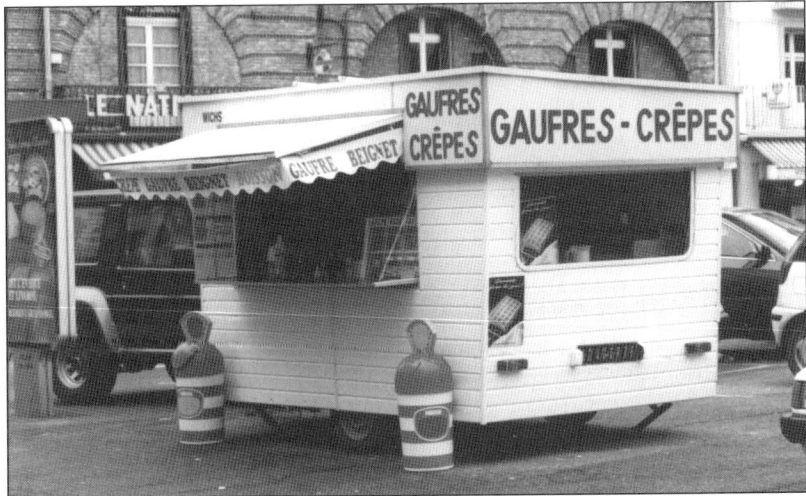

Could you pass the salt, please?
Pouvez-vous me passez le sel, s'il vous plaît?

beer	*la bière*
wine	*le vin*
draught beer	*une pression*
white wine	*le vin blanc*
draught beer (sm)	*une demie pression*
red wine	*le vin rouge*

Do you want something to drink?
Vous voulez quelque chose à boire?

I can't drink – I'm driving
Je ne peux pas boire – je conduis

Sandwiches

a ham sandwich
un sandwich au jambon

a cheese sandwich
un sandwich au fromage

a salami sandwich
un sandwich au saucisson

Please could I have a ham sandwich with no butter?
Un sandwich au jambon sans beurre, s'il vous plaît

How much is a cheese sandwich?
À combien est le sandwich au fromage?

Fish

anchovy	*l'anchois*
oysters	*les huitres*
cod	*le cabillaud*
prawns	*les crevettes*
eel	*l'anguille*
salmon	*le saumon*
lobster	*le homard*
sea bass	*le loup de mer*
monkfish	*la lotte de mer*
trout	*la truite*
mussels	*les moules*
tuna	*le thôn*

Meat, Game and Poultry

beefle	*boeuf*
rabbit	*le lapin*
bacon (diced)	*les lardons*
rib steak	*entrecôte*
calf's head (in jelly)	*la tête de veau*
sausage (spicy)	*le merguez*
chicken	*le poulet*
snails	*les escargots*
chopped meat/mince	*hâchis*
steak	*le bifteck*
duck	*le canard*
testicles	*les rognons blancs*
frog's legs	*les cuisses de grenouille*
tongue	*la langue*
hare	*la lièvre*
tripe	*les tripes*
kidneys	*les rognons*
veal	*le veau*
lamb	*l'agneau*
wild boar	*le sanglier*
pork	*le porc*

Could you explain what this is, please?
Pouvez-vous expliquer ce que c'est, s'il vous plaît?

What are today's specialities?
Quel est le plat du jour, s'il vous plaît?

I'm vegetarian – what do you recommend?
Je suis végétarien(ne) – qu'est-ce que vous me récommendez?

Could I have the bill, please?
L'addition, s'il vous plaît?

Do you take Visa?
Est-ce qu'on peut payer par Visa?

Excuse me waiter – there's a fly in my soup
Excusez-moi Monsieur, mais il y a une mouche dans mon potage

Further Information

K Baillie and T Salmon, *The Rough Guide to France* (1998). Informative, if slightly pricey, travel guide.

The Time Out Guide to Paris (1998). Easier to carry around than the *Rough Guide*, and contains lots of useful information on places to go.

Emmanuel Le Roy Ladurie, *Montaillou*. On one level a history of a 14th-century French village, on another a profound analysis of humanity's religious and social motivations.

Alfred Cobban, *A History of Modern France* (3 vols). A sensible, revisionist approach.

Simon Schama, *Citizens*. Controversial and idiosyncratic modern view of the French Revolution.

Simone de Beauvoir, *The Second Sex*. A literary and ideological revolution in itself.

Peter Mayle *A Year in Provence*. A light, entertaining view of the French, seen through the eyes of a resident Englishman.

Theodore Zeldin, *The French*. Including the essential chapter, 'How to be chic'.

Guy Maupassant, *Une Vie*. Intrigue and infidelity to a backdrop of the beautiful Normandy countryside.

Albert Camus, *L'Étranger*. Daring to be different can lead to trouble and jail.

Marguarite Duras, *L'Amant*. Winner of the prestigious *Prix Goncourt*, the story of a young French girl's passionate encounter in Indochina with an older man.

Victor Hugo, *Les Miserables* Valjean and Javert in an epic personal conflict during a time of political instability.

Victor Hugo, *The Hunchback of Notre Dame* Quasimodo and Esmerelda's tragic love story.

Alexandre Dumas, *The Count of Monte Cristo* A tale of false imprisonment, dramatic escape, adventure and revenge.

Alexandre Dumas, *The Three Musketeers* Classic swashbuckling adventure story set at the court of Louis XIII.

Useful website addresses

Education in France:	http://www.edutel.fr
French Culture:	http://www.culture.fr
Transport in France:	http://www.min-equip.fr
Tourism in France:	http://www.franceguide.com
	http://tourisme.gouv.fr
Prime Minister's Website	http://www.premier-ministre.gouv.fr
Education Links from Provence – Beyond	http://www.beyond.fr/links/edu,html
Guide to Paris:	http://infocities.com
France on the Run	http://www.worldmedia.fr/travel
Admi Net – France Sports	http://www.adminet.com/min/spo

SURVEY FORM AND COMPETITION ENTRY
Win the guide of your choice

We always like to keep in touch with our readers so that we can make changes or improvements to our books and guides.

You can help us by answering the questions below, and sending them back to the address below. We will enter your survey form into the World Study Guide draw which will take place on 31 July 2000. The first 10 forms to be drawn out of the hat will win an On Course publication of their choice.

1. *Where did you buy the France Study Handbook?*

....

2. *Have you read any other international course guides? If so, please say which ones.*

....

3. *How did you hear about the On Course guide? (bookshop, recommendation, advertisement…)*

....

4. *Did you book a course in France as a result of reading the On Course guide?*

....

5. *On a scale of 1 to 5 please indicate the level of importance that you attach to the following features of a course guide (5 very important, 1 not important):*
- Number of courses and colleges ☐
- Number of subject chapters ☐
- Price of the guide ☐
- Writing style ☐
- Essential information ☐
- Background country information ☐
- Ease of use ☐

6. *Do you have any suggestions for future World Study Guides?*

....

....

....

7. *Please tick your preferred prize from the following guides:*
- On Course – London's biggest and best course guide – Summer edition ☐
- On Course – Winter/Spring edition ☐
- What University? – A guide to British universities ☐
- What School? – Schools in the London area ☐
- World Study Guide, Britain Study Handbook ☐
- World Study Guide, France Study Handbook ☐
- World Study Guide, Spain Study Handbook ☐

Name: ....
Address: ....
Age: ....
Profession: ....

Rules:
1. All questionnaires must be returned by 31 July 2000 to qualify for the competition.
2. We regret to say that it will only be possible to notify the winners of the competition.
3. The judges' decision is final.

Please return this survey form to:
On Course Publications: Competition, 121 King Street, London W6 9JG, England
Good luck with the competition and thank you for taking the time to complete this survey

Index